# THE WAR OVER THE FAMILY

## Capturing the Middle Ground

Brigitte Berger is a Professor of Sociology at Wellesley College. She is the author of *Societies in Change* and *Childcare and Mediating Structures* and is a co-author of, among other books, *The Homeless Mind.*

Peter L. Berger is University Professor at Boston University. He is the author of *Invitation to Sociology, Pyramids of Sacrifice, The Heretical Imperative,* and *Sociology Reinterpreted,* among other books.

# THE WAR
# OVER THE FAMILY

CAPTURING THE MIDDLE GROUND

by Brigitte Berger

and Peter L. Berger

ANCHOR PRESS / DOUBLEDAY
GARDEN CITY, NEW YORK
1983

Library of Congress Cataloging in Publication Data

Berger, Brigitte.
The war over the family.

Includes index.
1. Family.   2. Middle classes.   3. Family policy.
4. Social change.   I. Berger, Peter L.   II. Title.
HQ734.B56   1983   306.8′5
ISBN: 0-385-18001-2
Library of Congress Catalog Card Number 82–45237

# CONTENTS

Preface   /*vii*

## I   THE FAMILY – IDEOLOGICAL BATTLEGROUND

1   Historical Evolution of a "Problem"   /*3*

2   Contemporary Alignments   /*23*

Excursus – Goshtalk, Femspeak, and the Battle of Language   /*41*

3   Contemporary Issues   /*53*

Excursus – Abortion and the Postulate of Ignorance   /*73*

## II   THE FAMILY – TENSIONS OF MODERNIZATION

4   The Family and Modern Society   /*85*

5   The Family and Modern Consciousness   /*105*

Excursus – Are We Decadent?   /*129*

## III   THE FAMILY – A REASONABLE DEFENSE

6   Assumptions of a Reasonable Defense   /*139*

7   The Family and the Individual   /*149*

8   The Family and Democracy   /*169*

Excursus – Father-Mother-Child   /*187*

9   Policy Directions – Capturing the Middle Ground   /*195*

Notes   /*217*

Index   /*237*

# PREFACE

*is it rhetorical book* *middle ground = myth*

In recent decades, in America and in other Western countries, there has been a vociferous debate over the history, the present condition, the prospects and, most important, the human and societal value of the family. This debate has been especially focused on what has been called, usually with derogatory intent, the "bourgeois family." This book is a contribution to the debate. Written by two sociologists, it seeks to use the resources of the social sciences in assessing the merits of various parties to the debate. The social sciences, whatever their uses, cannot produce judgments of value. Our own value judgments are very clear. We believe in the basic legitimacy of the bourgeois family, historically as well as today, both in terms of morality and in terms of the requirements of a free polity. Thus this book is unabashedly partisan. At the same time, our position is not extreme. We recognize some validity in most, though not all, the positions that have emerged in the recent debate. Our purpose is not to polemicize or to polarize but, rather, to build bridges. The subtitle of the book expresses our political intention. We are convinced that there exists a middle ground toward which most people instinctively gravitate in matters concerning the family. This middle ground is most plausible intellectually. It is also the position that has the best political prospects, certainly in America, very probably in other countries as well.

Part I of the book seeks to describe the contemporary ideological battleground. Part II gives our own social-scientific understanding of the family in the contemporary world, with special attention being given to modernization and its tensions. Part III develops what we consider to be a reasonable defense of the bourgeois family, in terms of the well-being of individuals and in terms of democratic values. We conclude with a general outline of the directions which, in our opinion, public policy should take in family matters. We do not pretend that any of this is exhaustive. We know that many questions are

left unanswered, that many details remain to be filled in. This is unavoidable. We hope that the major contribution of the book will be to
give heart to many individuals who have been dissatisfied with the
strident rhetoric coming from various sides and who are striving to express a position on the family that is both intellectually and morally
reasonable.

The nature of our collaboration should be specified. This book is,
in the main, Brigitte Berger's. It was her idea, the design and the central argument of the book are hers, and family sociology has been one
of her areas of specialization for many years. Peter Berger has contributed various theoretical perspectives, especially in the area of
modernization. He is also responsible for the four excursi in the book.
The basic approach, both intellectually and in terms of partisanship,
is common to the authors.

Brigitte Berger wishes to thank the Sarah Scaife Foundation for a
grant allowing her to take a leave from her academic position for the
purpose of working on this book, and to Wellesley College for granting this leave. She also wishes to thank Mary Strong for encouragement and advice.

We are very grateful to Loretta Barrett, our editor at Doubleday,
for her unstinting support and encouragement. We know that she
does not agree with everything we say here, which has made her sup-
portive attitude even more valuable. We have found her to be one of
those editors who understand their high responsibility as gatekeepers
(or should one say ushers?) in the theater of ideas.

Both of us have learned much from our association with the
Mediating Structures Project of the American Enterprise Institute,
1976–79, of which Peter Berger was co-director with Richard Neuhaus. We have also gained much from conversations with Michael
Novak and Nathan Glazer. We are also very much indebted to Robert
Woodson, to his National Center for Neighborhood Enterprise, to
Falaka Fatah, and to many other community leaders he has regularly
assembled through his unique program. Through these contacts, we
have learned to become more conscious of the middle-class bias inherent in much writing about the family, and we have learned how important the perspectives coming out of the black community are for a
balanced understanding of the role of the family. Finally, we want to
thank friends and neighbors in different cities, indeed in different

societies, who have given us ever-new confidence in the common sense of ordinary people and in the resilience of human beings in all sorts of circumstances in facing up to the challenges of family life.

Brigitte Berger                                    Peter L. Berger
*Wellesley College*                               *Boston University*

# I

# THE FAMILY
## Ideological Battleground

# 1

# Historical
# Evolution
# of a
# "Problem"

"The family has become a problem."

This observation is widely made today, in America as well as in other societies, to the point where it has become a commonplace. Needless to say, people who make the observation differ among themselves about the nature of the problem and about possible solutions; indeed, what is a solution to some appears as yet another facet of the problem to others. These differing perspectives and approaches will occupy us throughout this book. But before we delve into this cacophony of problem-pronouncers and problem-solvers, it may be useful to stop for a moment and ask what it means in the first place that something is seen to be a "problem"—or, in more precise language, that some phenomenon in human experience that used to be taken for granted becomes "problematized." And then it will be important to ask how the family, of all things, came to be seen in this light—an institution, after all, that has been around since the dawn of history, that was taken for granted for millennia, and that is surely the leading candidate for the status of basic institution in human society.

To say that any object of experience is a "problem" implies at least two perceptions. First, there is the cognitive implication that this object "sticks out" from the rest of experience, that it invites attention, and that it does so because there is something not fully understood and perhaps not quite right about it. Thus any part of our own bodies or of our natural environment can become a problem if it interferes with what we have come to regard as the normal course of events. We pay no attention to our breathing, say, until we have breathing difficulties; we do not perceive a particular tree as a problem until we develop anxieties that it may fall in on our roof. Human institutions are not the same as bodily or natural phenomena, but their problematization in the minds of individuals follows roughly the same logic—that is, an institution becomes the object of attention and concern because some difficulty arises in its role in the flow of social life. At least in modern times, however, there is a second implication to a declaration that this or that has become a "problem"—namely, that we ought to do something about it. In this sense (a specifically modern sense) death is not a problem, but illness is—because we believe, at least in principle, that science has given us the means to seek a cure for any particular illness even if death remains our ultimate fate. This practical, activist implication is especially important when an institution is declared to be a problem, since one peculiarly modern assumption is that society (unlike the body and the natural environment) is a human construction and therefore may be reconstructed if enough people think it should be.

The family has a history, as all human institutions do, and there have been instances in earlier times when the family has come to be seen as a problem, sometimes abruptly and dramatically. Still, the basic relations between the sexes and the generations have often gone undisturbed for centuries, indeed have remained undisturbed even through periods of great turbulence in other areas of social life. And since these basic relationships constitute, for most people, the most intimate core of their lives, there is a specially shocking quality to their sudden redefinition as public issues. Modernity, in particular has developed a keen sense of privacy, and modern individuals are particularly prone to being shocked when private matters come to be publicly exhibited. Sometimes, of course, this shock effect is deliberately sought. In the late 1960s, a young radical was up for trial before a court in West Germany and announced (apparently with little reference to the legal proceedings going on): "I have orgasm difficulties and I want the public to take cognizance of this fact." In a possibly unintended sense, this announcement could be taken as paradigmatic for both the problematization and the politization of the family, and indeed of the private sphere in general.

The French historian Philippe Ariès has argued persuasively that childhood as we now understand it was invented by the rising bourgeoisie of Europe.[1] As the bourgeoisie triumphed as a class, so did its ideals of child-raising. And as these ideals became institutionalized—in the law, the educational system, and in the thinking of individuals—a particular vision of childhood came to be taken for granted. What "stuck out" as a "problem," then, was any treatment of children that failed to conform to this vision. Such treatment, of course, was mostly meted out to the children of *non*-bourgeois parents, and a vast amount of energy was expended by well-meaning bourgeois men and women in attacking this problem, first through private charities and then through public policies. It is not much of an exaggeration to say that the origins of both social work and the welfare state lie in the missionary efforts by which the bourgeoisie sought to propagate its family ethos among the lower classes (as we shall see later on, this missionary impulse is by no means exhausted today). Subsequently, in the more recent period, with which Ariès does not deal, it turned out that many bourgeois children did not quite live up to the ethos either—at which point they, too, became a problem. In an analogous development, traced by the British sociologist Frank Musgrove, the adolescent was invented as a social type in the industrializing societies of the West in the 19th century.[2] Here, perhaps, the problem was invented right along with the institutional construct: The adolescent, by definition, exists in an uneasy biological borderland between childhood and adulthood. The problem of adolescence, consequently, has a considerable history, from its heroization in Romantic literature through century-long worries by countless pedagogues to the "identity crises" of the Age of Aquarius. But both the non-bourgeois child (or, more accurately, the child deprived of the advantages of a properly bourgeois childhood) and the adolescent can still be seen as problems, while the family as such (or that ideal vision of it from which these special cases "stick out") continues to be taken for granted.

Problematization clearly takes on a more radical quality when it proceeds from such special cases to the institution as such.

We may assume that there have always been individuals for whom the family became a problem, be it because they were the sort who always see problems where other people see none (the Socrates sort, as it were) or because they lived through difficult times (war, foreign conquest, natural catastrophes, or more personalized mishaps, all conducive to putting in question what had previously been taken for granted). But, on the level of ideas, a plausible time to take as the start of the currently operative problematization of the family is the Enlightenment of the eighteenth century.[3] The central goal of the Enlightenment was to free human beings from the shackles of tradition. Not surprisingly, the family was perceived as a problem for the realization of this project—it is, undoubtedly, one of the most traditional of institutions. For most Enlightenment thinkers—such as Locke, in England; Rousseau, in France; and Paine, in America—the project certainly did not include abolition of the family but, rather, its reform in the spirit of the new humanity to be brought about. The new political order that the Enlightenment sought to bring about was to be a great liberating agency, and education (still perceived as mainly taking place within the context of the family) was to provide training for the liberated citizens. The details of all this need not concern us here. But one important aspect of this Enlightenment reformism is still very much with us: The new political order was envisaged as a social contract between individuals—consenting adults, one is tempted to say—and it is individuals abstracted from all concrete collective bonds that Enlightenment idealism always focuses on. Both the individualism and the abstraction of liberal ideals to this day reflect the Enlightenment heritage—to the detriment of an understanding of the more "organic" institutions, of which the family is the foremost: Whatever consenting adults may decide to do in their private "life-styles," there are also those non-consenting children, who did not decide to arrive in this particular social locale and who experience their parents' life-styles as destiny, rather than as contracted choice.

In the nineteenth century, both in Europe and in America, the hopes for a liberating education were increasingly concentrated on the school, an institution outside the family.[4] In one sense, this entailed a loss of function for the family. But it would be quite mistaken to think that, therefore, the bourgeois family ethos lost ground. Quite the opposite was the case. Not only did the school itself become a powerful instrument for the propagation of bourgeois values—an instrument, moreover, which, after the passage of compulsory education laws, had behind it the full force of governmental coercion. But the bourgeois family itself gave birth to new ideological configurations, to further developments of its distinctive values. The nineteenth century, rather than the eighteenth, saw the full flowering of the new bourgeois sensibility—not accidentally, since the nineteenth century saw the triumph of the bourgeois class in one Western country after another.[5] Here, then, was the ideal bourgeois family come into its own, called by various names—"Victorian" in England, "Biedermeier" in Germany, and so on—but everywhere manifesting similar characteristics: an emphasis on high moral standards, especially in sexual matters; an enormous interest in the welfare of children, especially their proper education; the inculcation of values and attitudes conducive to economic success as well as civic peace; at least the appearance of religious faith; a devotion to the "finer things" in life, especially the arts; and last but not least, a sense of obligation to redress or alleviate conditions perceived as morally offensive.

One of the most important aspects of this development was a new role for women.[6] Bourgeois women, not their spouses, were the standard-bearers of the new sensibility, first of all within the home (where they tended to be very much in charge), but then more and more in the public arena as well. The latter was especially the case in the English-speaking countries. Bourgeois women in England and America were the shock troops of the various movements that sought to evangelize other classes with the blessings of the middle-class family ethos, be it through private good works or through marshaling the forces of politics for legislation and governmental action. The Protestant clergy were an important ally in this missionary enterprise. One recent author has spoken of this process of cultural change as the "feminization" of America.[7] This is a pretty accurate term, given the role of women in the process. The term *embourgeoisement* is equally accurate, referring to the class, rather than the gender, character of this development. In all of this, of course, the perceived problem belonged to all those families whose values and practices deviated from the norms of the new sensibility. Most prominent among these were the families of the working class, and it was to them that the alliance of ladies and clerics devoted most of their energetic efforts.

As already mentioned, the origins of modern social work, again especially in England and in America, are to be found in this vast missionary enterprise. George Bernard Shaw has left a vivid (and sharply satirical) portrait of this bourgeois evangelism in his play *Major Barbara*. In America, for many years and extending into the twentieth century, these efforts to redeem the lower classes were splendidly embodied in the Temperance movement, that near-perfect amalgam of bourgeois moralism, Protestant zeal, and more than just a touch of hysteria. It is very interesting, though, that the early socialists, particularly in England, very much shared in the underlying assumptions of this uplift operation—despite their supposed antagonism to the bourgeois class dominance and their reservations about religion. The Fabians illustrate this point very well.[8] The project was not to debunk or demolish the bourgeois sensibility; rather, it was to bring its putative blessings to the underprivileged. The working class, too, was to have culture, refinement, well-behaved children, and a sound education. In other words, the project was not to abolish but to redistribute the bourgeois family ethos. To be sure, there were always bohemians and other rebellious types who disdained this ethos as a whole. But throughout the nineteenth century they remained marginal to the major developments in Western societies, interesting subjects for literature and for opera librettos but of little cultural or political significance in the larger society.

Now, two things may already be clear from the above considerations. First: Among those who came to see the family as a problem, there developed a relatively negative faction and a more positive one, as it were. Some took a mainly negative view of the family, as an obstacle to the realization of true liberty, full individuality, and the like. Others took a more positive view, in which the family itself, albeit with some tinkering here and there, was evolving in such a way as to realize these ideals. This is important, because both these factions are still around today. And second: It is not enough to say that a problem has arisen; one must also ask *whose* problem it is. One person's taken-for-granted reality is another's problem, and vice versa. Thus it is safe to say that the working-class objects of all this bourgeois benevolence did not understand why their family life was sup-

posed to be a problem—at least in the beginning, before the missionary indoctrination had begun to take hold in some proletarian minds.
Then as now, when one hears the proposition that "the family [or this
or that type of family] has become a problem," one ought immediately to ask, "Says who?" Very likely, one will find that those who say
so come from a specific class location in society. And often one will
also find, as we shall see later on, that some of them have very concrete, indeed crude vested interests in the matter: Let it be suggested
at this early point in our argument that there are people who make a
living from allegedly solving certain problems—and who therefore
have a vested interest in propagating the notion that these problems
are very serious, very urgent, and (most important) insoluble without
their own expert assistance.

Among those who saw the family as playing an active and essentially positive role in the evolutionary process was Herbert Spencer,
the fashionable sociologist of Victorian England.[9] Spencer was a
*succès fou* in the English-speaking countries in his lifetime but has
been pretty much forgotten since then. But there also developed in
the nineteenth century an important viewpoint in which the family is
seen as a more or less passive reflection of broader historical forces. In
its Marxist form, this viewpoint is very much alive today. Marx himself did not write extensively on the family, but his disciples Friedrich
Engels and August Bebel did.[10] In this view, the family always takes
on specific forms due to the forces and relations of production. The
family here becomes a sort of barometer for the state of the class
struggle at any given moment of history. Thus the bourgeois family
reflects the objective class situation of the bourgeoisie, the working-
class family the situation of the working class. The Marxists, to be
sure, found much fault with both the bourgeois and the working-class
family—the former an embodiment of all the vices of the exploiting
class, the latter a victim of the same exploitation—but, by the nature
of their theory, they could not be bothered with reforms in this area.
The woes of family life could be cured only by the revolutionary
transformation of society as a whole. In the meantime, the Marxist individual may or may not have a liberated life-style in the area of private life (Engels did, while Marx was a stuffy bourgeois if there ever
was one), but these personal preferences were marginal to the overall

political project. This ambivalent relation of Marxism to all enter-
prises of personal liberation has also become a permanent heritage.

In America, the period after World War I was marked by the rise
of sociology as a new and (everyone thought) highly promising tool
for the solution of social problems. In many ways, the American sociologists were the successors of the clerical/"feminized" reformers of
the preceding generations—and in terms of personal background they
were often enough their direct descendants. The moral frame of reference, whatever the new scientific trappings, continued to be bourgeois, Protestant, and reformist, and the sociological imagination continued to be haunted by the small-town culture (the same culture
that, later in this century, came to be called "Middle America"), in
which these moral values were embedded.

American sociology in the 1920s, and to some extent still in the
1930s, was dominated by the department at the University of Chicago, and the so-called Chicago School produced a still astounding
volume of books, articles, and dissertations about every aspect of
American society but especially about the dynamic social reality of
American cities. The family was not the principal interest of the
Chicago School, but it entered into most of the School's analyses.[11]
The Chicago School viewed the family in the context of the urbanizing transformations of social life and in this context spoke about the
increasing isolation of the nuclear family—the term referring to the
shrunken unit of spouses and children deprived of the supports supposedly characteristic of the older, extended family. The emphasis
was on rootlessness. One might say that this view reflected what must
have been the experience of many of these sociologists themselves—
the children of bravely bourgeois homes, scions of small-town, Protestant, midwestern culture, suddenly transposed into the dynamic and
anonymous world of the big city—stranded in Chicago, as it were,
without cousins, without church picnics, without the comforting enve-
lope of a moral consensus. In this view, the ideals of the bourgeois
family were by no means devalued; on the contrary, if anything these
ideals were magnified in the perspective of nostalgia. The problem, in
other words, was not the bourgeois family but the process by which it
was weakened through the loss of the old kinship and communal supports.

In its specific American situation, the Chicago School took up once more what had been one of the basic themes of classical European sociology: that transformation of society which we usually refer to today as modernization. In France, Émile Durkheim described this as the passage from "mechanical" to "organic" solidarity; in Germany, Ferdinand Tönnies analyzed the same historical process as the change from *Gemeinschaft* to *Gesellschaft*. Both pairs of concepts contrast an earlier form of society, in which human beings were tied to each other by an absolute and unquestioned sense of belonging, with modern society, in which relationships are limited, open to revision, and increasingly specified through legal contracts. If one compares this view with the pre-sociological notions of nineteenth-century family reformers, it becomes apparent that the definition of the problem has expanded. It is not just the working-class family that is seen as the problem now (though this type of family may have peculiar problems of its own), but the middle-class family, too, is problematized because of its subjection to the disintegrative forces of modernization. Everyone in the caldron of the modern city is subject to the strains of social mobility, isolation, and anonymity; to that extent, everyone becomes part of the problem—except perhaps those folks back home on the prairies, left to their allegedly solidarity-rich cavortings under the elm trees behind the church.

One peculiar American phenomenon, of course, was that of mass immigration, very much in evidence in the Chicago of the time and given much attention by the Chicago sociologists. The Chicago School produced what is still today the most masterly study of the phenomenon, W. I. Thomas and Florian Znaniecki's *The Polish Peasant in Europe and America*.[12] Since the authors studied their subjects both in Poland and, after immigration, in America, the *Gemeinschaft/Gesellschaft* contrast was especially sharp. The immigrant family, of course, brought with it many of the old-country *Gemeinschaft* patterns, and for a while these dominated in the ethnic communities of the large American cities. But the forces of American urbanism began to exercise their disintegrative power immediately; with the second generation, or so it seemed, the old communal and kinship ties were already greatly weakened. It is probably fair to say that Thomas and Znaniecki, as well as the other Chicago sociologists, were ambivalent about the immigrant family. On the one hand, they were impressed with the solidarity-bestowing quality of this family type; on the other hand, the same family type was perceived as an obstacle to the immi-

grants' adjustment to American life. This latter perception was dominant in the thinking of educators and social workers, for whom Ameri-
canization (the "melting pot") was a powerful and then hardly
questioned ideal. Again, this ambivalence about the ethnic family has
remained a continuing theme, manifesting itself later on once again in
the controversies over the black family.

American sociology continued to view the family (as it did other
institutions) in the light of the dichotomies of traditional/modern,
rural/urban, ethnic/American. And in all of this, albeit ambivalently,
there continued to be a sense of loss. American anthropology, which
also developed impressively in the post-World War I period, contributed to this dichotomized perspective by parading a long line of primitive, peasant, and preliterate societies, all of them marvelously soli-
darity-prone and obviously different from the fragmented life-styles of
assistant professors at the University of Chicago. At the same time,
curiously, the family came to be defined increasingly as an arrangement between individuals, rather than as a meta-individual entity.
Thus Ernest Burgess, one of the masters of the Chicago School,
defined the family as a unit of interacting personalities.[13] To the extent that this definition is taken seriously, it becomes impossible to
conceive of the family as an entity transcending individuals. Where
such a conception may still be held onto, this could be seen as a
leftover from earlier times, *ipso facto* no longer relevant to the real social world. And sociology provided a concept for this, too: William
Ogburn's "cultural lag."[14] In this sense, then, sociology itself became
part of the problem, the diagnosis itself becoming a symptom of the
disease: If the sociological definition of the family sees only isolated
individuals in interaction with each other, and if this same isolation is
taken to be the heart of the problem, then sociology itself constitutes
an interesting contribution to the problem, however inadvertently. We
lack the knowledge to say to what extent sociology thus contributed
directly to the problematization of the family in individual lives, but
it is hard to believe that all these thousands of sociology courses,
taught to millions of American students since the 1920s, have had no
effects at all.

After World War II, the importance of the Chicago School in
American sociology greatly diminished, though many of its concepts
continued to be of influence and merged with newer approaches. In
the 1950s, the dominant school was that of so-called structural-func-

tionalism, of which Talcott Parsons was the most prominent theorist. It is interesting to see how the views on the family of this school both reflected and legitimated broad cultural trends going on at the same time. Like the Chicago sociologists, the structural-functionalists were not primarily interested in the family as such, but they paid a good deal of attention to the family as one important case in point of the larger societal processes they wanted to understand. Parsons himself, along with some collaborators, published a very influential book on the family, *Family, Socialization and Interaction Process,* which shaped the thinking of a whole generation of family analysts.[15] Compared to the Chicago School, Parsons' view of the family was certainly more upbeat. The emphasis was not on loss but on new functions understood in a basically positive way. This supposedly positive understanding, though, deserves closer scrutiny.

The argument runs something like this: The family has been greatly changed as a result of various modernizing processes. The most important effect of modernization is institutional *differentiation* —a key concept of Parsons', which means that functions earlier performed by one institution are now distributed among several institutions. Thus the family has indeed *lost* functions, notably economic and educational ones. This very loss, however, has *freed* the family for taking on new functions, some of which never existed before. These new functions centered particularly on the individuals in the family, their rights and their potential for self-realization. Thus marriage, while no longer essential for economic production (the modern economy functions independently of kinship structures) and for the socialization of children (largely taken over by the educational institutions), now becomes the locale for highly complex and emotionally demanding interaction between the spouses. In other words, in an ingenious way, Parsons brought to theoretical maturity the view of the family proposed earlier by Burgess: The family becomes a freely contracted arrangement between "consenting adults."

It would not be fair to Parsons to say that he paid no attention to the place of children in the family. On the contrary, he insisted that the rights and personality development of children were part of this new family function. But deepening emphasis on the family as a contractual arrangement between individuals inevitably de-emphasized the major *non*-contracting element in the situation: the children. The rearing of children frequently appears as a kind of afterthought in

this sociological literature. Parsons himself believed that the specialization of child-rearing functions was beneficial to children, because it
increased efficiency. Indeed, child-rearing became more and more of a
professional task outside the family—part of the institutional differentiation of modernity—and this process, supposedly in a benign way,
acted back upon the family itself. One phrase of Parsons', the "profes-
sionalization of parenthood," came to be widely used. It aptly described, and at the same time legitimated, what was going on in society anyway. It also, in a surely unintended way, undermined the
confidence of parents in their own child-rearing capacity.

If the school arose in the nineteenth century as an institution ancillary to the bourgeois family, the middle-class family in America
now became increasingly perceived as ancillary to the professional
child-rearing establishment. Who, after all, was to decide whether
parents were living up to their "professionalized" function? Well,
there was no shortage of candidates for this evaluative role: not only
sociologists (most of whom operated in the antiseptic milieu of
academia, at a safe distance, except for purposes of research, from the
messy world of nursery and school), but regiments of new experts on
child-rearing, education, and therapy. It is important to recall that
this same period also saw the massive expansion of psychology, psychoanalysis, and psychotherapy in America, generating a complex of
"helping" institutions which, from the beginning, paid very serious attention to children. The middle class was the main clientele of this
professional network, but via the equally burgeoning field of social
work (heavily influenced in the 1950s and beyond by psychoanalytic
ideas), these ideas on what constituted a "good family" were diffused
to working-class people as well—a slightly grotesque replication of
the bourgeois evangelism of the nineteenth century, with Major Barbara spouting Freudian jargon and masses of sociologists using the
latest statistical techniques to gauge the successes and failures of her
missionary efforts.

Needless to say, sociologists and psychotherapists make history in
only a modest way. All sorts of things were happening in society anyway, without the benefits of Parsonian wisdom. But the ideas generated in academia and in the clinical-counseling network found fertile ground in the larger societal changes, and in turn helped these
changes along. The 1950s in America were marked by what came to
be called a family renascence.[16] Undoubtedly there were many rea-

sons for this: the desires of the war veterans returning home, the new affluence of the postwar period, the heightened mobility (geographical as well as social) of large portions of the population, the rise of the new suburbs, perhaps even a new accessibility of birth-control techniques. Whatever the reasons, the 1950s fostered a positive view of the American family—or, at any rate, of its ideal or normative form. This view, of course, was, once again, a middle-class view, but it percolated down to other strata as well. The middle-class family was perceived as, essentially, a success story, particularly in terms of Burgess' and Parsons' notions about the primacy of the individual and his or her personal needs. The family became increasingly child-centered—and that was supposed to be good. Women were to find their mission at home, as mothers and as the intelligent, emotionally sensitive companions to their husbands—and if they did not accept this mission, the psychologists were ready to treat this reluctance as a neurotic ailment. In this new celebration of the family, what remained as a problem?

This question is not hard to answer: There was the problem, just indicated, of individuals (husbands and children as well as wives) who failed to adjust to the roles demanded of them in the successful family; this problem was the domain of the various therapeutic professions. And then there was the problem of entire social groups who failed to conform to the norms of family success; essentially, this was a continuation of the old problem of class and ethnicity, except that this problem was now professionalized by a sociologically and psychologically sophisticated social-work establishment. As far as the lower classes were concerned, middle-class families (and especially middle-class women) now underwent another Parsonian loss of function: to wit, the function of charity. This happened ever more, of course, as social work and the "helping" professions generally came to be increasingly included in the budding machinery of the post-New Deal American welfare state.

Already in the 1950s, however, there were some who questioned the success story. The new functions of the family, liberating and emotionally rich as they may have been, were also filled with a lot of anxiety. Especially the women, celebrated as mothers, wives, and "homemakers," were thrown back upon themselves into a kind of social vacuum. This was especially the case in the new, middle-class suburbs, where women were separated geographically as well as socially from the non-"homemaking" activities of their husbands and frequently experienced a sort of cage effect. Suburbia, and by extension middle-class existence as a whole, were soon interpreted as problems. The studies of suburbia by William Whyte and John Seeley (*The Organization Man* and *Crestwood Heights*, respectively) highlighted this new problem to a large (and by no means only academic) readership.[17] In other words, the success story of the new middle-class family, barely told, was already turning sour, in the opinion of many.

The critical voices, still relatively few and far between in the 1950s, turned into a crescendo of denunciation in the 1960s. This period is still very close to us, so it is probably premature to attempt a comprehensive explanation of what led to this historically unprecedented explosion of cultural self-criticism, even self-laceration, in America and (to a somewhat lesser degree) in other Western countries. In any case, it is fairly clear how this new radicalism affected views of the family. One way of describing this is to say that the definition of the problem was turned upside down: No longer were deviations from the norm seen as the problem, but the norm itself—that is, the normative American family—was perceived and denounced as the real problem. In other words, the problem was not maladjusted individuals or social groups but, rather, the "sick society," of which the "sick family" was an integral part.

If one were to identify one book that crystallized this new sensibility, it would be Betty Friedan's *The Feminine Mystique*, first published in 1963.[18] Again, of course, it is not our contention that this book by itself made history—not even best-selling authors have this power—but Friedan captured a spreading mood with great acumen and, having given it literary form, helped to diffuse and legitimate it. There was now a widespread rebellion against the family ideals of the preceding decade, against their "privatism" (Friedan coined the apt phrase of the "cult of domesticity") and their "repressiveness." Most of the social and cultural movements of the 1960s fed into this anti-family mood: the new feminist movement itself, of course, but also other movements of sexual liberation (including the gay and lesbian movements), the various cults of sensitivity and personal self-realization (subsumable under the heading of the "California syndrome"), the New Left (which was highly critical of American society as a whole and the normative American family along with the rest), and the rising black cultural self-consciousness (which rejected prevailing family norms as white impositions).

It later turned out that all this angry noise was far less pervasive in the larger society than it seemed at first blush. But those who wrote the books and articles about the family lived in those milieus where the tumult was greatest; not surprisingly, they tended to believe that the concerns of their spouses, colleagues, friends, and (last but not least) students were the augurs of a new age. In consequence, the view that the family was dying if not already dead gained wide credence, and for many who held this view it constituted good news. This attitude was pithily expressed by the radical social scientist Barrington Moore, who suggested that we should give the family a decent burial.[19] Radical feminists (such as Shulamith Firestone and Juliet Mitchell) and radical psychiatrists (notably R. D. Laing and his disciples) were all too eager to proceed with the burial, and the decency part of the procedure was hardly called for by their perception of the family as a nest of oppression and pathology[20]; "*écrasez l'infâme*" fairly describes their attitude.

We shall return later to the class-specific location and character of this radicalism. But, leaving a more detailed class analysis until then, it is clear that all these avant-gardes, even if one adds them all up together, constituted only relatively small sectors of the upper-middle-class population. Their influence, though, was much amplified by institutional processes that they themselves neither initiated nor controlled. There were, of course, the media, always in search of a good story—and the radical movements of the 1960s provided very good stories indeed. This was a generation of eminently videogenic revolutionaries. But, probably more important in the long run, some of the new radical ideas lent themselves to political uses by people who were not particularly radical in their own thinking or personal lives. The 1960s was the decade in which the American welfare state underwent its greatest extension, dwarfing the 1930s in its growth rate. Perhaps inevitably, this included a redefinition of miscellaneous private woes as public ones—and that means as problems to be dealt with politically. Many of the ideas proposed as radical innovations in the 1960s, at least in the area of the family, were really not all that new. What was new was, first, their embodiment in intense social movements, and second, their politicization. Thus the New Politics, finding a (so far) rather stable home in the left wing of the Democratic Party, included many of the radical ideas of the 1960s in its agenda. In the process, of course, the ideas had to be toned down and modified, but they retained enough of their original fervor to give continuing satisfaction to large numbers of erstwhile "movement people"—and this has remained so until today. Finally, insofar as some of the same ideas were adopted by the "helping professions," they, too, were now diffused into the lower classes of society. In this way, although the radicalism of the 1960s was a bourgeois affair *par excellence* (if one can still speak meaningfully of a bourgeoisie in the mid-twentieth century), it was carried far beyond its original class location by the powerful forces of the mass media of communication, the processes of party politics, and the (increasingly publicly funded and *ipso facto* politically reinforced) "helping professions."

If one wishes to look upon the radical movements of the 1960s as a cultural revolution, then one may say that in the 1970s, efforts were made to institutionalize that revolution. There were well-organized demands for sweeping changes in the family's social context through legislation and public policy. These demands were no longer made by radicals alone, but were supported or even initiated by other elements in society: activist sectors of the religious community, politicians and, most important, the professional combines regarding the family as their field of expertise. Now the "helping professions" not only claimed jurisdiction over the family, but they wanted to be put on the public payroll in the exercise of this jurisdiction. A new and large constituency for "family policy" began to take shape. By and large, the political results of this have been disappointing to this constituency, but successful in at least one respect: thoroughly alarming and mobilizing an opposition.[21]

Jimmy Carter deserves praise or blame for much of this development. Already in his presidential campaign, in 1976, he pointed to the alleged erosion of the family as an important national problem, and in his inaugural address he promised that his administration would do something about this. His running mate, Walter Mondale, had already made a name for himself in the Senate as a politician greatly concerned with family issues. Thus the Carter administration was well positioned to lift the family onto the national agenda. These developments in the government coincided (happily or unhappily, depending on one's point of view) with the mobilization of "family advocates" in the professional and academic world. In 1977 the Carnegie Council on

Children, originally formed five years earlier, issued an influential report calling for a national family policy.[22] The Family Impact Seminar, set up by the Foundation for Child Development, served as a Washington clearinghouse and sounding board for a mushrooming array of ideas and proposals as to what a national family policy should consist of. But the political center of all this activity became the White House Conference on Families (significantly changing its name early in its organizing phase from the singular to the plural—since it was impossible to arrive at even rudimentary consensus on what "the American family" was supposed to be). The meetings and discussions that were to prepare the agenda for the White House Conference became a veritable battlefield of competing interests and philosophies. Predictably, in the end no group was particularly happy with the project. Instead of the one great gathering at the White House that had been originally envisaged, the Conference finally eventuated in two regional meetings held in the summer of 1980, with results that even its most committed supporters (of whom, by then, there were not many) saw as meager.

Later in this book, we will look in greater detail at some of the major issues that formed the topics of these policy debates. Suffice it to say now that these debates over a possible national policy came to include a vast grab bag of concerns. Some of these were easily recognizable as issues traditionally related to the family—such as the manner in which the welfare system dealt with needy families, and the facilities available for children with special needs. But, in the wake of the ideological turmoil of the 1960s, the debates necessarily had to deal as well with new issues that had not been previously seen as pertaining to the family as such, notably the challenges to traditional norms posed by feminism and its allies in other liberationist movements, and the views of those (strongly expressed in the publications of the Carnegie Council) who took the family as a handy hook on which to hang their left-liberal agenda of radical structural changes in favor of more equality. And of course, the same political process became highly charged by emotional moral issues which, again, were only tangentially related to the family as such; among these, the abortion issue was central. It is fair to say that, as the Carter administration came to an end, the major consequence of its family interest was a widening skepticism about any notions of a national family policy, rather than greater clarity as to what such a policy might be. At the time of writing, it is too early to gauge how, if at all, present and future administrations will pursue this matter.

What also happened in the late 1970s, as already indicated, was the appearance of a strong, increasingly well-organized counter-movement, the so-called "pro-family" camp.[23] Like its radical counter-part, it, too, was an agglomeration of people of differing interests: anti-feminists, people concerned with the alleged evils of homosex-uality and of pornography, people concerned with the official secu-larism (or what they perceived as such) in American public life (the Supreme Court decision banning prayer in public schools continues to be a powerful issue here), parents just plain disgusted with the intel-lectual and social failures of public education, and, a core ingredient of this new coalition, the "pro-life" (read: antiabortion) movement. As with the radicals, the heterogeneous interests in this camp some-times ran in various directions and could not always be coordinated for political purposes. Nevertheless, this camp has gained remarkable coalescence around several issues affecting the family and family pol-icy, and it continues to exercise a powerful political influence, espe-cially since the 1980 national elections. Again, we will look at some details of this new phenomenon later in the book. For the moment, it is enough to point to the phenomenon, and perhaps to add that, in very broad terms, it resembles neo-traditionalist movements in other parts of the world (including the Third World countries). Here, too, viewpoints and values dismissed as "backward," "obsolete," or "no longer to be taken seriously" in the elite centers of the national cul-ture suddenly rally large numbers of people in a politically effective counterthrust against the putative blessings of "progress."

As we come to the present time, then, we can discern three major alignments on family issues in America: the radical-to-reformist coali-tion rooted in the movements of the 1960s, moderated somewhat by middle age and by the compromises of political horse trading but still marching under the old banners of liberation; the new "pro-family" camp, more brash and uncompromising by its very youth, marching in step with the general veering toward conservatism in the national mood; and thirdly, the combines of professionals, academics, and bu-reaucrats who make the family their field of expertise, advocacy, and management, more sympathetic on the whole with the first, rather than the second, movement, but inevitably more pragmatic because of both their alleged scientific spirit and their institutional interests. All these people share the very formal proposition that the family has "problems" or even *is* a "problem," but, of course, they vary sharply in their understanding of what it is that is problematic and what should be done about it. Indeed, the "solutions" of the first camp are an essential part of what the second camp sees as the "problem," and vice versa, while the family experts often have "problems" that nobody else on the scene is capable of perceiving. But such are the exigencies of pluralism and of democratic politics.

One final observation, before we turn to a closer examination of these contemporary alignments: What we have just described is an American constellation of ideas and social forces. However, there are similar alignments in other Western countries. As to the Third World (and, to a lesser extent, the socialist countries in the Soviet orbit), Western media, Western foundations and cultural exchange programs, and (perhaps more significantly than often realized) Western tourism have quite effectively exported all these "problems." Whatever may be its imperial fate politically, militarily, and economically, the United States continues to be the hegemonic *culture* in the contemporary world. The "problems" thought up by Ivy League intellectuals, New York media types, and Washington politicians today in the area of culture start worrying people in London and Stockholm a short time afterward, people in Budapest about the same time though in necessarily more subterranean fashion, and the modernized "with-it" crowd in Bombay or Jakarta not long thereafter. Such are the exigencies of being the "lead society" in the great drama of modernization (to conclude with another, often misunderstood but broadly valid term of Talcott Parsons').

# 2

# Contemporary Alignments

At first glance, the contemporary American situation appears to be characterized by a bewildering variety of positions on the family, some expressed in stridently aggressive tones, others put forth in what purports to be the calm voice of reason. Upon further investigation, the situation is disclosed to be simpler. In the main, there are three major positions represented on the scene: the position of those who continue to call for far-reaching, in some cases even radical, changes in the family; the "pro-family" position, very largely a reaction against the first position; and the position of various professionals, who claim to deal with the matter on the basis of their scientific knowledge. There are all sorts of variations within each position, but it is possible to speak of three major camps. We will call these the critical, the neo-traditionalist, and the professional camps. We will not conceal our serious reservations with regard to each one of these camps; while we believe we understand, and to a degree sympathize with, the underlying concerns of each of these three camps, we are also impressed by their severe shortcomings, and we are convinced that each position must be transcended both intellectually and in terms of public policy. In this chapter, though, we will not emphasize our own position. Rather, we will try to present an overview of the three camps, and then to place them in the sociological context of current class conflicts and cultural trends in American society. While the focus is in America, we would contend that roughly comparable alignments can be found in other Western industrial societies.

We have already seen, in the preceding chapter, that the family has been critically assaulted from various directions. Since the 1960s, however, a central place in the critical camp has been occupied by the new feminist (or Women's Liberation) movement.[1] This movement, too, is not a monolithic phenomenon, and it has undergone significant changes since its inception. A convenient event by which to date this inception is 1963, when Betty Friedan's *The Feminine Mystique* was published. This book was an indictment of the middle-class housewife's imprisonment in the kind of domesticity once described by Virginia Woolf as "the cottonwool quality of daily life." The solution was clear: to go out of the household into the world of work, in which a new identity could be found. The move was to be from private existence, within the confines of the family, to the public realm, where, supposedly, more-important things were going on. Thus freedom meant, above all, freedom *from* the family.

At the time, Friedan's position seemed very radical. In retrospect, it looks quite moderate, and indeed it has come to represent the more moderate wing of the feminist movement, as embodied in the National Organization of Women (NOW), which Friedan helped found. The position continues to be of central importance. It is not antifamily in intention. Rather, it insists on a larger field of action and a larger identity for women. Under attack is the self-abnegating wife and mother; this abnegation, it is supposed, is not only bad for women but for their spouses and children as well. It is important to see that, while Friedan was writing her book, women were entering the work force in unprecedented numbers. In the 1950s, 20 percent of all married women worked outside the home; by 1972, the figure had climbed to over 40 percent, with women with young children making up the bulk of the rise. As women thus moved into the labor market, they encountered massive and long-entrenched discrimination against them. Thus Friedan's message did not take place in a vacuum but was related to very real social changes and to realistic resentments of many women experiencing these changes in their own lives. This realistic base of the new feminist message helps account for its immediate, even incandescent resonance.

This position has both political and psychological aspects. Politically, it implies a struggle for equality in all realms of life. Psychologically, there is a struggle for personal self-assertion. Both aspects were quickly radicalized. By the late 1960s, there was a new feminist ideology, at the center of which stood the proposition that women are "the most oppressed of all people," in the words of Juliet Mitchell.[2] Kate Millett announced that "sexist oppression is more endemic to our society than racism," Shulamith Firestone that "sexism represents the oldest, most rigid class-caste system in existence," and Yoko Ono that "woman is the nigger of the world."[3] This was quite an escalation from Friedan's critique. Now it was no longer just a protest against this or that aspect of the contemporary role of women, but a reinterpretation of history and indeed of the human condition. The family now appears as an age-old evil. Heterosexuality is rape; motherhood is slavery; all relations between the sexes are a struggle for power. There came into prominence one huge outcry against being female. This outcry reached its peak in the early 1970s, then subsided somewhat, with the more radical feminists gathering in sect-like groups on the margins of the main feminist movement. But what remained of this radicalism was a recurring theme of total liberation, as an ideal if not an immediately realizable program, and a view of the family as the major obstacle to this liberation. New bonds of "sisterhood" were posited against the confining bonds of the family. There came into being a very vocal lesbian component of this radical feminism. It is impossible to gauge the magnitude of this, but quite apart from being relatively small in size it was important for the public perception of feminism: Feminists came to be widely perceived as women who hate men.

All branches of the feminist movement shared a strong missionary bent. "Consciousness raising" became a key feminist category. This ranged from national propaganda campaigns (around such issues as abortion and the Equal Rights Amendment) to cultural campaigns (such as the insistence on "non-sexist" or "inclusive" language) to therapeutic activities in small groups. In this manner, feminism met the requirement of many modern people to have an ideology that will span public and private concerns. In other words, feminism provided answers from the problems of bedroom and nursery to the big questions of national purpose. How effective has this massive propaganda been? It seems clear that the more radical versions of feminism have appealed to only small numbers of American women. But it also seems clear that the less extreme versions have notably influenced the views and attitudes, and probably the behavior, of large numbers of women, especially among the college-educated young. Equally clearly, there have been political effects, in terms of abortion, equal rights, and other causes pushed by feminists. As with most cultural or ideological movements, it is difficult to determine to what extent feminism *caused* changes in behavior or merely *legitimated* changes that were happening anyway. Thus divorce, pre- and extra-marital sex, and abortion are phenomena rooted in broad societal changes for which the feminist movement cannot be (as the case may be) blamed or praised. Clearly, though, many people *perceived* feminists to be responsible for these changes, and this perception contributed to the genesis of the neo-traditionalist alignment. At the same time, there is no doubt that most American women continued to believe in and to be behaviorally committed to fairly conventional performances of the roles of wife and mother. *Organized* feminism remained a relatively small phenomenon; between 1971 and 1981, membership in the major feminist organizations rose from about 75,000 to about 120,000— hardly an avalanche. This does not change the fact that many feminist ideas, albeit in moderated form, have become widely accepted in the national culture.

Whatever else feminism may have achieved, it brought about a widespread sense of the *relativity* of conventional family life. It greatly helped to give respectability to the notion of "alternative life-styles," which made traditional sexual and family norms appear as just *one of many* ways of organizing these human concerns. In this, feminism linked up with other challenges to these norms and to the "bourgeois family" as such—challenges such as the counterculture (with its ideals of communal collectivism), the gay movement (which increasingly demanded that its life-style be accorded symbolic and practical equality with the traditional heterosexual family), and the "singles" subculture (less of a movement than the other two but based on the social reality of an increasing and large number of young individuals living by themselves—and not so incidentally, a reality recognized and propagated by the advertising media). Also, all branches of the feminist movement latched on to the rhetoric of civil rights—and to its legal manifestations, as in the (logically rather remarkable) successful identification of women as a "minority" for purposes of affirmative action. To the extent that the "oppression" of women was perceived as endemic to the society, feminism developed an affinity with other attacks on the *status quo,* notably those of the New Left and the New Politics. Finally, the feminist emphasis on self-realization and the quest for a new identity was linked to other manifestations of the "new sensibility"—a general cultural trend, heavily infused with psychological and psychotherapeutic ideas, which may be called the "California syndrome" and which is best exemplified by the encounter movement. In all of these linkages, then, feminism appears much more than a movement for equal rights for women; rather, it has come to occupy a specific place in the cultural and political spectrum, giving it affinities (and, *ipso facto,* antipathies) to other cultural and political phenomena not intrinsically related to the issue of women's rights. Very broadly speaking, this cultural-political location is "on the left."

Both psychologically and politically, the critical camp seeks to realize a new identity for women. Politically, it seeks the legal ratification of the role of women as distinct from their traditional family roles, not only equal with men but in many respects identical with the latter (that is, all recognitions of differences between the sexes are defined as discriminatory), and also legal support for just about any alternative life-styles that individuals may choose to adopt. ERA has been a focus of much of this political activity, but (regardless of its fluctuating political fate) neither its success nor its demise will arrest the search for new causes on this agenda of equalization. Both psychologically and politically, the critical camp perceives the family as a deeply flawed institution.

The critical camp faces some built-in difficulties. First, since this camp has stressed the equality of all life-styles (read: all forms of cohabitation), it has found it difficult to avoid the label of "antifamily," and its attempts (belated) to get on the bandwagon of "profamily" sentiment have been unpersuasive.[4] Second, whatever its attempts at denial, the critical camp has appeared as hostile to children. Its enthusiasm for abortion and for day care have strengthened this impression, suggesting that here are people who want to prevent children from being born (to their opponents, of course, this means *killing* children), and, failing this, to dump children so that mothers can pursue their selfish programs of self-realization. The linkage of feminism with the neo-Malthusianism and the "zero growth" ideal of the New Left is relevant to this impression. If the critical camp has been widely perceived as anti-children, this also makes for its perception as anti-future: "liberation *now*"—and future generations be damned. It goes without saying that most representatives of the critical camp have vigorously denied such sentiments, but the perceptions are real nonetheless (and, one must admit, are not simply irrational, given the implications of the attitudes and positions of the critical camp). And third, there is a more subtle difficulty: The push for equality and self-realization has been above all a push of women into the world of work. This world, however, has become very problematic to many in it, men and women both. How are women to avoid enslavement in the "male" work ethic and its morality of selfishness?

A number of feminists have tried to deal with this third difficulty by saying that the drive for equality must not mean a "co-optation" of women into a "male" world of competitive self-destruction. Put differently, equality should not mean equal ulcers, equal cardiac failures, and so on. These considerations have led many feminists to identify with a broader notion of "liberation," with a push toward a more "humanistic" society as espoused by other radical and reformist (again, all basically "left") movements.[5] The trouble with this is that these movements have not been doing very well in America of late, so that feminism has come to be associated with political losers and discredited utopians. A deeper difficulty is that if these "left" transformations of society ever did come about, they would in all likelihood destroy the economic and social foundations for such "liberations" of women as have taken place, a point that, no doubt, is destined to be hotly debated in the years ahead and deserves the most assiduous attention of any responsible citizen.

The neo-traditionalist camp, whatever may be its positive value commitments, must be seen as essentially a backlash phenomenon.[6] It did not congeal as a visible entity on the cultural and political scene in the earlier period of feminist and other radical assaults on conventional morality. Thus, little was heard on the national scene of a conservative reaction in the 1960s (though, no doubt, there were many individuals who were dismayed). The appearance was that a growing number of Americans believed that some loosening of conventional morality was in order, that at least some of the new "liberating" thrusts were a good thing, and (perhaps most important of all) that the movements embodying these "liberations" were on the cutting edge of the future. There was virtually no opposition when, in 1972, the Supreme Court decided that an individual, married or single, had the right to obtain contraceptive information without "unwarranted governmental intrusion." The same lack of opposition greeted the

Family Planning Act, which, also in 1972, provided federal subsidization of birth-control clinics for all.

The galvanizing event for opposition came in 1973, when the Supreme Court barred the states from prohibiting abortions in the first trimester. Not only was this decision profoundly shocking for very large numbers of people, but it had immediate consequences of staggering magnitude. An avalanche of abortions followed the decision. Already in 1975 there were more than one million abortions, the majority of these performed on single women under twenty-five years of age. Thus, quite apart from repugnance against abortion as such, the decision was linked to the new sexual morality. In 1976 the Supreme Court further decided that abortion was a right of individual women, over which neither husband nor parent (except by delegation from the state) had a veto. This decision was perceived as touching on the very basis of the family as an "organic" entity over and beyond the individual. It should be noted that these truly revolutionary court decisions coincided with the period during which feminist rhetoric was becoming most strident, including the demand for total "reproductive freedom" for women.

At this juncture a vigorous antiabortion, or "pro-life," movement congealed, institutionally supported by the Catholic Church but by no means limited to Catholics. This also became the core of the "pro-family" movement, and the two causes coincided both in terms of organized activity and in the mind of the public. For example, *The Human Life Review*, founded in 1975 as a central organ of the antiabortion movement, from the beginning gave much space to general family issues. The protest was cultural as well as political: culturally as a mobilization against attitudes deemed to be anti-family; politically as a defense against moves to utilize the powers of law and government for the realization of such attitudes.

But while the neo-traditionalist camp was defensive in its origins, it soon went into an offensive stance. It also showed the capacity for very effective organization. The majority in the movement was, and continues to be, composed of parents of young children. Like the feminist movement, this, too, is a movement with many grass-roots branches combining into national organizations. By the same token (again, like the feminist movement), the latter are somewhat loose and compelled to reconcile sometimes divergent emphases. Local groups (going by names such as "Families in Action") are active in various causes, such as opposing the decriminalization of marijuana, monitoring libraries and TV programs for pornography, or opposing the public acceptance of homosexuality (as Anita Bryant did in Florida). Overarching these many local efforts, there is an alliance of national organizations: the National Right to Life Committee; "Stop ERA" (with Phyllis Schlafly as its main representative); "Happiness of Womanhood," or HOW (with auxiliary men's groups—of happy husbands, one surmises); "Feminine Anti-Feminists"; the League of Housewives; the National Pro-Family Coalition. Since 1978, when Schlafly's troops marched into a feminist-dominated women's conference in Houston, the opposition to ERA has been an important focus, and the political successes of this opposition have greatly encouraged the neo-traditionalist camp on other issues as well. In recent years, Moral Majority (the organization led by Jerry Falwell), the National Federation for Decency, and the Coalition for Better Television have captured public attention (and frequently caused public alarm). In sum, by the 1980 elections, the movement had powerful support from both state and national politicians, and it had succeeded in thoroughly frightening a lot of people. Since those elections, the movement has flexed a lot of political muscle (some of it, perhaps, exaggerated by awed media coverage). There were strong efforts to bypass the courts through congressional legislation against abortion; Senator Paul Laxalt, of Nevada, introduced the comprehensive Family Protection Act; and antiabortion riders were attached to various bills. The Family Policy Advisory Board exercised strong neo-traditionalist influence within the Reagan administration. And again, similar to the political fate of the feminist agenda, so too in the neo-traditionalist camp: regardless of the successes or the setbacks of the neo-traditionalist core concerns in the political arena, neither their success nor their demise will arrest the causes to which this alignment of groups is so deeply committed.

It is obvious that differing interests are in play here. What unites them? In terms of issues, there are mainly negative positions: *against* homosexuality and other sexual "revolutions"; *against* pornography, abortion, and ERA; as well as *against* other feminist equality causes (such as drafting women into the military). Subthemes on this negative agenda are opposition to forced busing of schoolchildren and opposition to "secular humanism" (some of it going back to the early 1960s, when the Supreme Court banned prayer in public schools). But beneath all these negative positions, it is very important to notice, there is a strong positive substance. People in this camp are *for* the traditional family and traditional roles within the family (between the sexes, between spouses, between the generations). They are *for* traditional notions of moral responsibility, not only in the areas of sexuality and family but over a wide range of social behavior. This affects such varied issues as the defense posture of the United States, policies toward welfare and crime, and attitudes toward the capitalist system. There is an important and powerful theme of American patriotism. In all of this, of course, the neo-traditionalist camp is in tune with a more ample conservative trend in the country.

As with the feminists, it is difficult to determine to what extent the neo-traditionalist movement has *caused* or has merely *legitimated* these cultural and political developments. Also as with the feminists, only relatively small numbers of people are active in organized groups. But, very obviously, there is a very much larger sector of the population that is in general agreement with the moral values of the neo-traditionalist camp, especially those values that espouse a traditional view of the family. It is also clear that many people, within and outside the organized groups, feel very intensely about these matters and see themselves as engaged in a historic battle with their adversaries. As Jo Ann Gasper (editor of *The Right Woman*) put it: "There is a war going on for the preservation of society and the pagans are already within the walls."[7]

But the neo-traditionalist camp faces some built-in tensions as well. There is a fundamental ambivalence about government in its positions. On the one hand, these people claim to be against government intervention in matters of private morality and family values. On the other hand, though, they do want government action on matters that concern them. The pornography issue reveals this ambivalence very sharply. But in the realm of the family, too, there is a tension between the position that state interference is undermining parental authority and the desire that the state help restore such authority. One might argue, from a detached vantage point, that parental authority that requires state support has already lost the battle. But, perhaps most fundamentally, the neo-traditionalist camp stands in tension with the realities of pluralism in America. It wants a public affirmation of moral values which, however widespread, are no longer *generally* held and are particularly no longer held in important elite sectors of

the society. Given the constitutional framework of the American
polity and the vocal adherence of the neo-traditionalists to this polity,
this is a serious difficulty. One may further ask whether these moral
values were *ever* held as widely as the neo-traditionalists believe or
whether, on the contrary, they may not be holding an idealized picture
of the American past. We strongly suspect that the latter is the case,
even though it is plausible to maintain that pluralism has greatly
increased in recent decades.

The professional camp differs from the other two camps just
discussed in that its character is the result not of ideology but of quite
hard vested interests. Needless to say, this is *not* to imply that professionals are only out for themselves or do not hold their views sincerely
—not at all. But the core motives in this camp are of a more practical
and *ipso facto* less ideological quality. All the same, if only because of
the professional training of these people, there are common assumptions and values in this camp too.

What is more, no more than the other two camps is this one to be
seen as a monolithic entity.[8] Rather, it has many components, some in
the public sector, some in the private. There are the older family professions, the heirs of "doing good" through social services and programs, both government-funded and private. Many of the people in
this group hold social-work degrees. Then there are the newer counseling professionals, whose approach is more therapeutic and educational than directly problem-solving. This includes the whole complex
of "family education," often linked to the school system. Then there
are researchers and theoreticians in academia. Then there are "family
advocates" and "child advocates," many of them lawyers (of the "public interest" type), most of them with a legal emphasis even when not
lawyers themselves. Finally, there are the politically oriented people
in policy institutes and seminars, such as those geared into action during the Carter administration. Obviously, all these people do not
speak with one voice, but certain commonalities are there all the
same.

The relation between the family and professionals has always
been difficult. There is a built-in tension between the belief in the
sacrosanct nature of the family and the claims of professional expertise. This tension goes back to the beginning of social work, in the
nineteenth century, but it increased with the ascendancy of professionals since the New Deal legislation and their augmentation through

the "Great Society" programs of the 1960s. It is fair to say that all this legislative history has been "pro-family" in intention, in that its avowed purpose was to strengthen the quality of family life. Already the Social Security Act of 1935 did this, by providing public help upon the loss of job, disability, or death of the breadwinner. So did the early welfare legislation, especially Aid to Dependent Children. And the same intention was undoubtedly present in the Great Society programs. But, intentionally or not, this body of laws (making up, in the aggregate, what we now know as the American welfare state) provided powerful handles for the intervention by professionals in the lives of individual families.

By the nature of modern bureaucracy, there is a tendency for such programs to proliferate. Ironically, some programs arise to deal with the unintended consequences of previous programs. For example, public housing was designed to strengthen families by giving them decent housing. Compared with where most of these families lived before, the aim of providing decent housing was quite successful. But, in the process, there was a disruption of the informal "support networks" of the old neighborhoods, creating new problems and the demand for new programs to cope with them, ranging from the problem of providing day care for the children of working mothers to the "treatment" of juvenile crime. The professionals, of course, have an interest in defining situations in such a way that their services appear necessary. Not surprisingly, this is what they did, with the family increasingly held to be incompetent to deal with its own problems. In the 1950s this alleged incompetence of the family was seen to be psychological. The radical critiques of the family in the 1960s (in which, incidentally, many professionals shared) focused more on social and economic issues, as did the Great Society programs for the poor. Despite all these efforts, the family problems to be remedied by all this intervention increased, rather than diminished. Professionals could readily cite statistics to "prove" their point—such as the rising rates of divorce, single-parent households, working mothers with young children, illegitimacy, runaway children, teen-age pregnancies, teen-age drinking and drug addiction, teen-age crime and suicide, child abuse and spouse battering, learning disabilities, and old people living alone. Each of these rates, supposedly, pointed up an urgent problem. And each problem, supposedly, was beyond the capacity of families to handle by themselves, thus necessitating continuing and new professional interventions.

What are some of the common perspectives on the family to be found in the professional camp? First, there is what may be called the "anti-organic" view. The basic unit of society is the *individual*, who has certain basic needs. Families provide social services to meet these needs. Sometimes they may do this well, but in principle the same needs could also be filled by other institutions: the state, professional agencies, and so on.[9] Second, in this view families are indeed providing *more* social services to dependent members as against other "service delivery" agencies—but not necessarily *better* services. This view is buttressed by references to families that are not capable of dealing with their problems and of individuals who have been harmed by their relatives, as in the areas of child abuse and "spouse battering."[10]

There is also a common sociological perspective in terms of the broad societal changes that have supposedly produced this family incompetence. We have looked at some of this sociology in the preceding chapter. It is argued that the changes brought about by industrialization, urbanization, and immigration have all tended to weaken the family's capacity to cope. Supposedly, the family has been particularly weakened in its capacity to care for its dependent members: small children, the handicapped, the sick, and the old. Because of a variety of structural changes—lower birth rates, decrease in size (that is, the decline of the extended family), instability (brought on by divorce, illegitimacy, and the hardships of single-parent households), the increase in the number of working women with small children, and rising expectations (especially by women)—the "pool" of potential care givers within the family has shrunk. But if the family is increasingly incompetent to deal with its dependent members' needs, there are also more subtle but nonetheless real needs of the nondependent individuals: psychological needs, educational needs, and the like. These needs take on a special form among the poor as well as ethnic and racial minorities. When all these needs are added up, the demand for professional help becomes formidable. As one author puts it, "We must deal with a more complicated reality, which includes proposals for mandatory daycare for children of welfare recipients, the licensing of all new parents, the diagnosis of 'behavioral disorders' in preschool populations, required parental education in public high schools, and the enrollment of infants in school-affiliated programs."[11] One does not have to be a member of the Moral Majority to recoil with terror from this Orwellian vista!

But even in its less totalitarian forms, this view of the family is inevitably antagonistic to what most people have always thought about this institution. The disenfranchisement of families by professionals in alliance with government bureaucrats becomes, in principle at least, unlimited: The professional-bureaucratic complex can legitimately intervene whenever the needs of any category of individuals could be better met outside than within the family. Such intervention, of course, is much more likely in the families of the poor, who, by definition, have more "problems"—and fewer means to resist the intrusions by the expert "helpers." The disenfranchisement of families reaches a certain logical climax when "parenting" is perceived as a paraprofessional role, for which the true professionals must offer "parent education" (even if they forgo the aforementioned desire to license individuals to become parents in the first place).

Since about 1975 there has appeared a more positive tone about the family among professionals. Some of it may be the result of research findings indicating that the family is a more resilient institution than many had thought.[12] Some of it may also be a politically defensive response to the mounting clamor of the "pro-family" movement. In any case, one may speak of a new group of professional champions of the family.[13] The family is now accepted, even celebrated, as the "basic social service." But it continues to be maintained that the family is under severe social stress. This stress is structural— that is, grounded in basic societal structures. It follows that, unless these structures are changed, help for families will remain superficial and ultimately futile. This approach (most characteristic of the Carnegie Council for Children) now links help to families to a comprehensive political agenda of a clearly "liberal-left" bent.[14] A "comprehensive family policy," of which the society is supposedly in urgent need, now includes attacks on the problems of income distribution, unemployment, environmental deterioration, as well as attacks on outmoded moral values in such matters as sex roles and the work ethic. It is not altogether clear what should be done with the concrete problems of families "in the meantime"—that is, until this great revolution is accomplished—but one gathers that the authors in question are much more interested in the grand revolutionary design than in the petty difficulties that bother most people. One revealing category in the discussion of family policy in these circles is that of "universal entitlements"—that is, a legally guaranteed equality of access of all families to the basic resources of the society.

There are great difficulties inherent in the perspectives of the professional camp. There is, first of all, a problem with the data on which this camp bases its position. The sociological interpretations about the decline of the family are open to question, and indeed have been questioned. There is a further empirical embarrassment in the fact that all the alleged weaknesses of the family are supposed to have become much worse in precisely the same period in which professional intervention has increased the most, leading some to the awful suspicion that the professionally prescribed remedies may actually be part of the disease. There is also a built-in tension between the habitual interventionism of the professionals and a professional ethos of respect for the values of other people. This tension is most acutely felt when the interventions are into the lives of culturally different groups, such as blacks and Hispanics, who fiercely resent what they consider to be some sort of cultural imperialism if not downright racism. Finally, the new champions of the family appear highly suspect in their enthusiasm for an institution for which many of them had little use before. Are they more interested in their own revolutionary scenarios or in the real needs of families today? We do not wish to make any pejorative judgments about the motives of individuals—let it be stipulated that everyone in this field is motivated by the most humane concerns. But the objective consequence of this notion of a "comprehensive family policy" is to harness the family to political purposes that, in themselves, have nothing whatever to do with the concrete problems that trouble ordinary people. One may add, of course, that the enthusiasm for radical social change, and also the overall approval of professional and state interventionism, runs counter to prevailing cultural and political trends.

The three camps we have been sketching in this chapter are, as we have seen, not exactly comparable. Two are defined in terms of ideological positions (antithetical ones, to be sure), one in terms of scientific and professional expertise. Also, the critical and professional camps have a good deal of affinity with each other (especially if one looks at the more restrained segments of the critical camp), and they have overlapping personnel. The neo-traditionalist camp is in sharp opposition to both of the other camps. All this will already have become clear. What remains to do here is to give some indications of how these camps relate to the class dynamics of American society.

In the preceding chapter, we drew attention to the missionary work of the bourgeoisie as it tried to "uplift" the lower classes to its own supposedly superior values and way of life—the Major Barbara complex, as it were. There continues to be a strong element of middle-class evangelism in the "helping" efforts of family professionals—except for the fact, of course, that the *contents* to be evangelized have changed greatly. Professionals, needless to say, always belong to the upper middle class—and their clients, especially in the public sector, are generally below them in socioeconomic status. There is by now ample evidence how allegedly scientific and professional judgments about lower-class people are shot through with prejudices and misunderstandings due to this class difference.[15] In the case of the family, there is cruel irony in this. In the 1950s, during the so-called "family renascence," middle-class social workers and other professionals were preaching the virtues of domesticity to their female clients: The good mother, it was maintained, stayed at home and devoted herself full time to the tasks of child rearing. Lower-class mothers who were economically able to do so were all too willing to follow such advice (which accorded with their own preferences anyway)—only to be berated in the 1960s and 1970s by the same professionals, who had now had their consciousness raised by the new feminist movement, for surrendering their autonomy as persons to the slavery of the household! And those lower-class women, unable or unwilling to follow these sequentially contradictory counsels, could at least be burdened with guilt—for being bad mothers in the first period and for being inauthentic persons in the second. Whatever one's general attitude to the propagation of bourgeois virtues, one must observe that it would help if the propagators did not change their minds about the nature of virtue every few years!

Generally speaking, of course, middle-class parents are in a much better position to resist disenfranchisement than those in the lower classes. The latter do not have the financial means, the recourse to legal or other advice, the verbal and organizational skills, and in some cases the plain self-confidence, to tell professional intruders to keep away from them and their children; if they are on welfare or subject for other reasons to state coercion, they have almost no defenses at all.

These people have become the powerless victims of professional-bureaucratic programs allegedly designed for their and their children's benefit, and they have often come under the total tutelage of various agencies with the arrogated and often state-enforced right to run their lives for them. It is no wonder that this has bred fierce resentments, most vocally among blacks and Hispanics in this country.

But the class implications of the three aforementioned camps are not exhausted by this continuing attempt of middle-class people to impose their values on other classes. There is another aspect, which we must at least briefly refer to. That is the aspect of the *new* middle class that has been on the rise in Western industrial societies in recent decades, commonly called the New Class, although "knowledge class" would probably be the better term to use.[16] Put simply, these are the people who derive their livelihood from the production, distribution, and administration of symbolic knowledge. They are not just the so-called intellectuals, who may be seen as an upper crust in this new stratum. Rather, the expanding "knowledge industry" (as the economist Fritz Machlup first called it) contains large numbers of people who could by no reasonable criterion be called intellectuals: the vast educational system, the therapeutic-"helping" complex, sizable portions of government bureaucracy, the media and publishing industries, and others. What these all have in common is that bodies of symbolic knowledge (as distinct from the knowledge of, say, the physical scientist or the marketing expert) are to be applied to indoctrinate ("educate"), inspire ("help"), and plan for other people. This group, certainly numbered in the millions in America today, fulfills the category of "class" in a number of specifics: It has a particular relation to the economic system (one important aspect of this relation is that a large portion of this group is either on the public payroll or is publicly subsidized), has particular collective interests (the most important being the maintenance and, if possible, expansion of the welfare state), and also has a particular subculture that is more than a direct expression of its vested interests. As especially Irving Kristol has persuasively argued, this knowledge class is engaged in a conflict with the old "ruling class," which is the business class.[17] Many events in American politics of the past twenty years or so make much better sense when one sees them in the context of this class struggle—which, like class struggles in the past, is primarily over power and privilege (and, to a lesser extent, over status, or prestige).

The details of this fascinating development cannot be pursued here. But it is important for the present topic. The professional camp is a "knowledge class" phenomenon of almost pristine purity—and therefore the imperialism of this camp is yet another expression of the power drive of this class. The critical camp, on the other hand, reflects ideas and movements that belong solidly in the subculture of this new class. Feminism, New Left, and New Politics, the encounter movement—all these are class-specific phenomena, all are products of the new class and have constituencies that primarily belong to the latter. If this is understood, the neo-traditionalist camp, whatever else it may be, is *also* a phenomenon of this class conflict. There is an unmistakable undertone of class resentment and class hostility in the rhetoric of the neo-traditionalists. Here are people who are fed up with the pretensions and the power aspirations of the New Class, and they are a politically potent alliance of *old*-middle-class ("business class"), lower-middle-class, and working-class components. In this perspective, the current war over the family is but one battle in a much larger conflict between classes in America (and also in other Western societies). It should be added that to say this is *not* to suggest that this conflict must be fought to the bitter end, with one class crushing the other. Indeed, barring catastrophic developments, such an outcome is unlikely. In Western democratic societies, both culture and politics have been marked by a mixture of conflict and compromise between classes, and this is the most likely scenario here also.

# EXCURSUS

## Goshtalk, Femspeak, and the Battle of Language

At the conclusion of his delightful history of expurgated literature in the English language *Dr. Bowdler's Legacy* (New York: Atheneum, 1969), Noel Perrin expresses the opinion that bowdlerism, the practice of changing language so as not to offend delicate ears, is a perennial phenomenon. He notes that there has been a great change in the canons of delicacy in recent times and that language which would have been utterly shocking some decades ago has now become commonplace. He then writes: "What then? Then it may be time for the new cycle to begin. Or a different cycle may by then be in full swing. Delicacy has never died, and never will. . . . It merely takes new forms." As an example of such a new form, Perrin cites the language of race: "If the rise of 'black' continues, 'Negro' itself may become obscene; perhaps it already has. If so, those of us who avoid the word will not seem prudish to ourselves, but sensitive—just as Americans in 1875 who avoided the word 'crotch,' say, felt perceptive."

Perrin's prediction has been validated beyond his wildest expectations. In the 1960s, of course, while Perrin was writing his book, America and other Western countries witnessed a veritable explosion of obscene language. It is important to recall that the Berkeley student rebellion, the *mater et magistra* of all the later student uprisings, began as the so-called Free Speech Movement—and "free speech" meant, among other things, the right to the public use of language previously deemed obscene. Archaeologists sifting through the literary debris of our age and finding themselves confused by the multiplicity of sources will have a good analytic tool for determining which source belongs to which side in various political battles, a tool for what historical scholarship calls "form criticism." The challengers to the status quo habitually used obscenity; their adversaries avoided it. Since much of the verbal outpouring of the mid-twentieth century will be very hard to understand a few centuries hence, this will be a very useful analytic tool for future scholars with the unenviable professional task of making sense of it.

Now, if anything is clear, it is that obscenity is a relative and socially constructed category. What is obscene in one place is ordinary language in another. In modern Western societies this has been especially true of different social classes: The language of one class is frequently not only difficult to understand or funny but downright shocking to another class. An important element of class subculture is class language, the details of which, of course, differ from country to country (England presumably wins the prize, at least among Western societies, for having raised class language to a level of obsessive perfection). And of course each such class language has a history which, if known, explains its peculiar features. What is more, there is nothing "natural" to these linguistic features; rather, they are the result of social constructions which, in principle, could have come out very differently. Thus, if one scrutinizes what was involved in the "free speech" issues of the 1960s, one comes on a surprisingly limited number of linguistic items, most of them being the substitution of short Anglo-Saxon synonyms for sexual intercourse and defecation. These, in addition to the profane use of religious terms, were also what troubled the expurgators of the nineteenth century.

A historian three or four centuries from now may well be puzzled by this: Why should it be shocking to say, "John fucked Mary," but perfectly proper to say, "John made love to Mary"? Do not the two verbal expressions refer to the same activity? Why, then, should the two synonyms have such different emotional, even moral connotations? Let us, across the generations and from the other side of the grave, instruct our future historian in some elementary facts about language (and let us hope that positivism will not have triumphed to the point that our explanation will be incomprehensible): The two verbal expressions are synonyms only in an instrumental sense; they are not synonyms at all in the symbolic freight they carry; and (most important instruction) language is as much a symbolic as an instrumental vehicle of communication between human beings. Now, in this particular instance the history leading up to this symbolic dichotomy is well known. One of its most masterful expositions (covering much more than language, to be sure) may be found in Norbert Elias' great work *The Civilizing Process* (originally published in German in 1936). Elias demonstrates how the bourgeoisie, in everything from table manners to speech, progressively "refined" life—that is, imposed controls on the expression of the "grosser" biological aspects of human activity. In Freudian terms, to which Elias gives credence, this has been a process of comprehensive "repression." All purely organic expressions have been subject to this process (one need only refer here to the general bourgeois cult of cleanliness), but the sexual and gastrointestinal systems of the human organism have been especially important targets. This "civilizing process," as Elias calls it, has had extremely visible behavioral aspects—from the complexities of bourgeois cutlery to the institution of the toilet—but, not surprisingly, all this "proper" behavior has developed its correlate in "proper" language. As suitably socialized bourgeois children refrained from defecating or urinating anywhere except in the "private" rooms set aside for these activities, so were they taught to speak about these activities, if at all, in the Latinate circumlocutions pounded into them by parents, tutors, and schoolmasters.

The bourgeoisie was an international class. The bourgeois revolution, begun in England and France, became an international movement. So did the "civilizing" mission of bourgeois culture. While, of course, this culture took various forms in various countries, its core features could be found everywhere. This was certainly the case in the matter of "proper" language. The "proper" circumlocutions were different in, say, American English, French, German, or Hungarian, but in all these languages children learned that "dirty" talk earned them parental anger, slaps, or worse. (Has any diligent historian made an inventory of words and expressions for which unfortunate bourgeois children had their mouths washed out with soap, often enough literally?) Regrettably, it cannot be our purpose here to delve more deeply into the comparative sociology of bourgeois language. Suffice it to say that the American bourgeoisie, or middle class, produced its own canons of linguistic propriety, rigorously enforced by an alliance of family, church, and school upon generations of children growing up to be respectable ladies and gentlemen (in the bourgeois, as against the old aristocratic, sense of these terms—aristocrats, by the way, always prided themselves on their freedom from these silly bourgeois inhibitions, but that is another story). Perhaps the great American Midwest developed this "nice" middle-class culture to its fullest perfection—generations of well-scrubbed and clean-talking boys and girls growing up in that vast territory between the Alleghenies and the Rockies, sneered and snapped at by the intellectuals of the two coasts (H. L. Mencken may be taken as the prototype of these cultured despisers of Middle-American rectitude) but ever again emulated by the unwashed multitudes aspiring toward middle-class status —learning in the process both to wash their feet and to wash out their mouths.

This world of middle-class culture still exists; indeed, of late it has become more militant. Perhaps, even in these times of austerity, some generous foundation will fund a team of diligent linguists, so that they can draw us a map of this culture. In its rawest form, the map will show the frequency distribution over the national territory of the use of the traditional circumlocutions. There still are all these people who say "gosh" instead of "God," "heck" instead of "hell," "darn" instead of "damn"—and who go about happily "making love" or at least "going out with" each other, who "step out for a moment" or "go to see a man about a dog" (not to mention the females of the species, who, assuming that they are not "in the family way," still "fall off the roof" every month). Such a map, arduous though its compilation would be, could greatly enhance our understanding of the social and cultural dynamics of the country. It will be a map of what we would venture to call *Goshtalk*. And, we would hypothesize, the map will also tell us a lot about other values and attitudes of which this language is symbolic, concerning issues ranging from national defense to the proper allocation of household chores. What is more, if our observations in the preceding chapter about the current class conflict in America are correct, the map will also indicate the points of strongest resistance against the power bid of the new knowledge class, which, more than any other major stratum (we leave aside such subgroups as professional soldiers, sailors, or streetwalkers), is the class that habitually "talks dirty."

In retrospect, as we have suggested before, the social and cultural eruptions of the 1960s marked the advent of this new class on the stage of American society. The Free Speech Movement, at Berkeley, in all its militant obscenity, was the opening salvo of this sociocultural warfare. It is hardly surprising that the counterrevolution takes on linguistic forms as well. The Goshtalkers have become enraged too. Their rage, of course, covers a considerable spectrum of issues (the list of concerns of the Moral Majority reflects the spectrum quite accurately). The campaign against pornography is the clearest expression of the linguistic symbolism involved in the current class struggle. To be sure, pornography is an issue in itself for these people. But the issue also stands for, symbolically, a wide range of other concerns. "Cleaning up America" constitutes an agenda that transcends this or that anti-pornographic campaign; the "clean America" toward which such campaigns aspire is an ideological whole, of which "clean language" is one of the important symbols.

This understanding of the situation goes far in explaining the zeal invested in anti-pornographic activities. A new bowdlerism is loose in the land. Vigilante bands pick through school libraries in search of offending books, picket motion-picture theaters, threaten television producers with boycotts, and bombard public officials with angry postcards. The Supreme Court, very sensibly, has spoken of different "community standards" in the definition of pornography or the toleration thereof. Peoria is not Manhattan. What must be understood, though, is that these community standards are not just a matter of geography. More basically, they are a matter of class, and the geography itself (as in the linguistic map we would like the National Endowment for the Humanities to fund in the interest of national consciousness raising) is primarily a function of class distribution. Those who perceive the new bowdlerism as being but one short step away from a fascist America, with book burnings moving up fast to the incineration of dissidents, are undoubtedly paranoid. As with most paranoias, though, there is a kernel of truth in this perception: Watch out, baby: These people are after much more than the way you talk! Along with smutty books and topless movies, they want to eradicate all sorts of other abominations of the new-class revolution, and while the success of these efforts would probably fit the notion of "fascism" rather poorly, it would certainly eventuate in a society very different from that heralded so fervently by the prophets of the Age of Aquarius.

The reassertion of Goshtalk and all it represents is an important feature of the war over the family that concerns us here. Imagine them facing each other, two typical representatives of the critical and the neo-traditionalist camps: It is as difficult to imagine the latter stepping out to take a shit as to imagine the former asking coyly to go to the bathroom. Pornography is a pivotal issue for the neo-traditionalists, because they correctly (albeit instinctively) understand that the language of their adversaries stands for much more than a rebellion against trivial conventions. Thus the battles fought over the new bowdlerism are skirmishes in the war over the family and, by the same token, episodes in the unfolding class struggle. Goshtalk is the language of an embattled bourgeoisie locked in conflict *not* with the working class so fondly fantasied about by academic Marxists (indeed, the American working class, except for carefully defined, all-male situations, is notoriously fastidious in its language) but with the rising knowledge class and its drive for power. Ideas are weapons. So is language. Linguistic victories are translated into political victories, and vice versa. Each book removed from a school library, each soap opera successfully purged from the television screen, is a battle won in the neo-traditionalist cause. And all participants in these events sense this, even if they lack the social-scientific concepts to describe their intuitions accurately. (It is ironic, incidentally, that most social scientists commenting on the same events have missed the point altogether. But that is yet another story.)

The political use of language is mirrored in perfect symmetry—with geometric precision, one might say—on the other side of the battle lines. Here, too, an aggressive and self-righteous bowdlerism is hard at work. The analogue of Goshtalk is the language which feminists are striving to impose on the public. Let us call it *Femspeak.*

Hardly anyone, of course, likes to admit the sociological relativity or the political function of the language deemed "proper" in a particular camp to which one belongs. Our Goshtalkers must suppose that their notions of what constitutes decent language are self-evident, natural if not God-given, and that therefore those who offend against it must do so out of malicious, indeed sinful, motives. Femspeakers similarly obfuscate, to themselves as much as to others, the real character of their own linguistic campaigns. Indeed, the very phrase "feminist language" is likely to arouse puzzlement if not resentment on the part of those who believe in the rightness of this language. In their mind, of course, there is no such thing; there is only the correction of the "sexist" language used by others; it is *the others'* language that is political language (and the alleged politics of sexism are dissected in endless analytic exercises by feminist authors); *their own* language, preferably called "inclusive language," is supposedly nothing but the cleansing of speech from the nefarious political manipulations of the sexist oppressor. As with all bowdlerizers, they, too, set about the job of cleaning everyone's mouth out with soap in a spirit of grim, unquestioning moral conviction.

As with the fighters against obscenity, these feminists are after a surprisingly small number of linguistic items. What is mostly at issue is the generic use of the masculine gender in standard English (the whole issue, of course, takes other forms or does not exist at all in other languages). Supposedly, saying "he" when one means a person of either sex, or using terms such as "man" or "mankind" to denote the human species as a whole, denigrates women and linguistically supports male dominance. Since the list of linguistic offenses is quite short, it is not difficult to observe the relevant tabus once one has grasped the principle. One just has to say or write "he or she" (perhaps randomly varied with "she or he" to avoid, heaven forbid, the suggestion that the sequence of pronouns has hierarchical significance), to use such "inclusive" terms as "the human race" or "humankind," or to employ neologisms like "chairperson" or "repairperson"). One's *bona fides* as a non-sexist is thus easily established, to the point where even an occasional stumbling relapse into standard usage may be graciously forgiven. Observing an individual—an academic, say, addressing a faculty meeting—carefully making his or her way through a minefield of possible lapses into the offending terms is a touching spectacle. It reminds one of nothing as much as the spectacle of a reformed drunk gingerly talking nice while giving testimony to his reformation at a Salvation Army rally.

All those feminist authors, of course, claim that standard usage has always been experienced by women as demeaning or excluding them. The evidence for this is typically anecdotal: some little girl, say, who thought that she was not invited to a party because the masculine pronoun was used in the language of the invitation. Let it be stipulated that little girls—and, we hasten to add, little boys—often have difficulties understanding the abstractions of adult talk. This is due to what child psychologists have called the concreteness of the child's thought. The evidence for the alleged suffering by adult women as a result of this particular feature of English is, at best, very dubious indeed. Virtually all of it is a retrojection into the past of what present-day feminists feel or have made themselves feel when they encounter the allegedly sexist elements in the language. These feelings, to be sure, are real enough. To admit this, however, in no way implies agreement with the elaborate theories of linguistic sexism erected upon them.

Sexist language is an invention of the feminist movement. Attributing it to Shakespeare, to the King James Version of the Bible, or to the way millions of people talk in those sectors of the society where feminist agitation has failed to make inroads is as meaningful as attributing blasphemous intent to an individual who says "goddamit"—or, for that matter, to attribute homicidal intentions to someone who says "drop dead." Taken literally, this is a theory that elevates infantile misunderstandings to the level of hermeneutics. But it would be a mistake to take this literally. It matters little, in the final analysis, that here is a theory of language that rests on little or nothing beyond the emotions of the theorists. What matters a lot is that the theory legitimates a linguistic offensive that is part of a general political strategy. In this strategy, every masculine pronoun purged from a text, every insertion of "person" as a generic suffix, constitutes a symbolic victory in the larger struggle. Once again, everyone involved in these affairs intuitively understands what is going on—which is precisely why emotions run so high on matters that to an outside and uninvolved observer might appear deafeningly trivial.

An example may help to clarify the point. (The example will, no doubt, offend the delicate ears of feminists. But if delicacy had been a strong concern of ours, we would never have started writing this book!) English is virtually alone among modern Western languages in not distinguishing the forms of address appropriate between more or less intimate individuals. Thus French distinguishes between people to whom one says, respectively, *tu* and *vous* (and even has the verb *tutoyer*, untranslatable into English, to denote the former case), Spanish has *tu* and *usted*, and so on. In modern Italian the intimate form of address is *tu*, while more distant individuals are addressed as *lei* (which happens to be the third person plural). Sometime in the 1930s Mussolini made a speech in which he castigated the use of *lei* as an effete, indeed effeminate mode of language. The purpose of the Fascist revolution, he said, was to restore vigor and virility to the Italian people. The good Fascist was direct in language as in action. The good Fascist, therefore, did not say *lei;* instead, he said *voi* (the second person plural). Now, from a philological or semantic point of view, this was sheer nonsense. The use of *lei* had never struck anyone as effete or effeminate; it was, quite simply, standard Italian. But, needless to say, the situation changed dramatically after Mussolini's speech. From then on, everyone became highly conscious of the matter (if you will, everyone's consciousness was raised). The use of *lei* became a sign of reactionary, perhaps even subversive, attitudes. The use of *voi*, preferably in a self-righteous and highly audible manner, was evidence that the speaker (or writer) was a Fascist in good standing. Indeed, it became the verbal equivalent of the Fascist salute. Put simply, what before Mussolini's pronouncement had been an apolitical and unreflective element of the common language now forced itself on everyone's consciousness as a highly political symbol.

Feminists, eager to wrap themselves in the mystique of the civil rights movement, like to compare so-called sexist language with the linguistic etiquette used to denigrate blacks. The comparison does not withstand close scrutiny. The language etiquette of race relations in America, especially in the South, was understood by everyone *at the time* as having the purpose of humiliating blacks. Whites understood this, as did blacks, and outside observers wrote about it as far back as the nineteenth century. Thus, to call adult blacks by their first names or to deny them the use of such honorific titles as "Mister" and "Miss" was part and parcel of a linguistic degradation ceremony (to use Harold Garfinkel's apt phrase) that was in the consciousness of all participants in the situation. Racist language, in other words, was *not* an invention of the civil rights movement, retrojected into the past prior to the advent of that movement. If one wants to stay within the context of American English, a better comparison would be one suggested by the aforementioned failure of English to distinguish between intimate and distant forms of address. Imagine a movement arising in America with the avowed purpose of creating greater intimacy between all members of society. Let us call it the Intimatist movement. One of the theorists of this movement writes a book developing the point that the use of "you" to address both one's closest friends and the most casual acquaintances is one of the most dehumanizing characteristics of American speech: A language that fails to distinguish such fundamental differences between human relationships, this theorist tells us, is not only a symptom of alienation but an active cause of it. Therefore, the good Intimatist never says "you"; instead, he (or she) always says "thou." Nonsense? Of course—from a philological or semantic point of view. From a political point of view, though, it will cease to be nonsense in the exact degree to which the Intimatist movement gains influence and power in the society. We will not pursue this little fantasy any farther—the censorship imposed on textbooks and government handbooks, the boycotts directed against allegedly alienating language in the public media, not to mention the new avenues of employment for retired Episcopalian priests giving rush courses in Elizabethan syntax and writing guidelines for editors—"lift up thy voice like a trumpet, and shew my people their transgression"—as to the outside observer, he shuddereth and keepeth his tongue in dreadful silence. . . .

And so, here too, the bowdlerizers are let loose in the land (not the Intimatists; we're back with the feminists). Like their neo-traditionalist cousins in faith (albeit a different faith), they rummage through school libraries, scrutinize television programs with inquisitorial alertness, harass nonconformists in classrooms or political meetings, and try to mobilize editors of books and periodicals in the service of "proper" language. The more ambitious among them invade the nursery with their language tabus (a whole new set of linguistic no-nos for the toddlers of the knowledge class to learn) and rewrite the classics in their deplorable idiom. And (how could it be otherwise, given the state of religion in our time?) there is a new phalanx of Malcolm Muggeridge's category of demented clerics translating the Bible and the Christian liturgy into the language of *Ms.* magazine. All of this activity, of course, takes place in a spirit of unquestioning and self-righteous certitude. Bowdlerizers are not given to skepticism, moderation, or humility.

"Non-inclusive language," then, is the pornography of the critical camp in the war over the family. Actually, we need not quarrel with *this* particular phrase. It does indeed "include" some—the activists and the fellow travellers of one camp; by the same token, both symbolically and behaviorally, it "excludes" those on the other side.

Both Goshtalk and Femspeak include *and* exclude. The basic purpose of all ideologically charged language is to draw boundaries, and if possible to expand these boundaries. As we have pointed out before, the same boundaries, to a considerable extent, are also boundaries of class. The expansion of Femspeak beyond its original more or less sectarian circles, therefore, must be understood as part of the cultural imperialism of the new knowledge class, seeking to impose its language, values, and political control over other classes in the society.

Probably it would serve no useful purpose to enter in detail into the linguistic contributions of the third camp discussed in the preceding chapter, the professional camp. Since that camp is less overtly political, its use of language is much less militant. There is no real equivalent of pornography and therefore of bowdlerizing in this camp. However, there is one important linguistic feature of this particular encampment that should at least be mentioned, and that is the obscurantist use of allegedly scientific terms. The two major sciences from which professionals in the family field draw most of their language are sociology and psychology. Both have been disciplines with luxuriant growths of esoteric neologisms, which are appropriated by long and sustained study (cynical observers might say that this appropriation of a secret language is one of the major goals of graduate study in sociology and psychology) and are typically incomprehensible to the outsider. This very fact has a political function. It enhances the claims of the professional to superior wisdom and therefore to status, high income, and possibly even political power in specific societal areas. Professional language also draws boundaries, though they are not ideological ones: The boundaries are between the professional insiders and the laity outside. Doctors used to speak Latin so that their patients would not understand them. Sociologese and psychologese serve roughly the same purpose. One difference is that today there are millions of college students taking sociology and psychology courses. These people acquire at least a smattering of the language of these disciplines and, up to a point, acquire along with the language the capacity to interpret their own experience in its terms. Thus the laity, at least in college-educated America, suffers from "relative deprivation" and "regressive reactions," experiences "affective cathexis" and "libidinal displacement," and hungers for "role models" and "love objects." It may be doubted whether any of this linguistic dexterity helps them in the day-to-day problems they face in their personal lives. As far as the war over the family is concerned, the major function of professional language has been the aforementioned legitimation of professional ambitions for privilege and power—a very dubious contribution from the viewpoint of everyone else.

The relationship between language and society is dialectical. That is, language reflects social reality; language also shapes social reality. This dialectical character of language becomes especially clear in situations of political conflict such as the one that concerns us here. This should be understood by any analyst of the situation. Such understanding may also be helpful as one tries to find one's own linguistic stance amid the clamor of clashing jargons and ideologies. The final aim of this book is to find a reasonable middle ground amid the current alignments in the war over the family. This aim also determines our linguistic stance: We are tired of all the varieties of bullshit that have assailed us in recent years. We believe that a rational and humane view of the family is essential for the future of mankind. We even believe (most audacious article of faith) that sociologists should write in English.

# 3

# Contemporary
# Issues

There are many issues, in the political sense of that term, that can be seen as part of the contemporary debate over the family. Some of these (such as, for instance, issues related to the care of children) have been seen as pertaining to the family for a long time; others (such as the current linkage by some of concern for the family with a policy of income redistribution) would not previously have been seen in this context. It is also clear that here, as in any other area of social life, the politicization of issues tends to polarize and to do away with nuances: Politics, especially politics in a democracy, tends toward bold, simple propositions, around which people can mobilize for action. Also, politics allows issues to become symbolic of interests that are not necessarily related to them; we have already made the point that some of the issues in the current war over the family are symptoms of deeper disjunctions and conflicts in American society, especially disjunctions and conflicts related to class. Thus it can be argued that the political struggle over the Equal Rights Amendment has been symbolic in a fundamental way of the conflict between the new "knowledge class" and other classes in the society, a conflict that in itself has little if anything to do with the rights of women. It is not possible in this chapter to deal exhaustively with all these issues. What we will do instead is discuss some of the most central issues, putting them into the context of the previously discussed ideological alignments. At this juncture we will hold back on our own view of these matters, leaving that for later presentation; in other words, at this juncture our main concern is description and sociological "placement" of salient "family issues."

An underlying issue, recurring in just about any discussion of the family today, is that of "gender roles." By this, of course, is meant the roles that society assigns to men and women. The debate is over the correct understanding of what these roles are and, more hotly, over what they ought to be.[1]

Once again, it pays to be sensitive to the implications of language. It is noteworthy that in an earlier period social scientists used the phrase "sex roles" for precisely the same set of questions. For example, anthropologists would discuss in great detail the differences in "sex roles" between, say, American society and this or that traditional culture. Since the advent of the new feminist movement, the phrase "gender roles" has become more favored. Why? The answer, we think, is quite easy. "Sex" is an essentially biological term, while "gender" is a term previously used mainly in connection with grammar. To say "sex roles," then, might be construed as implying that these roles are based on biological differences between men and women (though, it should be stressed, that this was certainly not the intention of the aforementioned anthropologists; quite to the contrary). To say "gender roles," on the other hand, immediately suggests that the role differences between men and women are just as arbitrary as the assignment of gender in many human languages. After all, even the most dedicated feminist will admit that the respective physiologies of the two sexes are not arbitrarily imposed by societal fiat. But it is certainly arbitrary that the French language assigns the masculine gender to the sun and the feminine gender to the moon, while the German language reverses these gender assignments. We have no objection to the use of either phrase, if properly defined, but it is important to understand that the usage "gender roles" is, in the present ideological context, already "Femspeak" in its tonality—and will be heard as such by all who are clued in to the situation.

Be this as it may, the debate is over the nature, the role, the needs, and the rights of *women;* men, children, and other participants in the drama (such as gays) have mainly come into the debate as those with whom women must necessarily contend in society. Even as far as women are concerned, the questions about them are not new;

indeed, some are age-old. But the new feminist movement, as of the 1960s, introduced a vast intensification and amplification of the issue, and also a new emotional vehemence that has invited retaliation in kind. Prior to the 1960s, and for quite a long time, there had been widespread agreement (certainly among social scientists) that the traditional role definitions are no longer fully applicable and that some modifications are necessary. But now a much sharper crystallization of contending viewpoints has emerged. For our purposes, we may distinguish four major viewpoints: the view that differences between men and women are indeed innate, and thus lead necessarily to the differing role assignments given to the two sexes traditionally; the view that the role differences are overwhelmingly the result *not* of biology but of sociocultural constructions which, in principle, could be radically changed; the view that women are innately superior to men; and the view that the innate nature of women is indeed different but also equal. To some extent, some of these viewpoints overlap, both logically and politically, but it is useful to distinguish them analytically.[2]

Feminists demand "equal rights" first of all in the public sphere. Such equality has been traditionally denied precisely on the grounds that the differences between men and women are innate, perhaps God-given, and basically not changeable by deliberate interventions. Very likely, such a view of the matter continues to be widely held in the general population, especially in its non-middle-class sectors. And the same view, of course, has been taken up by many in the neo-traditionalist movement.[3] Feminists, logically, have argued that existing inequalities between men and women are *not* based on innate differences but, rather, are due to the sociocultural environment, to socialization, and to the imposition of institutional patterns by society. Thus, again logically, feminists have tended toward an animus against biology, or at least against any biological approaches to the issues of interest to them. There has been a great deal of research by feminist scholars designed to undergird this preference for "nurture" against "nature" (to use earlier terms in the debate of social scientists and biologists on such questions) with scientifically tenable data. All of this research has focused on the nature of women—such as research on sex differences in glands, hormones, and chromosomes; on differences between the sexes in body size, maturation, visual acuity, hearing, taste, motor skills, sensitivity to pain, and resistance to disease; and more psychologically oriented research on differences in IQ, aptitude, achievement, and personality.[4] By now there is enough literature on these topics that (leaving aside the methodological doubts one may have about such notions) one may speak of a "feminist biology" and a "feminist psychology"—and of course a "feminist sociology." It is perhaps ironic that the bulk of this research has underlined sex differences; it is also impressive that feminist researchers have conscientiously reported these findings, although this must often have been disturbing. But of course the debate has continued as to how these differences are to be explained and evaluated, so that the same research findings can often be used to legitimate opposing ideological positions. For example, data show that women, even if given a choice, will gravitate toward traditionally "feminine" occupations. Such data can be interpreted in a neo-traditionalist vein: The traditional occupational differences are based on innate differences between the sexes, and therefore any changes in the traditional job hierarchy would be self-defeating and in vain. But the same data can also be interpreted (and are being so interpreted by feminists) as having the opposite implication: The existing system of occupational stratification consistently undervalues the occupations chosen by women; therefore, the traditionally "feminine" occupations must be "upgraded," in terms both of status and of levels of remuneration; this is the program currently known under the heading "comparable worth"; an (often unspoken) assumption here is that, if these occupations are sufficiently "upgraded," they will no longer be primarily "feminine."

The mainstream of the feminist movement consists of those who vocally assert that gender roles are a function of the sociocultural environment.[5] This view is the presupposition of most feminist efforts at legislation and government regulation. Thus, the feminist position on equal employment opportunity and affirmative action presupposes that differences in the ratio of male and female representation in any occupation must be the result of discrimination. Say, for example, that women are underrepresented (in terms of their proportion in the general population) in the engineering profession. This fact must *not* be explained by some innate disinclination of women to become engineers. Rather, this can only be the result of discrimination, either immediate or long-lasting. That is, it is either argued that the engineering profession, beginning with its training institutions, is consciously discriminating against admitting women or, if this cannot be shown, it is argued that the sociocultural environment as a whole has impressed on women the prejudice that they cannot or should not become engineers. In either case, remedial interventions by government are in order; in the latter case, of course, additional remedies (in the final analysis, a reformation of childhood socialization as a whole) will be called for.

This idea that, barring sociocultural barriers, women would make choices very much like men's in all areas of public life (at least there) is also an underlying presupposition of the movement for an Equal Rights Amendment to the United States Constitution.[6] It is just this presupposition that has mobilized opposition to ERA, since it has struck large numbers of people as an attempt to enshrine a biologically absurd principle in the highest law of the land. ERA has a long history, having first been introduced in Congress in 1923. It has always been in conflict with quite different women's concerns (some also labeled "feminist" in their day), notably the long-lasting efforts to have protective labor laws for women. ERA cleared the Senate in 1972, after which the opposition became vehement and well-organized. And although the political fate of the Equal Rights Amendment has its ups and downs—as recent history so clearly shows—the ERA movement provides the clearest expression of the vision of gender roles being the result of the sociocultural environment; it is a strongly, often fanatically anti-biological vision, a proclamation of the faith that the biological makeup of women is *not* their destiny. Thus ERA is aimed at any social arrangement that gives special rights to men, but, by its inherent logic, it must also threaten every law or other social norm that gives special protection to women. The same vision also gives primacy to the public sphere, with the domestic sphere (the major locale of the private lives of most individuals) being frequently treated as an obstacle to be shunted aside in the quest for public equality. We have already referred to the symbolic character of this particular issue: More, perhaps, than any other feminist issue, ERA symbolizes the class conflict in American society, to the point that an ERA button is as much a badge of membership in the new knowledge class as it is an expression of this particular political sentiment.

In sum, this important wing of the feminist movement tends to deny that there are any innate differences between men and women. Where such denial is impossible, notably with regard to the unique capacity of women to bear children, there is still the aspiration to equalize the resultant differences by political intervention. Feminist efforts for child-care legislation are the best example of this.

A very different view prevails among the minority of feminists who believe that, far from being equal with men, women are the superior sex.[7] For them, the ideal state of affairs is some sort of matriarchy. They, too, can cite miscellaneous data as evidence for their position (such as data on women's greater longevity and resistance to diseases). The intellectual problem, for them even more than for the socioculturalists, is how this natural superiority of women has come to be reversed in human society. Various historical theses are designed to explain them, some generally interpreting history as one long drama of men overthrowing and repressing women (interpretations in the tradition of Bachofen and other nineteenth-century "matriarchalists"), others maintaining that it was capitalism which reduced women to cheap labor at home as well as in outside work (in this case following the Marxist tradition, notably the one started by the influence of Morgan on Engels). For this group of feminists, ERA is only the first step toward a new matriarchy. When it comes to matters of public policy, therefore, they tend to agree with mainline feminists. The differences come out sharply in matters of the private sphere. The idea that heterosexual sex is, *ipso facto*, rape is perhaps the clearest example of this. There have been big debates on these differences within the feminist camp, sometimes threatening the unity of the camp even in the public-policy arena. Also, of course, these radical positions have fueled opposition to feminism in general.

Finally, there is the view that could be called "differential-egalitarian."[8] People holding this view will be in agreement with main-line feminists on such issues as equal opportunity and equal pay. But they will reject the denial of all innate differences between the sexes and the notion that gender roles are nothing but a function of the sociocultural environment. Consequently, they will be skeptical of ERA. The discussions on the question of whether women should be drafted into the military and on the question of whether male standards should be applied to women in industry have brought out this more nuanced position on gender roles. The position requires, logically enough, special protective laws for women. Because of this, people holding such a position find themselves in an often uncomfortable alliance with the neo-traditionalists, although the philosophical beliefs and the general social attitudes may be quite different in the two groups. All the same, this *ad hoc* alliance between neo-traditionalists and those who affirm "equality in difference" surfaced after the Senate's approval of ERA, in 1972, in numerous hearings and debates in the states considering ratification. This alliance has been a major factor in the changed political climate for ERA as well as for other feminist issues.

In a quite unexpected way, the question of how *to define* the family has become an issue in itself.[9] It has often been observed that human beings have difficulty defining the subjects that are closest to them: One does not feel the need to define what one takes for granted every day. Of all those subjects, as far as social institutions are concerned, the family is closest, most taken for granted (as the English word "familiar" eloquently expresses), and therefore rarely defined. As the family becomes a political issue, however, it is "raised into consciousness"—that is, made the focus of deliberate attention and reflection—and in this process definition becomes necessary. We have seen the importance of labels and definitions in the case of "gender roles." It should not surprise anyone that the question of how to define the family—which means, basically, how one is going to speak about it—has been entangled in acrimonious and ideologically charged debates.

The year 1980 was to be the "Year of the Family," to be celebrated by a White House Conference on the subject. It was during the endless seminars and colloquia preparing this Conference that the question of definition surfaced dramatically. During this preparatory period, a radical semantic shift took place in the definition of the family. Indeed, this shift may perhaps be regarded as the most important if not the only accomplishment of an otherwise abortive undertaking. Whatever else this process of public disputation achieved, it succeeded in changing linguistic usage within the federal bureaucracy and in segments of the public. The change was from speaking about *the family* to speaking about *families*. At first glance this may seem an innocent shift, from the singular to the plural, perhaps a much-needed recognition of American pluralism. Upon closer scrutiny, the shift reveals itself as anything but innocent: It gave governmental recognition to precisely the kind of moral relativism that has infuriated and mobilized large numbers of Americans.

The taken-for-granted definition of the family in American culture, of course, was not merely descriptive but charged with positive value. It was, in other words, not an antiseptic social-scientific statement about individuals living together under certain conditions, but a strongly normative statement about the nature of the bonds linking these individuals. This normative view assumed that family bonds established a unit that transcended the individuals constituting it—a view, needless to add, with deep roots in the religious traditions of Western civilization. While this normative view changed over time (as, for example, by the rise of modern notions of individual choice and "romantic" love), it continued to serve as an ideal for the great majority of Americans and was strongly supported as such by the law. The ideal could be translated into an image, which in turn served as a model for the actions and aspirations of countless individuals who could, so to speak, "fill in" the image by their own lives. The image can be easily described: a married couple and their minor children, living together in their own home, forming an intimate and protective environment, providing nurture and care to the individuals concerned. Until very recently, this culturally established image was supported not only by church and state but by the media and by family professionals. Any deviation from this powerful image tended to be perceived as abnormal and unfortunate, making for the counterimage of the "broken family." The latter was the special object of attention for family professionals.

Later in this book we will examine the way in which this image of the family was shaped by the forces of modernization acting upon the Judeo-Christian tradition, especially in the nineteenth century. Suffice it to say here that the peculiar forces of modernity created considerable stress for this normative view of the family from the beginning. As the twentieth century unfolded, it became increasingly evident that there had come about a wide discrepancy between the ideal image and the social reality. Empirically, there was clearly now a great variety of family types as well as family norms. The social sciences, of course, were busy documenting this fact. Today there exists what one observer called an "impressive diversity" in this area. Families differ depending on where their members are in the life cycle and on their spacing of children. But, more basically, there are large numbers of childless couples, one-parent households (due to separation and divorce, as well as the timeless factor of a spouse's death), remarried couples with children from antecedent marriages, not to mention an increasing number of couples cohabiting without formal marriage, and so-called "singles households." All of these types of households, of course, do not fit into the ideal image of the family. In addition, family patterns vary greatly by ethnicity and race, and by socioeconomic status (or class). The picture has been further complicated by new norms of family life in specific groups, notably the advent of so-called "open marriages"—probably not a very large phenomenon in terms of actual numbers but looming large in the public consciousness. Since many of these changes reflect moral as well as demographic shifts, the recognition of them within a definition of the family obviously became a moral issue over and beyond any social-scientific efforts at adequate classification. Thus the definition of a married couple without children hardly presented a moral question to anyone, but it became an altogether different matter when homosexual or lesbian couples demanded the right not only to raise children but to be recognized as "a family."

By the mid-sixties, as the discrepancy between the old ideal and the contemporary reality was noted in public discourse, there was also a shift in the conceptualization of the family by experts. Various professional groups contributed to this shift. The anthropologists had for quite a long time emphasized the great variety of family forms in various cultures and thus helped to bring about a sense of relativity concerning the modern Western form. It would be an interesting topic of research to explore the degree to which books like Ruth Benedict's *Patterns of Culture* and Margaret Mead's *Male and Female,* frequently required reading in college anthropology courses, affected the thinking about the family of the large number of students taking these courses over a period of decades. Psychologists, especially those in the psychoanalytic tradition, emphasized the "incubator" effect of the (allegedly) isolated nuclear family, which was presented as a pathogenic institution, stunting or repressing or neuroticizing the individuals caught in it. Quite apart from the specific negative notions about the family propagated by many psychologists, there was the (perhaps inevitable) focus of psychology upon the individual *as against* the institutions in which he finds himself. This focus very naturally led to an approach to the family as one of the institutional structures against which individual personality must assert itself. As to the sociologists, they oscillated in their approach to the family. On the one hand, in the tradition of the Chicago School, they stressed the disintegrative effect upon the family of modern processes: urbanism, institutional differentiation, technologization, and bureaucratization combining to deprive the family of its traditional functions in society and eroding the old bonds of solidarity within it. On the other hand, sociologists (notable among them Talcott Parsons, the grand theorist of so-called structural-functionalism) maintained that the modern family had acquired *new* functions. These were supposed to be primarily emotional functions, for adults and children alike. For more optimistic sociologists, especially those in the structural-functionalist school, there had taken place a very positive trade-off: The family had been deprived of some of its old functions (such as its productive role in the economy and its educational functions for older children), but this deprivation was actually liberating, allowing the family to take on new functions turning upon mutual affection and the development of sympathetic individuality. Part of this positive trade-off was also supposed to be the takeover of old family functions by new institutions, such as the modern educational, child-care, and therapeutic institutions. It should be recognized that such sociologists as Parsons were anything but social revolutionaries; on the contrary, they tended to celebrate the family *status quo* in American society. However, the shift from a normative to a functional conceptualization had a relativizing effect in itself (in that, it may be argued, sociology is very similar to anthropology in its, often unintended, effects on people's thinking), and the positive attitude to the deprivation of the family of many of its old educational and "caring" functions served to legitimate the new professionals in their bid to claim jurisdiction over this or that area of traditional family life.

By the mid-1960s, as a cultural revolution was spreading across Western industrial societies like wildfire, there began a great debunking of what the anthropologist R. Birdwhistell called the "sentimental myth" of the family. Various political and ideological trends came together in this demolition job. The New Left was interested in exalting the public sphere over against all forms of private life, in having women return to the sphere of work, in collectivizing child-raising, and in "non-repressive sexuality." The feminists, wanting to liberate women from domesticity, were against the privatized and child-centered "bourgeois family." Populationists were against the "frightful reproductive potential" of the family. And the professional complexes, growing in power (mainly by government support) and legitimated in their role by the functional definition of the family, were obviously interested in proclaiming the inefficiency of the family in providing "services" that they had a claim to.

Under the onslaught of these combined forces, the definition of the family changed. Ira Reiss, a sociologist at Yale, led the slide down this slippery slope with his widely cited 1965 article in which he defined the family as "a small kinship-structured group with the key function of the nurturant socialization of the newborn."[10] But even that most basic function was challenged by academics caught in the grip of the new egalitarianism. For instance: "It is idle to talk of a society of equal opportunity as long as that society abandons its newcomers solely to their families for their most impressionable years."[11] Not surprisingly, people who think that way are tempted to correct this "injustice" by means of public policy. The "rediscovery of the family" in the late 1970s, to which we have made reference earlier in this book, has not discouraged those who see greater professional dominance as the solution to "the problem of the family": The family as an "endangered species," of course, is supposed to need professional help more than ever before.

All this furor led to the redefinition of "the family" into "families" by the White House Conference. The official new definition was supplied by Ira Hutchinson in his position paper for the Conference, which was subsequently adopted.[12] The old image of the family, consisting of husband, wife, and two children, was found to be myopic and limiting. American families are far more diverse than this old stereotype would suggest. If this diversity is taken into account, one can no longer speak about "the American family" but must, rather, speak about "American families." It is important to note that the *empirical fact* of diversity is here quietly translated into a *norm* of diversity. In other words, norms and values, as well as the wishes and hopes, of many people are simply bypassed by this definition. Put simply, *demography is translated into a new morality*. This is not the place to discuss the methodological errors of this procedure. It should simply be stated that there is no intention here of criticizing individuals such as Hutchinson for their contributions *qua* social scientists. After all, they did not invent the data on which they based their statements. The problem came (here as in other areas of social-scientific research) when normative conclusions were directly drawn out of a set of statistical data often not by the social scientists themselves but by those making political use of their findings. In any case, the new conceptualization of "families" was instantly acceptable to the entire range of interests mentioned above: For the various groups of ideologists, it legitimated insistence on "alternatives" to the "norms of Middle America," and for the experts and bureaucrats dealing with family, it legitimated the need for professional services in this situation of diversity.

For exactly the same reason, this redefinition (and the whole White House Conference program from which it came) mobilized the neo-traditionalist "pro-family" camp. The more sophisticated members of this camp do not deny the *facts* of diversity cited by experts like Hutchinson. But those very facts constitute the problem for them. It is *against* the empirical diversity that they want to uphold the old image of the family and to seek government support. All the constituent parts of this camp, as we have enumerated them before, have mobilized against the redefinition of the family. The efforts to publicly enshrine the old normative definition have reached a certain climax in the Family Protection Act, introduced by Senator Paul Laxalt, of Nevada. What is to be "protected" here, of course, is precisely the old, normative definition of the family.

The sentiments behind this movement were very clearly stated by Senator Laxalt himself: "For years we have been debating on the terms of those who want to remake society. Now those groups will have to explain why they oppose the traditional idea of the family."[13] And another spokesman of the neo-traditionalist camp, rejecting the shift in the definition of the family made by professionals, put his position as follows: "There are no 'new family forms.' Nor are American families 'changing.' Rather, disruptive human relationships existent since the beginning of social life, but always discouraged or restrained in healthy and growing societies—homosexuality, unsanctioned sexual cohabitation, and promiscuity—have been elevated to family status by a simple semantic change. And normative standards—far from being parochial, oppressive, or pathological—are in fact the very defining elements of all culture. Without 'single standards' guiding human acts such as mating, reproduction, and the nurturing of children, social life rapidly falls prey to anarchy and nihilism."[14]

In other words, the recent shift in the term "family" is seen to have stripped the word of any coherent meaning. In the neo-traditionalist camp, this is understood as a change that is far from innocent, but is a portent of social disruption and decay. And this is why the debate over the definition of the family is far from a mere sideshow.

The issue of abortion has galvanized more passion, on both sides, than any other issue in the area under consideration here.[15] This should not be surprising, in view of what is at stake here. For the one side, what is at stake is the fundamental right of a woman to have control over her own body and her own life. On the other side, what is at stake is the very purpose of society in protecting the life of even its weakest member. Clearly, there is an enormous cognitive gulf between the two sides, in terms of the understanding of the nature of the human person: Is the fetus a person—yes or no? This is a *cognitive* issue, logically prior to any discussion of *norms*, for the norms of each side, one may assume, would be readily acceptable to the other side, provided the cognitive issue were resolved: The most ardent pro-abortionist does not recommend infanticide in the exercise of a woman's right to control her own life, which presupposes that an infant has a different status from a fetus; and the most fervent anti-abortionists do not dispute a woman's rights over her own body, but what they do dispute is that a fetus is simply part of a woman's body.

The language used in the debate over abortion has systematically obfuscated this fundamental cognitive divide. This is already evident in the appellations used by each side to describe its own position: "Pro-choice" versus "pro-life." Pro-abortionists demand a woman's right to choose for herself—which begs the question as to whether, in the case of an abortion, she is choosing only for herself and not also for another human being. Anti-abortionists claim to be defending human life—which presupposes agreement as to when the life of a human individual begins. Both appellations, of course, have powerful emotional connotations. "Choice" is one of the key concepts of modernity, as we have argued elsewhere.[16] To be modern entails a vast expansion in choices and thus in the control of human beings over their own lives. Conversely, to be "anti-choice" suggests a deeply reactionary and obscurantist attitude—a suggestion used to the hilt in pro-abortion propaganda. And "life," after all, is one of the most potent words in the language. One can hardly say anything worse of political antagonists than that they are "anti-life." As part of the language battle in this area, it is noteworthy how carefully words are chosen by each side. Pro-abortionists will always use language that avoids suggesting a human status for the fetus; anti-abortionists will regularly say "child" instead of "fetus." Anti-abortionists, by the logic of their own position, must, then, speak of "murder" to refer to abortion and, in view of the number of abortions now taking place in the United States (more than one million annually), of "genocide." Little room for compromise would seem possible under these circumstances, and the debates over other family issues seem mild by comparison.

This cannot be the place to trace the history of abortion in Western societies. Suffice it to say that until the 1960s abortion was rarely if ever a political issue. Performing an abortion was a criminal act; if there was an issue at all, it was that of the incidence of this particular crime. Today abortion is a legal act in a large number of countries: not only in the United States, but in Western Europe, the Soviet bloc, Japan, China, India, and other countries in the Third World. The general world trend appears to be in the direction of liberalization. At least in this country and in Western Europe, the liberalizing trend was in large measure an achievement of the new feminist movement. Feminists were concerned to "demystify" health questions for women, particularly those related to childbearing. The book *Our Bodies, Ourselves,* published in 1971 by the Boston Women's Health Book Collective and reprinted many times since then, stated the position of the movement in exemplary fashion. It is very important that it declared women's health problems to be a public issue—a significant shift into the political arena of matters that had previously been considered part of private life. Generally, feminists came to list "reproductive freedom" among their political demands, subsuming under that phrase abortion along with birth control and other health matters. In this undoubtedly the new feminism was in line with the so-called "sexual revolution" sweeping the Western world during this period, implying the rightfulness of free, especially guilt-free, sexual expression. Freeing women from the burden of unwanted pregnancies was a logical part of this message of liberation; not so incidentally, the same message had considerable appeal to men in their always-potential role of unwilling fathers.

In the 1960s and early 1970s a number of court decisions and acts of legislation greatly expanded access to contraceptives, both by abrogating earlier proscriptions and by positive measures. Thus there appeared to be an intrinsic logic to the historic Supreme Court decision, *Roe* v. *Wade,* in 1973, which in effect legalized abortion on demand in the earlier period of pregnancy throughout the United

States. The most important "philosophical" aspect of this decision was to declare that the fetus, minimally in the first two trimesters, was not "a person" in the eyes of the law and thus not subject to the protections of the Fourteenth Amendment. It is precisely this "philosophical" point that served as the rallying cry for the opposition, which passionately insisted on the human quality and therefore the human rights of the fetus. But as opposition grew, so did the practice of abortion, increasing rapidly in numbers after 1973. To those viewing abortion as the killing of a human being, the rapid increase in the number of abortions, under the umbrella of law and widespread moral approval, was naturally seen as a societal problem of monstrous proportions, indeed as mass murder taking place under the aegis of the supreme law of the land. In view of this perception of the issue by large numbers of Americans, the accusation by the other side that these people were engaged in "single-issue politics" missed the point entirely: Given this perception, what single issue could be more important than a million murders per year?

Through the 1970s the anti-abortion opposition became increasingly successful in influencing public opinion and the political process. In this, of course, it was part of the much larger neo-traditionalist movement described before. But it is important to see that the "pro-life" movement today is a coalition of quite various groups, not all of which can meaningfully be described as neo-traditionalist. It is also important to see that the movement is by no means simply a Roman Catholic one, although of course the strong position on the issue taken by the Roman Catholic Church has been a crucial support for it. Blacks have been prominent in the movement, some maintaining that the pro-abortionists were, wittingly or unwittingly, intent on reducing the black population of the country. Conservative Protestants and Orthodox Jews are just as adamant as Roman Catholics in opposing abortion, as are Eastern Orthodox Christians. What is more, many quite secular individuals, especially in the health professions themselves, have come to find the casual attitude toward abortion morally repugnant. The anti-abortion movement has been very well organized and has had great political efficacy, and by now there have been various legal and political attempts to reverse the 1973 Supreme Court decision. One of the most successful attempts to date has been the so-called Hyde Amendment—an amendment to an appropriations bill for the fiscal year 1977 prohibiting the use of Medicaid funds for purposes of abortion (including the promotion or encouragement of abortion). If this has been an important victory for the anti-abortion movement, it has also made it vulnerable to attack: Since Medicaid funds were involved, pro-abortion partisans could argue that the measure discriminated against the poor. In this as in other cases, the abortion issue has become entangled with other political issues dividing the electorate.

As this book is being written, the two camps are in a political deadlock. Either side can point to successes and defeats. Clearly, the future course of the debate will hinge on the future of the political climate in general, but it seems unlikely that either side will win a decisive victory in the forseeable future. Public opinion polls show a population very much divided on the issue, though class differences are important; again, the "knowledge class" appears to be the most strongly pro-abortion segment of the population. The pro-abortion camp is in a defensive stance, seeking to protect what they have won in the recent past. The anti-abortion camp has an agenda comprising several steps: passage of the human life bill in Congress, for which only a simple majority would be needed but which would not stop a multitude of legal challenges; passage of a power to protect life bill in Congress, which would limit court jurisdiction over the issue, a measure of very doubtful constitutionality; and finally passage of a human life amendment to the United States Constitution, obviously a difficult and drawn-out political project. As the political and legal battles over abortion go on, every other issue pertinent to the family is inevitably drawn into this controversy—a fact that one may deplore on grounds of logic but that is probably inevitable politically.

The issue of "children's rights" does not involve ideologized language as visibly as the preceding issues discussed in this chapter, but it, too, reveals a cognitive gulf between the parties to the debate. And here, too, a very profound philosophical or anthropological question is touched upon, namely: What is the nature of a child? Or, even more simply: What is a child? Only if that question were answered satisfactorily, would it be possible to hold a well-founded position as to the rights of the child. The political debate, however, swirls wildly around this question without answering it. In this, at least, it resembles the debate over the issue of abortion. The question is particularly irksome because, as we shall see in greater detail in Part II, ideas about childhood changed in history along with ideas about the family; what is more, various classes and ethnic groups hold differing views about this matter. Being a child, like being female, is obviously based on specific biological characteristics of the human species. But biology provides no clear indication of the age at which a child passes into adulthood, even less of the qualities and thus the rights of the individual, given the status of being a child. All these matters, rather, are subjects of societal definition (or, if one prefers, of social construction). Thus the current debate over the issue is also a debate about the kind of society to be constructed in this particular period of history and inevitably touches on other ideological visions dividing people today.[17]

Western legal tradition has long held the view that children, unable to represent themselves before the law, were in most cases adequately represented by their parents. The same legal tradition has strongly protected the rights of parents to the care and custody, and to some extent at least the rearing, of their children. Only in specific cases, where parents are unwilling or unable to exercise the proper representation of the child's best interests, is the state to enter *in loco parentis*, be it through its own initiative or through being directed to do so by a court of law. In recent times, however, this view of the role of parents has been attacked from two sides, which logically are quite distinct if not antagonistic: from the "helping professions," some within and some outside the machinery of the modern welfare state, who seek to apply their own notions of the best interests of the child *against* parents; and from those holding a liberationist ideology of self-determination for children. The latter view protests against the child's status as his parents' "chattel" and likens children to other historically oppressed groups; its avowed goal is to emancipate children from parents as well as from the state.[18]

In general, the notion of children's rights has moved from "protection" to "prevention," the latter term meaning that children are not only to be protected from harm in the more obvious sense but to be assured all sorts of services that will allegedly prevent harm at later stages of their lives. This shift, of course, has enhanced the importance of the professionals providing these services. The child is now put in the legal position of an individual *demanding* his rights, against the state as well as against his own parents. In the case of adolescents (and in particular those bureaucratically designated as "persons in need of supervision," or "PINS") it can be argued quite plausibly that they may benefit from having their rights recognized independently of their families. The issue is clearly much more difficult in the case of younger children; at the same time, the issue is more urgent in the latter case, since it is precisely younger children who are most vulnerable to neglect or abuse. But younger children cannot be expected to represent themselves and to make decisions for themselves, as is recognized by all but the most doctrinaire liberationists: How, say, is a two-year-old child to exercise his rights of self-determination? Younger children, then, are always dependent on adults; the question is *which* adults are to be recognized as representing the children's best interests. As a result, there is something misleading about the phrase "children's rights." In practice, the question resolves itself, when it refers to younger children, into a conflict between parents' rights and the rights of miscellaneous professionals; in other words, what is at issue is a quarrel between differing categories of adults. This is evident in the battle lines as they are currently drawn. On the one side are those who advocate parents' rights, more or less along the lines of Western legal tradition; on the other side are those who advocate increased state intervention, via this or that professional group. The advocates of children's rights inevitably tend to be on the latter side. The legal profession, in fidelity to its own tradition, may be said to have a strong bias in favor of parents' rights, and it has yielded only reluctantly to the other side on specific matters relating to the welfare of children. This legal tradition has been reinforced by a number of recent Supreme Court decisions, such as in *May* v. *Anderson* (1953), which declared that one of the most precious personal liberties was a parent's right to the care and custody of minor children, and in *Yoder* v. *Wisconsin* (1972), which affirmed the right of Amish children to challenge certain provisions of the state's education laws.

Recently, the issue of children's rights has been raised with particular intensity in connection with neglect and abuse.[19] In such cases, of course, even traditional legal ideas accept the notion that the state must intervene to protect children against their neglectful or abusing parents. The difficult question is to decide just what kind of behavior constitutes neglect or abuse if one moves beyond the more obvious cases of a physical sort (say, letting a child starve or brutally beating him). In 1977 data, for example, it is indicated that only 4 percent of cases of neglect or abuse reported annually (which add up to hundreds of thousands of cases) are of this gross physical kind. Yet every year more than 450,000 children are separated from their parents by state action, 150,000 of them coercively, the rest with "voluntary" consent by their parents (a very dubious term, since parental consent is frequently achieved under threat of prosecution). This means, quite simply, that in the great majority of these cases children are taken away from their parents for alleged neglect or abuse of a nonphysical kind. This fact becomes especially grave when class, ethnic, and racial factors are taken into account. When the term "neglect" is applied to poor families, it commonly refers to quite elusive matters: Homes are deemed to be "dirty," nutrition to be "substandard" or "not wholesome," or (even more elusively) parents are found to be "non-caring" or "hostile." Sociologically, one must ask here to what extent such judgments involve the application of upper-middle-class and white values to social strata with different values. Beyond this, one must ask whether the "standards" of the white upper-middle class, and more specifically its professional component, are really so superior (not to mention "scientifically" supported) that the state should impose them coercively on the rest of the population. These questions have been asked with particular animus by blacks and Hispanics. Since the majority of children in foster care belong to these racial minorities, the issue has become embroiled in racial animosity and politics.

Enough has been said to indicate that the "child advocacy" camp is not without its own vested interests. Broadly speaking, these interests are very similar to other interests of the "knowledge class" discussed before. The other camp, assembled under the banner of "parents' rights," is constituted by the same generally neo-traditionalist coalition involved in the other issues discussed here (though obviously there are individuals concerned with only one issue and with little interest in other issues taken up by this coalition). Here, as in other issues, there is mounting resentment against the disfranchisement of families and against the professional/bureaucratic groups that engage in it. Religious aspects are important in some parts of the country, as in the battles between the educational establishments of various states and parents wanting their children in nonconformist religious (usually Evangelical Protestant) schools. Quite a few cases reflecting these battles are now in the courts.[20] This issue touches logically and politically on the issue of anti-religious values and pornography in the media—which is perceived by many people in terms of the protection of children against nefarious influences abroad in the society. In this way the issue of children's rights has become a battleground between much larger forces locked in social conflict. And in this of course it is typical of the issues discussed in this chapter.

To repeat: The purpose of this chapter has not been to give a detailed presentation of these issues thrown up by the current war over the family. This would have required a vastly lengthier treatment. Rather, our purpose here has been to show how each one of these issues involves acute value conflicts within the society. We have also indicated how each of these conflicts, far from taking place in some rarefied sphere of philosophical discourse, also involves very mundane vested interests, most of them pertaining to class. In sociological parlance this means that many of the values in contest are "ideological"—that is, serve as legitimations of specific vested interests and as weapons of political strategy. This aspect of the matter will be further explored in the following excursus.

# EXCURSUS

# Abortion
# and the
# Postulate
# of Ignorance

Both sides in the abortion controversy agree at least on one thing: that abortion is a strategically important moral issue. We agree with this too. But it does not seem to us that abortion properly belongs to the topic of *family* policy; it raises fundamental questions of human and civil rights that touch on every political issue and not just on "the problem of the family." Consequently, we do not propose to return to the issue of abortion later in the book, when we try to outline our own position with regard to family policy. But the abortion issue raises some general questions about moral judgments in the political arena, questions that are relevant to other issues as well. In raising these questions, we must deliberately step across the line that separates sociological analysis from political ethics; the reader should have no difficulty in recognizing when we do this; he should also recognize that, while we claim a measure of competence as sociological analysts, we have no more ethical competence than any other thoughtful citizen in a democracy. It is of the essence of democracy, though, that citizens communicate their thoughts to each other.

Sociologically speaking, the abortion issue reveals a highly significant rupture in the moral fabric of contemporary Western societies. More specifically it discloses a phenomenon that may aptly be called "moral pluralism." The association with the well-known phenomenon of religious pluralism is intentional. It can be said, even with a degree of self-satisfaction, that Western societies in general and the United States in particular have gone very far in solving the difficulties of religious pluralism. To be sure, there are still areas of sharp conflict (Northern Ireland is an obvious case of this), and even in religiously "pacified" societies there are disputes that arouse passions and hostility (such as in the ongoing disagreements over the precise implications of the separation of church and state in the United States). Still, after centuries of bloody religious wars, massacres, and persecution, most countries of North America and Western Europe have attained a historically rare (though not unique) state of civic peace between a large number of diverse religious groups. The observation that this need not necessarily last (one need only point here to the deep-seated poison of anti-Semitism in the collective psyche of Western man) is pertinent and suggests caution and vigilance but does not in itself detract from a justified sense of political achievement. So far, so good. But what is appearing now is a related but distinct phenomenon, that of *moral* pluralism. We would contend that this presents a problem of grave proportions and one that may not be easily solved by the mechanisms set up to "contain" religious conflicts.

These mechanisms all relate to what in America has been called "denominationalism." A denomination, as Richard Niebuhr has taught us, is a religious body that has given up (in practice if not in theory) its claim to monopoly status. In other words, a denomination is a religious body that recognizes, at least implicitly, that other religious bodies have a right to exist in society as well. The religious history of the United States has ongoingly expanded the range of religious groups included in this zone of interdenominational peace—first within the major Protestant churches, then including more marginal Protestant groups (such as the Quakers), then going on to include Catholics and Jews, and finally accepting into this civic ecumenism not only every conceivable religious expression known to man (some coming from outside the Judeo-Christian tradition) but coherent expressions of nonreligious world views (a point made clear, for instance, by the federal courts in ruling on what are acceptable grounds for conscientious objection to military service). To be sure, there have always been fringe cases that put this civic ecumenism to the test (for instance, the Mormons in the nineteenth century, some of the so-called "cults" today), but the social mechanisms of denominationalism and the legal system protecting them have been very successful in meeting these tests, eventually if not at once. Put simply, denominationalism has been a very successful historical experiment.

One reason for this, suggested by retrospection, may well have been that until very recently virtually all the groups entering the denominational "market" had a common moral heritage (derived of course from the Judeo-Christian tradition). This common morality allowed the resolution of religious differences within a framework of civic order. Indeed, as has been argued (among others) by Will Herberg and Robert Bellah, this common morality became a central ingredient of a "civil religion," which transcended the individual denominations and was "established" socially if not legally. This is not the place to speculate why this common morality can no longer be assumed in the way it once was. A possible reason for this may be the overall process of secularization, relativizing moral convictions as well as undermining religious certitudes. Another reason may be the sheer multiplication of groups clamoring to be recognized as legitimate partners in the officially protected religious system. Be this as it may, we now face a new situation, and the issue of abortion illuminates that situation very sharply.

Let us just ask the following questions: How likely is it that the "pro-choice" and "pro-life" camps will become "moral denominations," analogous to, say, Episcopalians and Presbyterians? Can one imagine someone expressing a "moral preference" for abortion as he may express a "religious preference" for Presbyterianism? Or could one say, "I happen to be pro-life," as one says, "I happen to be Jewish"? A sociologist could not responsibly say that such an outcome is impossible; it is plausible to say that it is improbable. And the reason for this is simple: Unlike many if not most differences between the major religious rivals in Western history, this moral difference touches directly on an important area of actual conduct in social life, therefore demands legal regulation, and therefore makes it very difficult for people amicably to "agree to disagree." Indeed, as far as American history is concerned, two important moral issues in the past support this assessment: the issues of slavery and of prohibition. Both issues divided the society down the middle, both involved moral convictions with unavoidable behavioral and legal consequences—and neither could be solved amicably. Those who were convinced that slavery was an intolerable moral evil achieved victory only after the bloodiest war in American history. Those who had a similar conviction about the use of liquor were led to a milder form of coercion, which eventually failed but not without tearing deeply into the fabric of moral consensus.

Sociologists should not be surprised by this. One of the basic insights of sociology was expressed classically by Émile Durkheim when he observed that society was, above all, a moral community. Such a moral community, and what he called its "solidarity," is maintained by an ongoing consensus. Wherever that consensus breaks down, coercion must take its place. If the breakdown is at the edges (sociologists speak of "deviance" here, as in the case of the criminal who "deviates" from the norms of society), the moral community at the center is preserved by coercing the offender responsible for the breakdown (thus society has institutions to apprehend, try, and punish criminals). But when breakdown threatens the center itself, the ordinary instruments of "marginal" coercion fail to solve the problem. More-massive coercion becomes necessary. This is always a difficult matter, doubly so in a democracy, whose very political legitimacy depends upon consensus.

Our data indicate that the American population divides almost evenly in its views on the morality of abortion; the situation in Western Europe appears to be quite similar. As we have tried to show, this division is not sociologically random but is heavily influenced by factors of class and ethnicity, which makes it even more serious. How can the moral consensus of society be maintained if half the population views the other half as actual or potential murderers, and is in turn viewed by that other half as violating the fundamental human rights of women? The debate between the two sides is passionate, based on theoretically contradictory doctrines, and generally contemptuous of compromises. It is only logical, then, that each side seeks the coercive support of state power—the "pro-choice" side no less than the "pro-life" side. Is it conceivable that either will succeed in this? Yes, it is. Depending on how one estimates the likely course of the current class struggle, one will bet on one or the other side. The law, in other words, may continue to uphold abortion against those who consider it murder, deepening their alienation from the society;

or the law may reverse itself and proscribe abortion once again, thereby creating a new explosion of "crime" for which the prohibition era provides a good preview. A sociologist must believe that "victory" would be Pyrrhic in either case. For this reason, if not for weightier ethical ones, it is very important to ask what chance there is for a new consensus to be generated, a consensus that may not include everyone but that could command that "vital center" (to use Arthur Schlesinger's happy term) on which democracy depends.

Let it be quickly admitted that we are not in a position to give a definite answer to this question; we must also admit that we are not overly optimistic. The most we can do is to suggest some changes in attitude that might provide at least a starting point for a new consensus. While this is admittedly an exercise in hope (not to say wishful thinking), the hope (or the wish) is at least an informed one.

It is not difficult to say how a new consensus is *not* likely to come about. It is not likely to come about by one side's converting the other outright; the moral chasm is too deep for that. Nor is it likely to come about by the courts' pronouncing the wisdom that will rally all sides. The American legal system, especially through the institution of the Supreme Court, has always tended to give the courts a role of moral oracle for which they are singularly ill-fitted. To be sure, there exists what Hans Kelsen (the founder of so-called "legal positivism") has called "the normative power of facticity," which means here that the law can indeed create facts that in turn affect people's normative thinking. But this can happen only on the basis of an already existing moral consensus; it cannot create such consensus *de novo*. In other words, in the normal course of events, the law expresses and codifies morality, but it cannot create morality. In this case, the Supreme Court created very new facts in the matter of abortion by its 1973 decision. But these very facts, far from creating a new consensus, provoked the most bitter moral warfare. Finally, it is very unlikely indeed that a new moral consensus can be established on the basis of science. The current debate over abortion has brought forth a large number of scientists expounding on such things as the DNA code, brain waves, and other biological properties of the human fetus. But, relevant though all this scientific information is, it cannot by itself answer the underlying question of when a human person comes into being—as little as it can answer the question of when a human person ceases to be, that crucial question at the other end of the life cycle.

These are metaphysical questions, not scientific ones. It makes as little sense to turn to scientists as to jurists to provide answers. (Most scientists, incidentally, agree with this proposition. So do many jurists.)

If one were to look for likely *institutions* that might take the lead toward a new consensus, religious and educational institutions would appear to be the most plausible ones, at least in theory (in practice, most of them are far too much entangled in the current *Kulturkampf* to play such a role). But changes in the moral climate of a society are often much more diffuse, less institutionally channeled. What, for example, was the process which, in the eighteenth century, led to a new moral consensus to the effect that judicial torture was an intolerable practice? Or, in the nineteenth century, that children should not be subject to the full rigors of the criminal law? In both of these examples the process can be traced, and it involved various institutions, but it was possible only because large segments of society acquired a new vision of the nature of being human and therefore of the limits of humanly tolerable acts. If a new consensus on abortion is imaginable at all, something like this would have to happen here. We would suggest two elements for such a *prise de conscience,* both at least bordering on the religious (and how could they not, given the metaphysical dimensions of the problem?): a revival of awe and a recognition of ignorance.

Birth and death are two of the greatest mysteries of the human condition. They posit the two fundamental metaphysical questions: Where do we come from, and Where do we go? The brief flicker of individual consciousness between birth and death is what the mystery of human existence is all about. Long before it constitutes a problem for theoretical thought (be it in myth, theology, philosophy, or science), it is an occasion for terror and awe. Human beings have succeeded in at least containing the terror by various means of religious faith and philosophical detachment. They abandon awe at the peril of their humanity. Abortion, in its relation to the mystery of birth, is therefore a truly awesome subject. It is the pro-abortion party that has offended most grievously against this imperative of awe. In "demystifying" abortion along with other aspects of sexuality, it has "demystified" human existence as such—or rather, tried unsuccessfully to do so, because the mystery reasserts itself by the undeniable facts of our experience. What is more awesome than the genesis of a new human individual out of all those antecedent physiological contingencies? And what act, therefore, could be more awesome than a deliberate interruption of this genesis? Even very insensitive parents are overcome with awe at the moment of their child's birth—a new human being appearing in the world, the result of their own act (however unreflected or even frivolous that act may have been all those months before), all the accidents of their own biographies suddenly transformed into necessity by this totally new reality. What before *was not*, now *is*: The newborn child, needless to say, insists upon this reality in the most clamorous way possible. Perhaps even very sensitive people can perform or go through an abortion without awe because the fetus is not capable of the same sort of insistence. It exists, or ceases to exist, behind the "screen" of a woman's body. And this, of course, is why pro-abortion advocates are so infuriated when their opponents parade color photographs of fetuses or (as happened at least once) dump fetuses literally in their laps. In other words, a doctrinaire pro-abortion position is only possible for morally sensitive people if the "screen" is maintained. It functions then as a reality screen and, by the same token, as an instrument of "false consciousness" (we are not very fond of this phrase, but if it applies anywhere, it applies to this kind of reality-avoidance).

The anti-abortion party is morally superior at least in this: that it does not try to avoid the awesome reality involved in the matter. In our opinion, it forfeits much of this moral credit by insisting on certitudes that, in fact, none of us possess. In other words, if we would recommend a revitalization of awe to our "pro-choice" friends, we strongly suggest a recognition of ignorance to our friends of the "pro-life" party (and, it so happens, we do have friends in both camps).

One of us (Peter Berger, in *Pyramids of Sacrifice*, 1975) has argued before that most public policy decisions are governed by a "postulate of ignorance"; that is, it must be postulated that those who make the political decisions do not possess the information which, in theory, would be necessary for truly informed decision making. This argument was made in the context of a book dealing with Third World development, but the postulate applies in principle to any area of public policy. Social scientists are in the business of pointing up those vast zones of ignorance and then of saying that "further study is required." Leave aside here that social scientists have an obvious vested interest in "further studies" being made—and funded; in most cases, a disinterested observer would agree that more information could be very useful for the policy maker. But it is a very rare case in which the political process in question can be halted until all these "further studies" have been completed (in the case of development studies, this would be many decades—by which time many Third World countries would have fallen into irreversible catastrophe). Thus the policy maker, or the individual advocating this or that political program, is almost always in the position of having to make decisions in a state of considerable ignorance. It follows from this that special attention should be paid to what was called the "calculus of pain"—that is, given the fact that we do not fully understand the situation and that therefore we cannot foresee the consequences of our proposed policies, we should try to assess the human costs of the latter, both in the present (which is usually easier) and in the immediately foreseeable future (which is more difficult but at which one can at least take a stab if the time frame is not too large). The moral implication of this is that policies that exact a high price of human pain in the service of a future that nobody can be sure about should be minimized as much as possible.

The postulate of ignorance applies to the abortion issue as it does to any other issue involving public policy. Thus it is safe to say that the judges involved in the 1973 decision were unaware of the class dynamics of the issue and did not foresee the furious social conflict that their decision would unleash. But this particular issue involves ignorance at a much deeper level as well, and it is the recognition of *this* level of ignorance that we particularly miss in the anti-abortion camp. It is ignorance about the very foundations of human being: We do not know what human nature is, and therefore we do not know when a human being begins (and, by the same token, when a human being ceases to be). Now, we are fully aware that there are religious groups who claim to know, by virtue of divine revelation or traditional authority. Certainly the Roman Catholic Church has made this claim. For those who find such a claim believable, there is no problem. They are the *beati possedentes* of truth and, as such, are morally certain in their war on error. We do not find ourselves in this enviable position. We also think that most of our contemporaries are similarly under-privileged; indeed, data suggest that large numbers of Roman Catholics are as uncertain about this as we are, notwithstanding the self-assured stance of their bishops. We would venture to say that, for most people in modern Western societies, thinking about and making moral judgments about abortion must take place under the postulate of ignorance. It follows, minimally, that any new consensus on this issue will emerge from common reflection about uncertainties, rather than from shared certitude.

It may be useful to spell out the quality of these uncertainties a little further. The extreme cases, here as elsewhere, help to clarify this. Very few people who do not base their moral judgments on allegedly inspired certitude would find it believable to say that a fertilized ovum fifteen minutes after conception constitutes a human person entitled to all the protections of the law. Curiously, even those who would say this and who regard the abortion of this fertilized ovum as an act of murder are unlikely to want the act punished as if it were murder in the ordinary sense; it would seem that even they would look upon such an abortion as murder of a special sort. On the other hand, very few people who are not complete fanatics on the pro-abortion side would maintain that a fetus carried for nine months is a human person fifteen minutes after delivery but *not* fifteen minutes before. This side of doctrinaire certitude, then, it would seem that our ignorance diminishes as we approach the beginning and the end of the normal period of pregnancy; our ignorance is greatest when a reasonable dividing line is to be drawn through this period. It seems to us that both a moral and a practical lesson may be drawn from this fact.

Morally, the "calculus of pain" applies here in a double sense. Since we do not know at what point in the nine-month cycle the fetus should be regarded as a person, we must take cognizance of the pain inflicted on the fetus as a putative person. To that extent, the anti-abortion position is justified. However, as the pro-abortion side has argued persuasively, we cannot ignore the pain caused not only to mothers but to others (notably fathers and siblings) by an unwanted pregnancy carried to term. There is no need to summarize the copious literature on this subject; let it be stipulated that a child that is wanted and prepared for enters the world under greatly more favorable circumstances, both for himself and for his family, than a child whose appearance in the world adds miseries of all sorts to the lives of his parents and siblings. If this is so, then we cannot assent *either* to the kind of position expressed in the Supreme Court decision of 1973 *or* to the position that would proscribe all abortions (with the possible exception of those necessary to save the mother's life). Both these decisions assume that the postulate of ignorance does not hold, and both deal with the calculus of pain in a morally one-sided way.

We readily concede that the practical lesson from the foregoing considerations does not eventuate in a clear-cut policy conclusion. Nor are we competent to enter into the manifold social and legal ramifications of the sort of intermediate position our considerations would point to. (We can only refer here, with great appreciation, to the work done in this area by Daniel Callahan and the Hastings Center he directs.) We do have an idea, though, of the general policy direction suggested by all this. While it would not proscribe all abortions, it would tend to set a fairly narrow time frame (certainly not beyond the first trimester and probably below it) as the period when abortion is to be permitted. In other words, the law should, as far as possible within the bounds of concern for the mother and other family members, lean to the side of conservatism in presuming at what point the fetus is to be regarded as a person. But within the time frame set, the decision on whether to abort or not must be left to the pregnant woman, in consultation with whomever *she* chooses. The reason for this should be clear enough: If the fetus is presumed to be a person, neither the mother nor any other individual has the right to kill that person. But if the fetus is presumed *not* to be a person, it must be presumed to be part of the pregnant woman's body, in which case no one else has the right to make decisions regarding it.

We also do not know the chances of a new consensus, along these lines, emerging out of our uncertainties. A presupposition for this would have to be an abandonment of many of the attitudes now exhibited by the major contestants in the debate. The stance of dogmatic arrogance, the shrill tone, the habit of mutual excommunication from the ranks of the truly humane—all these would have to be abandoned. Those on both sides and those in the middle would have to begin listening to each other with an openness that is now widely absent. The revitalization of awe, as we have described it, might provide the basis for such a new attitude. A central theme in the Judeo-Christian tradition is that redemption comes from forgiveness, rather than self-righteousness. This theme will serve those among us, Jews and Christians, for whom the tradition continues to be a source of moral insights. But there is, as it were, a secular equivalent to the theological notion of grace. It is the discovery of humility by those who know the extent of their own ignorance.

# II

# THE FAMILY
## Tensions
## of
## Modernization

# 4

# The Family
# and
# Modern
# Society

The various viewpoints concerning the family that we discussed in the preceding chapters have contradictory implications for the way in which this institution is to be understood today. There is the view that the family and its values are in a steep decline. This decline is variously interpreted in terms of its causes—broad social trends or specific ideological movements or changes in religion and morality— but most of those holding this view agree that the alleged decline of the family is harmful both to the individual and to society. This viewpoint can be summed up in the proposition that the family is in decline because of decadence. There is also the diametrically opposite point of view to the effect that changes in the overall society have revealed the outmoded character of the family. Supposedly, the family as it is now constituted will not be able to deal with this situation and will either disappear or have to be radically refashioned. And this is supposed to be a good thing, because of the allegedly harmful, pathogenic effects of the family in its peculiar, "nuclear" form. Here, too, there is the idea that the family is in decline, but the opposite implication is drawn from this assumed fact. The decline of this supposedly harmful institution is cheerfully applauded. In between these two opposite interpretations is the more moderate view (probably held by the majority of family analysts) that social changes have had a massive impact on the family, which has shown itself to be a remarkably robust and adaptable institution but which is nevertheless in a state of crisis. Data on divorce, the rise in single-headed households, and the like are used to undergird this idea of crisis. And as we have seen, all three interpretations of the current state of the family can be used to demand government intervention, albeit for differing reasons and in differing ways.

It is not difficult to see the common *empirical* base of these three viewpoints, despite the great and (between the two polar views) contradictory interpretations: The family is in bad shape—and that is a terrible thing; the family is in bad shape—and that is just great; the family is in reasonably good shape—but it has very serious problems, and these will get worse unless something is done about them. What is interesting is that spokesmen for these various viewpoints have accused those holding other views of "mythologizing" the family, in the present or the past or both. Thus those holding the "decline and decadence" view have been accused as having fallen prey to the myth of "the classical family of Western nostalgia."[1] Those believing in the "bad is great" thesis have been accused of seeking mythological solutions that have no chance of success. And the moderates in the debate have been faulted for not understanding that they themselves are part of the problem, because they do not take with becoming seriousness the concerns of the other two parties. In consequence of these all-around accusations of "mythologizing," the watchword for much recent work on the family has been (logically enough) "*de*mythologizing." Every aspect of the academic as well as the popular understanding of the family—its nature, history, present function, and future course—should be subjected to revisionist scrutiny. But there is a cheering aspect of this "demythologizing" thrust: It has indeed produced some very valuable research, which indeed helps us to acquire a "revised" understanding of many facets of the family in modern society. Perhaps ironically, this "revisionism" puts in question precisely some of the common empirical assumptions mentioned above.

The most important "revisions" have been due to new historical research. The 1960s and 1970s have produced a considerable body of new research into the origins and early development of the family in the modern world.[2] This has yielded interesting insights of various sorts. But the insight most revelent to our present topic is this: The notion that the nuclear family is an exclusive product of modernity can itself be shown to have been a myth. This is all the more important in that, as we have indicated above, the alleged problems of the nuclear family (most of them ascribed precisely to its "nuclearity") constitute the common empirical base for all the major participants in the current debate over the family. It is perhaps noteworthy that the most recent revisions of this view have been a case of historians debunking sociologists. In any case, what has happened is that the demythologizers have themselves been demythologized.

Recent research into the history of the family, both in Western Europe and in northern America, shows that the nuclear family, far from being a product of modernization processes (such as urbanization and industrialization), *antedates* these processes *by centuries*. This means that the extended family, for which there has been so much nostalgia, has not existed in those parts of the world at least since the high middle ages. Thus, for example, the brilliant study of Montaillou, a fourteenth-century village in what is now southern France, by Emmanuel Ladurie, makes this point very clearly: The families described in this study show striking similarities with the nuclear type discovered by sociologists as specific to modernity.[3] Even more interestingly, there is some evidence that this nuclear family was common in *Western* Europe, while *Eastern* Europe did indeed have the sort of extended family that Westerners have been so nostalgic about.[4] One could perhaps develop a theory of nostalgia out of this paradox. For our purposes, though, it suggests a striking hypothesis: It could well be that the nuclear family is a *precondition*, rather than a *consequence*, of modernization. This hypothesis, needless to say, would stand on its head many of the assumptions that sociologists have operated with since the 1920s.

The central idea of the nuclear family, of course, is that a household consists of only a married couple and their children. Thus most of the historical data just referred to concern the membership of households.[5] It is this facet of family life that has been found to be dominant all the way back to Montaillou. The presence of servants in the more-well-to-do households has tended to obfuscate the nuclearity of the family structure. With servants, of course, a pre-modern household would have many more members than the typical middle-class family today—but the addition of the servants to the nuclear unit of spouses and children can hardly be called an extended family. What is more, this pre-modern nuclear pattern did not break down under the impact of modernization. On the contrary, it appears as a *continuing* structure (one is tempted here to employ the Marxist term "infrastructure") of Western societies before, during, and since the great transformations of modernity.

It cannot be said that the earlier views of the relation of the family to modernization have been irrevocably falsified. However, the new research suggests that the family in the West was not, as had been thought before, simply a passive recipient of modernizing changes but, rather, an active participant in the modernization process. It is also much more plausible to say now that the peculiar family type of Western societies has been one of the factors *fostering* modernization.[6] Looked at cross-culturally, it then appears that the pre-modern family can be *either* a block to modernization, as sociologists had so often assumed and as they may have been right in assuming with regard to non-Western patterns, *or* a conduit for modernization, as the new research suggests. In the latter case, one important contribution of the family to the modernization process may have been the protection of individuals against the dislocations and transformations taking place in the larger society.[7] The Western nuclear family was small and mobile enough to allow individuals to participate in modernization, and at the same time tightly knit enough to make this participation humanly tolerable. But even the non-Western, extended family patterns have a considerable capacity to survive in urban-industrial settings and indeed to provide individuals protection and succor in the face of modernizing changes. This is suggested both by studies of immigrants to America (especially from Eastern Europe) and by studies of the family in various Third World societies today.[8] In these cases what often takes place is what could be described as a very "creative schizophrenia": The individual in the modern urban-industrial situation can be "modern" at work and "traditional" at home, alternating between these two worlds of his life in a manner that is not only quite comfortable but actually productive. To be sure, this kind of alternation between worlds also produces tensions. But it is possible that analysts, especially social scientists, have overemphasized the negative aspects of these tensions, overlooking their creative potential.[9] It is still an open question, though, *how long* such "creative

schizophrenia" can be maintained, and we are open to the possibility
that those who have argued for the convergence of family types all
over the world as a result of modernization may be proved correct in
the long run.[10] One of the most important cases in this regard is modern Japan, where for a long time a "creative schizophrenia" between
modern and traditional spheres of life was successfully maintained—
and where analysts disagree on the continuing viability of this
synthesis.[11] But a pursuit of these broad questions would exceed our
present purpose.

In any case, in Western societies, it now appears, the impact of
urbanization and industrialization on the family has been greatly
overestimated.[12] Thus new research suggests that there has *not* been a
decline of family ties (including ties to kin beyond the nuclear family
unit), *not* a mounting isolation of the family in the urban situation,
*not* a general loss of functions of the family (but rather, a transfer
of functions). On the contrary, when one looks at the strength of
family ties and the importance of those ties to the individual, one is
struck by the remarkable continuity over the recent centuries of
Western history. As one analyst recently summarized these findings:
"In a period of rapid and radical change in most aspects of economic
and social life, it is odd that in many ways the European family
should have changed so little."[13] To be sure, this statement loses
some weight if one distinguishes between classes within Western
societies, but it remains correct in suggesting a major modification in
the earlier view, which understood modernization as having hit the
family like a convulsive cataclysm.

We should not go overboard on this. Major changes *did* take
place. There have been the separation of work from the home, the
transformation of housework by technological innovations, the disap-
pearance of servants, the revolution brought about by effective
methods of birth control—to name just a few. It is important therefore to find an explanatory model that will include both change and
continuity in the modern Western family.

We believe that modernization theory broadly understood is capable of doing this. However, we must distance our own position
from those who understand modernization primarily in terms of structural and functional changes, with ideation in all its forms reduced to
a dependent variable. Curiously, this reductionist bias is common to
both sociologists who consider themselves structural-functionalists

and to Marxists.[14] We can agree with *some* of the theoretical presuppositions of both schools. Thus we can agree with William Goode that "explanations for social behavior must be found in the social structure.[15] We can also agree with the Marxists that the "mode of production" of any society must be given primary attention in any explanation of social change. But our own version of modernization theory puts much greater stress on ideas, values, and structures of *consciousness* as factors in social change. This does not make us "idealists." Rather, we see social change as the result of the *interaction* (or, if one prefers, of a *dialectic*) of institutions and consciousness.[16] To which of the two sides of the interactive, or dialectical, process is attributed causal primacy will depend not on some theoretical *a priori* but on the empirical evidence concerning the situation under study. Thus it can be plausibly argued, in a Marxist vein, that the onset of industrial production dramatically transformed all aspects of social life, *including* consciousness. But this particular "mode of production" did not suddenly appear in history as a total innovation. It was the result of a long historical process—which included far-reaching changes in human consciousness. If industrialization caused great changes in consciousness, the advent of industrialization was in turn rooted in specific changes in consciousness (which, if Max Weber was right, may go back as far as the origins of the Judeo-Christian religious world view). And the future course of industrialization may in turn be affected by changes of consciousness. As to modernity, it is a constellation of structures both in the institutional order and in human consciousness, and the interrelation of these structures must be analyzed anew in each empirical situation.

This is highly relevant to our understanding of the relation of the family to modern society. We must distinguish between modern institutions and modern consciousness. It is quite correct that modern institutions produce modern consciousness. Thus, as the family is subjected to such modern processes as urbanization and industrialization, family values, norms, and concepts undergo changes. This does not mean, as we have indicated before, that all premodern forms of ideation simply disappear; with whatever modifications, or even with very few modifications, these traditional structures of consciousness may survive long into the modern period. But what is more, we can find (both historically and today) that modern structures of consciousness antedate their "realization" in modern institutions. Logically, of course, this had to be so in the beginning. Thus modern science and (at least by implication) modern technology had first to appear in the minds of innovative individuals before they began to be realized in the transformation of the external social world. But even today there can be a "cultural lag" in the opposite way from the usual sociological understanding of this phrase—that is, modern institutions may "lag behind" the appearance of certain elements of modern consciousness. A good example of this is the effect on consciousness of even a very minor injection of modern mass communication into a traditional situation, in consequence of which modern ideas begin to circulate in this situation *prior* to any concrete institutional change.[17] In just this way, the new historical research on the family suggests that the Western nuclear family, long before the advent of modernization, fostered mind-sets and values that were instrumental in bringing about institutional modernization, perhaps even in a very decisive way.

More specifically, the new research suggests that at least *one* of the sources of modern "rationalization" (to use Max Weber's term) may have been the peculiar Western nuclear family. If so, the reason for this is probably to be sought in the patterns of socialization in such a family: in the closer relationship between parents and children, in greater parental influence, and in greater individuation (always as compared with non-nuclear, or extended, family types). The most dramatic way of putting this would be to say that modernity did not produce the nuclear family but, on the contrary, the nuclear family produced modernity. Let us hasten to add that we do not believe in such simple, monocausal explanations of social change. But the dramatic reversal of the usual formulation of the relationship has a certain heuristic use, as a corrective to the conventional view.

In any case, we are persuaded by those historians of the family who argue that a society might become modernized before becoming industrialized and that this was probably the case in Western Europe in the sixteenth century if not earlier.[18] This would mean that modern structures of consciousness were fostered by the European family and that these structures were necessary, or at least very important, preambles to the industrial revolution that followed a considerable time later. We shall pursue the question of the relation of the family to modern consciousness in greater detail in the following chapter. For now, the most important point to be made is that one ought to move away from the conventional, one-sided view of the relation of the family to modernity in all its aspects. With this important reservation, we can now look at the institutional changes that have affected the family in the West. We have already looked at some of these in the first chapter, but a summary will be useful at this point in our argument.

The economic changes have been, if not paramount, of very great importance. The rise of wage labor, at the very beginnings of modern capitalism and prior to the coming of the industrial revolution, changed the relation of the household to economic production. Already in the late middle ages one can discern differences in family patterns between peasants and the classes out of which, later, the bourgeoisie was to emerge: the quasi-urbanized artisans and merchants. Family life among the latter appears to have been more open, individuated, and less ritualized than among the peasants. In the same way, there were differences between peasant families continuing to work their own land (whether owned or tenanted) and peasant families whose members hired themselves out for wage labor. When industrialization did come, of course, the nature of work was changed fundamentally. Most important, productive work was progressively taken out of the household. The family changed from being a unit of production to being a unit of consumption, with far-reaching consequences for its values and bonds. Also, with the industrial revolution, for some classes, there came about an increase in real *per capita* income, vesting earning power in the individual as detached from the family, further encouraging economic independence, mobility, and individuation. Again for some classes, this also meant a rising standard of living, from which the family derived immediate benefits. Greater material well-being, in these classes, allowed for new interests to develop within the family, including the "luxury" of new attitudes to spouses and children. Changes in socialization patterns were probably the most important aspect of this.

The "invention of childhood," as described by Philippe Ariès and other historians, was one of these "luxuries."[19] Beginning with the urban classes and the bourgeoisie that sprang from them, there appeared a new tenderness toward children, an interest in their development, and a prolongation of the period considered proper to childhood. Beginning in these classes, children came to be removed from the family for purposes of education. The school, as a separate educational institution standing over against the household, came into being. Later, of course, increasingly as a matter of state policy, this bourgeois pattern came to be extended to the entire population. These changes can be interpreted as a "loss of functions" for the family, if compared with its earlier character as an economic and educational institution. But, as Talcott Parsons correctly pointed out, the same changes can also be interpreted as a "freeing" of the family for other, partially new functions. These latter, however, belonged mainly to the private sphere; to some extent, at least, the family as an institution became "privatized."

The political changes were just as important, or nearly as important, as the economic changes, in their impact on the family. If capitalism and industrialism were the potent new realities in the economic area, the rise of the modern state was the immensely powerful new political reality. The feudal system, from top to bottom, was essentially an organization of households, and was aptly legitimated in familistic images. With the modernization of government, the household lost political functions. Patriarchal power within the household was progressively restricted. But, more fundamentally, *the individual,* abstracted from all family relationships, increasingly became the basic political unit, first as subject, then as citizen. Increasingly this affected women as well as men, culminating in the demand for universal suffrage independent of sex or family status. Parental control over the lives of children diminished not only with the development of independent educational institutions (increasingly administered and coercively recruited for by the state) but with the proliferation of economic opportunities not dependent on parental arrangements and with the progressive extension of political rights to individuals of all social classes. Of course, even today parents continue to be the "gatekeepers" of certain opportunities for their children—by "purchasing" the right kind of education, by other forms of financial support, and by contacts and influence. But, compared to earlier times, this parental control over the future of children is greatly attenuated. With the reduction of control, probably inevitably, came a reduction of authority. Where previously parental authority (especially, of course, the authority of the father) was taken for granted, it now rests on the relatively feeble pillars of personal affection, and must be ongoingly "renegotiated." In consequence, there appear new forms of intergenerational conflict, sometimes very intense in quality.

Finally, the declining influence of religion, as a result of the peculiarly modern phenomenon of secularization, also impacted upon the family. In the medieval world view the family was ultimately legitimated in terms of its connection with the sacramental apparatus of the church. The weakening of this legitimation could not but reduce the authority of the family. To a considerable extent the church as an institution was also "privatized." Other institutions now competed with it in providing moral guidance and authority for individual life. The most important institution doing this was, again, the modern state, increasingly arrogating to itself the final authority in the determination of the obligatory moral standards for society. One might say that, in a certain analogy to the economic change, the family became a consumer, rather than a producer, of moral values. To be sure, to put it this way tends to exaggerate the *degree* of change; the family continues to be a very important source for the moral constitution of individuals; but, compared with earlier periods, there has been a good deal of change in this area as well.

We must now look in somewhat greater detail at the most important feature of modern social change in terms of the history of the family—to wit, the victory of the so-called bourgeois family. As just argued, the great social transformations that are part and parcel of the modernization process are deeply rooted in the history of Western civilization—not only in its peculiar social, political, and economic structures but, above all, in its beliefs and values. And as more recent historical research emphasizes, these great changes appear to be rooted in the practices and values of many small groups, predominantly in rural and provincial communities. As these changes occurred, formerly backward areas were turned into bustling commercial and manufacturing centers—in England (notably in the Midlands), Scotland, France (notably around Lyon and La Rochelle), and in parts of the Netherlands, Germany, and Austria. It appears in this perspective that the cataclysmic changes that transformed Europe were the end products (one is almost tempted to say, the marginal products) of a specific way of life, in which the family played a paramount part. What was this specific way of life, and which strata of the population were its "carriers"? The answer, by now, is fairly clear. The "carrier" class of the great revolution was that middle stratum that later on came to be called the bourgeoisie, and the specific way of life underlying the revolution was what we now know as bourgeois culture (though, as we have seen, this has historical antecedents that could only awkwardly be given this designation).

The bourgeoisie already existed in embryonic form in the medieval social order, grew slowly over centuries, spread in ever larger measure to other social strata (both above and below itself), and reached the working class by the end of the nineteenth century. An essential element in this process was a particular type of the family. This type can be viewed as a significant deviation from the "common human pattern"—to use the apt term coined by Jan Romein to designate broad cross-cultural patterns of human life. The distinctive features of this deviation became more pronounced over time, as they visibly benefited those who adhered to it.[20]

One of the basic features of this deviant family type was the separation of the public and the private spheres—or, if one prefers, the *invention* of private life rooted in the family. This innovation already appears in merchant and artisan strata of the late middle ages, especially in urban or urbanizing areas (as Max Weber already saw). As this deviance developed, a great rupture appeared in what had been the common pattern. Until this rupture the household had been an economic as well as a conjugal unit. The master of a craft, for instance, presided over a "family" consisting not only of his wife and children (and whatever other blood relatives shared the household) but also of a fluctuating number of servants, journeymen, and apprentices, all living together. Thus his functions as husband, parent, and head of the enterprise tended to be fused. In this example, an urban household did *not* deviate significantly from its rural cognate; households of this type are common in peasant societies all over the world. This type of family functions very well in situations (again, very common cross-culturally) where there is no, or only a very rudimentary, public authority providing the security of social order. This (as we today conceive it) public function was provided by the family, disciplining its own members and "negotiating" the rules of order with other, similar families. It is important that the members of one family consist of blood relatives and others not so related; that is, membership in a family is determined not only by descent or marriage but by the sharing in a common economic enterprise. All these individuals were bonded together in an "almost perpetual community of life."[21]

In a household of this older type, life was "ungraded," in the sense that individuals of all ages participated in the same activities. Childhood, in other words, was not yet relegated to a distinctive and increasingly segregated category of life. Work was loosely organized, without the regulation of schedules so characteristic of modern life. In all likelihood, most people worked considerably less than they do today. (We will not pursue here, as tangential to our main topic, the interesting implication that, if this historical research is valid, the notion that modernity has brought about a quantum leap in the availability of leisure time would be false.) And, very important, privacy in the modern sense was virtually unknown. Life was communal in most respects, and only very rarely did or could individuals withdraw into solitude from this common web of living. Our modern sense of shame about such activities as elimination (to be engaged in increasingly in the privacy of the "privy") and sex, and, last but not least, our attitude toward death are very much related to the rupture of an earlier, communal way of life.[22]

The family and the economy changed in tandem. As early as the fourteenth century, in the very early stages of European capitalism, there emerged trading associations no longer based on domestic cooperation only. These trading associations were marked by two important features: the formation of capital based on the pooling of funds by several families, and the separation of economic activities from family life dictated by this. Concomitantly, a distinctive private sphere began to come into being, separated from economic activity and (necessarily) giving new prominence to the interaction between the members of each family. Also concomitantly, contractual relationships gained in importance, since the larger economic units could no longer be held together by an informal "patriarchal" authority. The ancient role of the father began to be undermined. The limits of allegiance implicit in the very notion of contract liberalized social life. This has been a commonplace of sociological theory for a long time (central, for instance, to the views of modernity of Émile Durkheim and Ferdinand Tönnies, as well as of Henry Maine). But, less commonplace, the same liberalization affected life within the family as well. Sons became contractual partners of their fathers, increasingly with equal rights. They were no longer bound to live in the parental household or, if they did live there, to work in the parental enterprise. Individuals thus began to gain economic independence from their families. To a lesser extent, this is also true of daughters, who tended to be "silent partners" but who came to acquire the legal right of withdrawing their inherited capital from the parental enterprise. This new kind of extra- or supra-familial enterprise was increasingly protected by the law. Thus the legal recognition of companies with limited liability separated personal or family funds from business capital, further solidifying the separation of private and public spheres.

As these processes matured, the old unity of the household was dissolved, with enormous consequences for the family. The individual became increasingly independent of the family. Privacy and individualism developed together. And, in consequence, the interaction within the family also had to change dramatically. With the loosening up of what Philippe Ariès has called the "density of social life" in an earlier period, and with the emergence of a distinctive and family-centered private sphere, individuals within the family were "liberated" to experiment with novel and even revolutionary roles. This "liberation" affected the relations between spouses, and between the latter and their children.

As the family became "liberated," it became "domesticated"—a historical correlation all the more important to emphasize, as the two terms are widely perceived today as antithetical. Philippe Ariès has been very influential in our understanding of the process of "domestication," basing himself on French sources from the fifteenth to the end of the seventeenth centuries. While Ariès' views have been criticized by other historians, there are some aspects of his perspective that are difficult to challenge. The emergence of the concept of childhood in its modern sense, with the removal of children into a separate category of life and the introduction of "age grading" into the family, is probably the most important aspect. The rise of education consequent to this "invention of childhood" is another very important aspect, allying family and school in a grand "conspiracy" to remove the child from adult society. Then there is the development of a new sensibility in the family, strongly linked to children and their education but then spreading far from the nursery and the schoolroom in its new notions of love, morality, and propriety. And Ariès was almost certainly correct in seeing all these changes as occurring first and foremost within the rising bourgeoisie, thus giving empirical validity to the common phrase of the "bourgeois family."

However, much of what Ariès described belongs in a larger picture of societal change, over and beyond the French history on which he concentrated. Also, his critical view of modernity reduced him to a mocking tone when describing the new bourgeois domesticity; a very different attitude to the latter is possible, even while granting the validity of most of Ariès' data. In any case, the larger picture into which these data should be fitted is the transformation of Western society by the economic and political forces of modernization. Although the domestic family emerged in the West during the sixteenth and seventeenth centuries among the merchant and artisan strata of the towns, and somewhat later in the landed nobility, its most vigorous expression was in the eighteenth century in the class of small producers working their own property—the class from which the bourgeoisie of the industrial revolution sprang.[23] This *petite bourgeoisie* managed most effectively to merge the new family values with the new ideas of private property and individualism that legitimated its social aspirations. In saying this, we are not at all implying a quasi-Marxist understanding of the family values being nothing but ideological constructions in the service of class interests; rather, we understand the relationship, in Max Weber's sense, as one of "affinity" between ethos and class interests, with each influencing the other. During this period, the new family ethos was often linked to religion: Puritanism, Presbyterianism, and later Methodism in England and the American colonies, Calvinism and Jansenism in France, Pietism in Germany. And we agree with Weber in his understanding of the role of Protestantism in the genesis of modern capitalism—though Weber could not have known the equally important role of the family, as uncovered by recent research.

At least since the late-eighteenth century, the history of the West is, in a very basic sense, the history of the bourgeois class and its culture. The great historical transformations of the subsequent two centuries, which, in the aggregate, have produced what we now know as modernity, have been overwhelmingly the products of this class. Since for about half of this period, since the triumph of the bourgeoisie in the nineteenth century (in the major countries of the West, that is), this class and its culture have been identified with the *status quo* against which every rebel worth his salt would define himself, it is all the more important to understand the revolutionary character of this class in its deviation from age-old human patterns. (It may be remarked here, incidentally, that Marx understood this much better than many of his present disciples.) It is very important *not* to confuse this new, culture-producing bourgeoisie with the bourgeoisie of seventeenth- and eighteenth-century France, who made their entry into the court of power as of the reign of Louis XIV. This older bourgeoisie did not create its own culture and ethos but was imitative, in virtually all aspects of life, of the ruling aristocracy. This was derisively described, in his famous *Memoirs*, by Louis, Duc de Saint-Simon, who can be said to exemplify the aristocrat looking down on the social climbers of his age. This older, as it were culturally derivative bourgeoisie, was very different from the "new" bourgeoisie, which was originally predominantly Protestant. It was these people and their descendants who developed "an ethos, a culture peculiar to the industrial bourgeoisie."[24] *This* culture created the modern world. One of its major characteristics was a fine balance between revolutionizing activity in the larger society (the public sphere) and a zone of domesticity (the private sphere) into which the individual could ongoingly withdraw—for rest and recreation, as it were. The bourgeois family, we would contend, has been the pivotal institution making this balance possible. In this lies its most fundamental relationship to modernity, at least in the shape this has developed in the West. And for this reason the future of modernity is very much linked to the future of the family.

We will return to this point in later chapters. For now, to continue the historical sketch, we would emphasize once more the character of the early bourgeoisie as a community of dissenters. Dissent always requires forceful legitimations, without which the dissenting individual simply lacks the self-assurance and courage to defy the existing structures. This is why the religious qualities of the rising bourgeoisie were so important. Especially Protestantism, in its more unbending varieties, provided these people with an almost unshakable confidence in the righteousness of their values, culture, and political causes. It goes without saying that this often had an aspect of rigidity and fanaticism, inevitably so. It so appears to the retrospective today; it also looked that way to many observers at the time (such as good, moderate Catholics). Revolutionaries are not given to moderation. They pursue their aims with a minimum of self-questioning. This same single-mindedness was expressed in the pursuance of the bourgeois virtues—such as hard work, simple living, and moral propriety—within the bosom of the new bourgeois family.[25] If this produced "repression" in the children growing up in this milieu, it also gave them an inner resilience we can only look back to with wonder. To understand history, here as elsewhere, is to appreciate trade-offs.

If the historical perspective outlined in this chapter is valid, as we are inclined to think, then it no longer holds that the bourgeois family was the *product* of the industrial revolution; instead, it must now be understood as one of the important *preconditions* of this technological cataclysm. To say this, however, is not at all to deny that, once the industrial revolution was under way, there were far-reaching effects back upon the family. As industrialization proceeded through the nineteenth century in the major Western countries, the bourgeois vision of life was given the facility to penetrate ever-wider sectors of society. In the area that concerns us here, the bourgeois family and its norms became the standard for *all* classes. This was the beginning of the "evangelistic," or missionary, phase of the bourgeois family ethos, to which we referred in an earlier chapter. And increasingly this ethos was coercively spread, not only by the voluntary efforts of well-meaning bourgeois individuals and institutions, but by the power of the state.

Within the bourgeoisie itself, the rise in standards of living made possible by industrial technology progressively transformed the household. This had a very important consequence for the way of life of bourgeois women. Sheila Rothman has described this very well for American society in the last decades of the nineteenth century: "Almost every technological invention in the period 1870–1900 significantly altered the daily routine of middle-class women. During these years, city after city, responding to the demands of engineers and real estate promotors, constructed and extended water and sewage lines. . . . By 1890, even moderate-priced homes in many cities were equipped with hot and cold water, water closets, and bathrooms."[26] This technological transformation of the household leaped forward of course with the advent of electricity, the effects of which are still continuing today with gadget after gadget. All of this led to an extraordinary reduction in women's menial tasks, to be sure first in higher-income households but in the twentieth century penetrating massively into the working class. With this, the bourgeois "liberation" of women took on a new character, one of far-reaching and enduring physical comfort. By now, needless to say, this physical comfort is taken for granted by everyone above the poverty line—and claimed as a basic human right by those below it. On the basis of this physical comfort, every sort of life-style innovation and experiment.

But what was diffused to all social classes was not only the external accoutrements of bourgeois life but, more important, its peculiar vision of family life. This vision can be spelled out without much difficulty.[27] Family life is supposed to be attractive. Thus the home becomes a major focus of concern and attention. The home is supposed to be "nicely" furnished, comfortable, an expression of the "good taste" of its inhabitants. Living space is separated by function, and there is special space (typically, the living room) in which the family does things together. For the working father (and, later, the working mother), the home becomes the locale of withdrawal from the tensions and worries of the job, a place of refuge and renewal, where the "real life" of the individual can unfold.

Naturally enough, as the home became more attractive and the key locale for the "self-realization" of the individual, sociability came to be centralized there. In other words, sociability moved out of the streets, out of public places; it, too, became "domesticated." This has been criticized as a distortion of social life, as a diminishment of the public sphere, just as the increase of physical comfort and its accoutrements has been attacked—the former as "privatization," the latter as "consumerism." Such criticism is plausible on the basis of specific values—such as a classical vision of the primacy of the public, or an ascetic ideal of personal, life. We are not interested at the moment in challenging these values (though we are skeptical of them); the point here is, rather, to emphasize that both affluence and domesticity have been very important ingredients in what, for generations, was experienced as the "liberating" quality of bourgeois life.

The new bourgeois ethos, while being diffused, retained its central features as these were formed in an earlier period. The concern for children remained in the foreground. Linked to this, there was the concern for education, both as a general social value and as applying specifically to one's own children. The intimate life of the family remains as the focus of personal values and identity, both for men and women. The idea of romantic love continues as the major motive for marriage. The relation between spouses is to be one of intense mutual affection and respect. Within the household, at least, the woman is seen as equal if not dominant. In view of the recent feminist interpretation of this process, the last point ought to be stressed. To be sure, the domestic sphere came to be seen as women's "proper place." This is now frequently interpreted as an economic, and in consequence sociopolitical, disenfranchisement of women. With the modern organization of work, it is argued, men working outside the household were paid, while women performed unpaid work within the household. Ivan Illich has coined the phrase "shadow work" for this type of unpaid labor: "The woman, formerly the mistress of a household that provided sustenance for the family, now became the guardian of a place where children stayed before they began to work, where the husband rested, and where his income was spent."[28] This interpretation rests on the unstated assumption that only paid work is to be considered as supplying status. Almost certainly, this is a projection onto the situation of very new perceptions by intellectuals, which did not prevail at all in an earlier period and still do not prevail in wide areas of society. On the contrary, for many women, especially below the upper middle class, this alleged "disenfranchisement" is precisely what they consider to be "liberation" from the discontents of work in the marketplace.

Be this as it may, in the bourgeois vision of the family the woman is paramount in the home.[29] It is her domain. The husband/father continued for a while as a figure of power and authority in the household, but this status was very successively undermined by the emancipated bourgeois wife/mother, increasingly in conjunction with outside experts such as clergy, doctors, and teachers, more recently psychotherapists and counselors of various types. Today, where this family vision continues to hold, the family regime is largely a regime of women, and the old paternal ideal is the subject of caricature, rather than realistic perception (as, say, American soap operas of the 1950s vividly expressed). It is ironic that just this father figure of diminished and comic status should become the object of feminist wrath. The woman of the bourgeois family has, above all, a "civilizational" mission, both within and beyond the household. Within the household, the woman is the "homemaker"—companion and helper to her husband, supervisor and "facilitator" of her children's development and education, arbiter of taste, culture, and all the "finer things of life." But this civilizing mission also extends beyond the home, into social and cultural activities of an "edifying" nature, and (especially in America) into reformist politics. The role of bourgeois women in the building of cultural institutions (museums, libraries, symphony orchestras, and so on) and in political reform (take, for example, such organizations as the League of Women Voters) has been staggering in its society-wide impact. Far from being imprisoned within the family, we would argue, bourgeois women have been prime builders of bourgeois civilization.

Perhaps it should not surprise us that some women became disenchanted with this role, quite apart from the feminist movement as such. Civilization-building is a weary-making task, with its own psychic costs. In the (somewhat misleading) language of the critics, it can become tiresome to be "on a pedestal." Also, the very values of the bourgeois family ethos, from the beginning, had within them the seeds of their own destruction. Individualism, brought forth within the family, would turn against it. Education would free itself of its family linkage and burgeon into powerful institutions with an anti-family animus, or at least with vested interests antagonistic to those of the family. The experts who started out as allies of the bourgeois family would develop interests and viewpoints of their own that put them at odds with the family. Again not surprisingly, these disintegrative developments became intense in the upper middle class (the original social location of the bourgeois family ethos) just after the patterns of that class were effectively diffused to the lower classes. If one prefers a different language, "decadence" always sets in first in the higher strata of society, those strata whose "virtues" originally shaped the society. (The same phenomenon could be observed in the aristocracy of the *ancien régime*, as it weakly tried to defend itself against the vigorously rising bourgeoisie.) Thus today, ironically, a more "intact" bourgeois family ethos can be found in the working classes of most Western societies than in that upper middle class which is still identified with the "bourgeoisie" by its radical critics!

The diffusion of the bourgeois family "downwards" is itself a fascinating topic of historical research.[30] There have been few well-documented arguments as yet as to the precise nature of this process. But it can be confidently stated that by the middle of the twentieth century the main features of the bourgeois family ethos, as outlined above, had spread to virtually all classes in Western societies. Especially the women of the lower classes saw in this ethos the great promise of their own fulfillment and "liberation" from the drudgery of low-prestige and low-paid jobs. In these classes, too, women more than men have been the great "civilizers." This can be seen, for instance, in the black family in America, which has been misleadingly characterized as a thoroughly disorganized and pathogenic social milieu.[31] One of the final ironies of our contemporary situation is this: that the "helping professions," offsprings of the bourgeois family ethos, are now trying to police the lower classes in the name of values quite antagonistic to that ethos—those same lower classes whose vision of the good life is mostly closer to the old bourgeois patterns than the vision of the professionals! It is as if, in truly "decadent" fashion, the bourgeois ethos had turned upon itself.

# 5

# The Family
# and
# Modern
# Consciousness

The recent history of the Western world, we have argued, is closely bound to the rise of the bourgeois family. More specifically, we have argued that this type of family, with its very distinctive features, has been the chief "carrier" (to use Max Weber's term) of modernization. This, of course, is not to deny that a multitude of historical forces have shaped the process of modernization; any monocausal explanation of history or society is uninformed, incomplete, and in the end wrong. But we believe that the family has been a "motor" of modernization in a way still not perceived by most historians and social scientists. The latter continue to perceive the family as, in the main, responding to changes outside itself, to see it as a passive object of history, rather than as an active agent. In this view, the bourgeois family must adjust itself to the changing economic and political forces outside itself; in this effort of adjustment, the inherent flaws and weaknesses of this family type are revealed; unless the family can overcome these and adjust itself to a changed society, the family as an institution will perish.

In the preceding chapter, we have tried to show why this view is to be questioned. We must now delineate the implications of this active view of the family for an understanding of the contemporary situation. This will reveal a further important phenomenon—to wit, that the bourgeois family, which played such a crucial role in producing the modern world, has now, paradoxically, become the locale of *de*modernizing forces. To understand this, it is necessary to look at the family not only on the institutional level but on the level of consciousness. Specifically, the important (and, as will be seen, paradoxical) relation of the bourgeois family to modern consciousness must be brought into focus.

Our theoretical presuppositions on this relation of the family to modern consciousness are based on the sociology of knowledge.[1] We cannot digress here on the details of this theoretical approach. We must stress, however, that the approach is neither "materialistic" nor "idealistic." That is, we are *not* presupposing that consciousness is an epiphenomenon, fully determined by "underlying" causes of a material sort; but *neither* do we assume that, finally, ideas are the final causes of historical change. Rather, we understand the relation of society and consciousness to be a dialectical one, in the original meaning of that term: Social institutions and formations of consciousness *interact*, cause each other, in such a way that neither can be explained without the other. In this instance, we argue, the interaction is complex and strangely ironic.

The bourgeois family has been the matrix (a singularly apt word in this context!) of a variety of values, norms, and "definitions of reality." Put differently, the bourgeois family has engendered specific structures of human consciousness. These structures, however, have not been contained within the family only. By virtue of their very nature as modes of relating the individual to the world, they have transcended the family and penetrated other spheres of institutional life: the economy, the political order, and a variety of other institutions. This penetration has been crucial for what has rightly been called the bourgeois revolution. Marx understood this very well when he described this revolution as "the victory of family over the family name."[2] The bourgeois revolution, which initiated the whole drama of modernization, has totally transformed society. In the course of this transformation, such powerful forces have been released that it is often difficult to trace them back to the seemingly parochial social locales in which they originated. One may use Marxian language here by saying that these revolutionary forces have become "alienated" from their source. The Marxian term is useful in showing how the modern world, itself the product of the bourgeois family, now confronts the latter as an alien, "reified" reality. In the face of this reality, the family now seems dwarfed, impotent, in the thralls of external forces utterly beyond its control. Thus the family appears as the victim of the very forces that it gave (and still gives) birth to.

Ever since the Marxian attack on the bourgeoisie as the exploiting class of capitalism, mostly negative connotations are evoked by the adjective "bourgeois." Even today, few self-respecting scholars will use the word without distancing themselves from the reality it purports to denote. Needless to say, this was not always so. Such divergent thinkers as John Locke, Friedrich Hegel, Alexis de Tocqueville, and John Ruskin used the word in a positive way. And it is good to recall that Marx himself evinced great respect at least for the early bourgeoisie as the great fashioner of the industrial revolution. It is all the more important to transcend the evaluative connotations of the term in order to disclose its phenomenal contents, especially those that refer to the level of consciousness. Thus Benjamin Franklin, one of the best-known adulators of "bourgeois man," describes the latter in terms of frugality, enterprise, decency, common sense, abstinence, discipline, reliability, politeness, respect, and fairness. Each of these terms could easily be translated into a pejorative. Thus the anti-bourgeois vision portrays these traits as selfishness, pettiness, narrowness, avarice, competitiveness, bigotry, inequality, oppressiveness, and a generally uninspiring philistinism. Yet it is quite possible to perceive both sets of terms as describing the *same* reality; if so, it is also possible to describe that reality in nonevaluative terms.

As far as the bourgeois family is concerned, of course, the same double vision prevails. In one vision, the bourgeois family is a natural unit of parents and children, united by love, mutual respect, trust, and fidelity, based on religiously inspired values and giving a distinct moral quality to this basic unit of social life. In the other vision, the bourgeois family is a narrowly constraining cage, turning its members into mere instruments of production, profoundly destructive of the personalities of women and children (and, perhaps to a lesser degree, of men), and generally cutting off its members from participation on the larger concerns of society. Can these contrasting visions be over-

come in a clearer understanding of the root characteristics of this family type? We think so. But before proceeding to this matter, a few
clarifying observations about the term "bourgeois" itself are appropriate.

When we speak of the bourgeoisie as the principal "carrier" of
modernization, we are not thinking of the early bourgeoisie, which entered the stage of history in the late-sixteenth and in the seventeenth
centuries. As we have argued before this early bourgeoisie was intent
on accumulating wealth and gaining political power, and in its
successes in these areas it certainly laid the foundations of what later
became the bourgeois revolution. But it was still an *haute bourgeoisie*,
its *hauteur* betraying its quasi-seigneurial ambitions. Both life-style
and world view were still very much derived from the aristocracy,
with which this early bourgeoisie vied for wealth and power. That is,
the later and highly distinctive bourgeois self-consciousness was as yet
lacking or very weak. A self-reliant, self-conscious bourgeoisie appeared later, and it had different origins. It evolved out of the large
stratum of small merchants, artisans, and the increasingly educated
"clerks" whose services became part and parcel of the push toward
modernity. This was a *petite bourgeoisie*, quite different in life-style
and world view from the early bourgeoisie. It is this new class, with
its "petty-bourgeois" values and practices, which created a peculiar
family life and a culture that came to dominate the Western world.

This new bourgeois world view and the morality that went with
it had important religious roots, especially in the Protestant countries.
This fact, as is well known, is central to Max Weber's theory of the
relationship of Protestantism and capitalism. The same "Protestant
ethic" was centrally related to the new bourgeois family. The latter,
more than any other institution, facilitated the process by which this
morality, in Weber's words, "strode into the market-place of life . . .
and undertook to penetrate just that daily routine of life."[3] It was in
the bosom of the bourgeois family that the Protestant virtues, with
their affinity to capitalism, were nurtured. Weber describes these virtues: anti-traditional, abstemious, disciplined, dynamic, individualistic,
and above all, rational. Individualism and rationalism may be considered as decisively important themes in this moral formation. Both
were rooted in specifically Protestant religious attitudes and beliefs.
As the modern world became secularized, these themes inevitably
weakened in plausibility.

The modern world is the result of a long and all-pervasive process of rationalization. Capitalism, as an economic order, is only a part of this process. Weber concentrated on capitalism, but his view of the latter's origins is as relevant to modernity as a whole, of which capitalism is but one (though very important) institution. Equally important to the constellation we know as modernity are science and technology, with their distinctive forms of rationality, and rational law, political order, and bureaucracy. All this is generally accepted by analysts of modernity. What is much less discussed is the process of rationalization in the private lives of individuals, as it developed within the bourgeois family.

Rationalism refers to a mind-set oriented toward *control*—to wit, toward controlling the world by rational calculation. And individualism refers to both the belief in and the psychological reality of *autonomy*—to wit, an attitude on the part of the individual of independence, self-assertion, and if necessary dissent *vis-à-vis* society. In the Protestant ethic, these two phenomena (which, looked at abstractly, could well appear in separation) were closely linked in what Weber called "inner-worldly asceticism"—a discipline of life geared to purposes within this world (as against the quest for salvation in another world) and marked by hard work, frugality, and endless effort. Protestantism, especially in its Calvinist version, gave birth to this social-psychological constellation for peculiar religious reasons. The anti-magical, radically transcendent orientation of Protestant faith had the consequence of freeing the world from supernatural interventions (as in the sacramental world view of medieval Catholicism) and thus laying it open first to the rational inquiries of the scientist and then to the imposition of rational controls by both the engineer and the entrepreneur. Further, the peculiar solitude of the Protestant religious experience (as against Catholic communalism) fostered an austere individualism, which could never relax and which led to a lifelong striving for perfection. These virtues were built into the socialization process as it was established in the bourgeois family in Protestant countries.

This family type provided the social context for the formation of highly individuated persons. Put differently, it provided for the socialization of autonomous individuals. This type of human being has been aptly described by David Riesman: "Those who are capable of conforming to the behavioral norms of society . . . but are free to choose whether to conform or not."[4] In traditional parlance, these are individuals with "character." For such people, tradition is no longer the sole yardstick of conduct. A personal stand not only may but must be taken in situations in which this is morally demanded by conscience, even if this stand arrays the individual against accepted convention. Luther's "here I stand, I can do no other" is the prototypical formula of this ideal of autonomy. The individual is to be *both* free *and* responsible, guided only by a specific (originally, of course, religiously grounded) "internal self-piloting process," as Riesman calls it. If it is the individual who is ultimately responsible for his actions, over against any group to which he belongs, then it is of the utmost importance to raise children in such a way that they will become "men of conscience." The autonomy of the individual must be asserted even against the family, if need be; on the other hand, only the family can be the social context within which such individuals can be formed.

Since this type of individualism has been subjected to much criticism in the recent past, and since in the course of this assault it has been regularly pictured as old-fashioned and traditional, there is a need to recall how revolutionary it was when it first appeared. When the individual is responsible for himself and for his career in this world, he becomes the center of life in what then was a totally novel way. The hierarchical world view of medieval society is decisively breached. Hierarchy is always conservative in its social and political consequences; conversely, the breakdown of hierarchy introduces a new element of social and political dynamism. There are to be no more barriers, natural or social, to the advancement of the individual, provided the latter follows those virtues that have proved to lead to success. In Benjamin Franklin's words, "Help yourself, and God will help you"—an anti-traditional dictum if there ever was one. *Any* individual, regardless of the accident of his birth, is now liberated to advance himself.

The virtues enjoined by this bourgeois-Protestant morality are, in principle, accessible to everyone: hard work, diligence, discipline, attention to detail, frugality, and the systematic (not sporadic) cultivation of willpower. And the obverse vices can be avoided by everyone (not just by saints or geniuses): idleness, thoughtlessness, intemperance, vanity, and self-indulgence in all its forms. In other words, the bourgeois-Protestant morality was, from the beginning, a democratic and egalitarian one. *These* were the virtues that the bourgeois family forcefully inculcated in its children, and it is a peculiarly short-sighted vision that perceives the forcefulness of this socialization as "authoritarian" or "repressive."

An important apostle of this ethic in mid-nineteenth-century England was Samuel Smiles, known for a series of tracts on such themes as "self-help," "character," "thrift," and "duty."[5] These tracts were explicitly addressed to men from the "humbler ranks" of society, who were enjoined to improve their position by following these virtues, pointing out that their happiness and well-being as individuals in after-life must necessarily depend mainly upon themselves—upon their diligent self-culture, self-discipline, and self-control—and, above all, on that honest and upright performance of individual duty which is the glory of manly character[6]—the phrase "after-life" referring here *not* to life after death but to the career of the individual in society after he takes these wholesome teachings to heart. What must be emphasized in all this is that this kind of individualism relies completely upon "strong character"; thus *the* question is how such a "character" is to be formed. No wonder, then, that the family, the character-building institution *par excellence,* moved to center stage! Only "strong families" could shape "strong characters," and this the bourgeois family set itself to do—with, one must say, remarkable success.

In view of more recent criticisms, it should be emphasized that in this ethic, economic success in itself is not a virtue. Rather, the virtue lies in individual responsibility and performance of duty. In other words, this is not at all a morality that legitimated greed. It placed a major burden on the successful and the rich: to earn ever again a "state of grace" by resisting the temptations and vices of wealth. The systematic quality of this life-style should also be emphasized: The "little things" in life, the ordinary and seemingly unimportant details of everyday events, matter as much as the "great things." One may call this orientation typically petty bourgeois, as against the "magnanimity" of the aristocratic and *haut-bourgeois* ethos, but the word "petty" should not necessarily be understood in a pejorative way. Rather, behind this morality lies the primarily Protestant conviction that God is present in even the smallest things of this world, which for that reason deserve the most careful and reverential attention. Once again, this can be done only by individuals of strong "character." In Smiles's words: "The man who can withstand the weight of riches, and still be diligent, industrious, and strong in mind and heart, must be made of strong stuff. For people who are rich are almost invariably disposed to be idle, luxurious, and self-indulgent."[7]

Smiles was English, but very similar sentiments can be found in other Protestant countries, notably in America and in Germany.[8] Thus, for example, this ethic is succinctly expressed in a famous poem by Theodor Fontane, the nineteenth-century Prussian writer:

> Gaben, wer hätte sie nicht?
> Talente—Spielzeug für Kinder.
> Erst der Ernst macht den Mann,
> Erst der Fleiss das Genie.[9]

(Gifts—who has them not? Talents—toys for children. Only seriousness makes the man, only diligence the genius.) Everywhere, religion provided the ultimate foundation of these moral strictures for everyone and the balancing force in social life. Without this religious foundation (one can see in retrospect) this morality was bound to lapse progressively into implausibility. This is why the fate of the bourgeoisie, its ethic and its family form, was very intimately tied to the fate of religion. And those who perceived this, often intuitively and in an inarticulate way, were better sociologists than those "progressives" who fervently believed that the bourgeois virtues could be divorced from the religious world view that had originally engendered them.

As we have observed before, the bourgeoisie invented a new world of childhood. It was in that class that the family was sharply separated from work and that the household became a segregated locale for child rearing. It was in this setting that the formation of "strong characters," of autonomous individuals imbued with an ethic of responsibility, could take place.

One of the questions that intrigues social historians revolves around the origin of the bourgeois concern for the welfare of children.[10] Demographers differ as to the details of this. Our inclination is toward the view that the falling infant *mortality* rates, which began to occur at the end of the eighteenth century, rather than the falling *birthrates*, which did not occur until the end of the nineteenth century, are the more important causal factor. The reason for our position on this is that the new world of bourgeois childhood antedates by a good century the great decline in birthrates. To understand this factor, an exercise of the imagination is helpful. One must imagine the psychological implications for parents of a situation in which, when a child is born, the strong probability is that this child will never grow into maturity, indeed that the child will die in the first three years of life. This situation, which still prevails in a large number of places in the Third World today, was the normal one for most of human history —and not only for the poor, for infant mortality ravaged the families of the rich almost as much (if not more so at least in early-nineteenth-century France, according to Donzelot). In such a situation it is only natural that parents would "armor" themselves against investing too much emotion in small children and that they would refrain from overexerting themselves in efforts to prepare such children for a future they would probably never live to see. To say this, of course, is not to impute to these parents lack of love or affection, or to arrogate to ourselves some superior humane status; on the contrary, the psychological assumption here is that parents, everywhere and at all times, loved their children[11]—and that, for this very reason, they had to act in such a way as to reduce the destructive onslaught of grief when it all too predictably occurred. The decline in infant mortality changed all that. Now it began to make sense, rationally as well as emotionally, to treat even very young children as inheritors of the future—and we know from child psychology how very important the earliest years of life are for the formation of personality. Once again, the bourgeois family was the locale of this demographic revolution—not because there were fewer children (bourgeois families in the seventeenth and eighteenth centuries had very many children) but because fewer children died. And that latter fact can be ascribed to the aforementioned bourgeois ethic of discipline and attention to a careful management of life, including the management of child care. Hygiene ("cleanliness next to godliness") was an important element of this. An alliance between mothers and doctors was one outgrowth.

The rising bourgeoisie, in contradistinction to the aristocracy, emphasized upbringing as against innate endowment. Aristocrats (this seems to be a cross-culturally intrinsic feature) tend to think in biological terms—an individual *is* his "blood"—and this often leads to an attitude toward procreation not too different from the attitude one has toward the breeding of fine animals. The bourgeoisie, by its very origins, cannot aspire to be an elite of "blood"; rather, it is an ethical elite—that is, its status depends on the successful cultivation of certain values. That, however, is necessarily a matter of upbringing and education. In other words, while the aristocracy emphasized inheritance, the bourgeoisie emphasized environment—specifically, the environment in which its children grew up. By the end of the nineteenth century, this bourgeois "environmentalism" had become dominant, especially in the United States. Thus children were perceived as wax or blank paper, to be molded or "written on" by their educators.[12]

This education was to be primarily the task of parents. There developed a pronounced distrust of servants in terms of their influence on children, and this distrust extended to tutors (still the mainstay of aristocratic education). Defoe, for instance, regarded tutors as "murtherers of a child's moralls."[13] Increasingly, parents were the adults in whose company children spent most of their time—in itself a powerful socializing agent. For a while, before the school began to "expropriate" the family of its educational functions, most education took place within the home; it was, so to speak, domesticated. This domestic education brought the young more immediately under parental control—and conversely, children became the center of attention within the bourgeois household. It was believed that only parents were properly aware of the unique characteristics and individual needs of their children and therefore that parents knew best how to bring up those children. The main burden of raising and educating the young child fell on the mother; educating the older child and the adolescent, especially in the case of boys, was deemed to be more the father's task. Both boys and girls had intense and sustained contact with their parents, who served as the principal initiators into the world of adulthood.[14]

Maria Edgeworth, an English writer of the nineteenth century, tells how her father did not allow his various activities to interfere with his educational task. On the contrary, these activities "assisted in affording him daily and hourly opportunities for giving instruction after his manner, without formal lectures or lessons. For instance, at the time when he was building or carrying on experiments or work of any sort, he constantly explained to his children whatever was doing or to be done." This easy, informal association of the children with the concerns of the household caused "animation [to] spread through the house by connecting children with all that was going on, and allowing them to join in thought or conversation with the grown-up people of the family. . . . Both sympathy and emulation excited mental exertion in the most agreeable manner."[15] William Cobbett writes in the

same vein: "The paying of the work-people, the keeping of accounts, the referring to books, the writing and reading of letters; the
everlasting mixture of amusement with book-learning, made me, almost to my own surprise, find . . . that I had a parcel of scholars
growing up about me."[16]

We may make allowance for selective memories and for the likelihood that in many bourgeois households things were less ideally ar-
ranged. The fact remains that, by the evidence, domestic education
made it possible to socialize precisely the sort of responsible, competent, and morally sensitive individuals that bourgeois values demanded. This centrality of the child-raising function transformed the
family from within and did so in terms of a comprehensive rationalization. That is, the transformation had its roots not primarily in
external forces acting upon the family but in the values the family imposed upon itself. And this had to have a rationalizing effect: Since
*everything* the parents did came to be related to the great educational
mission of the family, *everything* had to be disciplined in accordance
with that mission. Put graphically, if one did not do certain things "in
front of the children," one would find that not much time or space
was left in which one was free of this constraint!

This rationalization extended to the body as well as the mind. The
bourgeois family paid much attention to health care. It tended to experiment with various methods designed to produce strong bodies
able to resist the many childhood diseases—again, by the evidence of
the results, with some success. The physical living arrangements of the
family were similarly rationalized. Every aspect of the child's life was
carefully *planned,* and this in itself was a powerful rationalizing
factor.[17] Thus the child was carefully protected at the same time that
he was to develop into the autonomous individual of the bourgeois
ideal; this has been aptly termed a pattern of "protected liberation."[18]
In this way, the restructuring of the family for purposes of child rearing fostered and socialized rationality, and this rationality inevitably
carried over beyond the family into other areas of life.

The class aspect of all this should again be stressed. The old
upper classes, the aristocracy, long resisted these patterns, as did the
working class. It took the latter as much as a century to develop a
comparable family ethos—mainly, of course, under the influence of a
bourgeois-inspired and bourgeois-managed compulsory educational
system. For a long time, working-class childhood was one of "super-

vised freedom," rather than of "protected liberation."[19] But, for those
working-class families who adopted the bourgeois family patterns,
this became a very important factor of upward social mobility. That
is, a bourgeois-type socialization produced individuals who had the
attitudes and skills by which they could hope to rise into the bourgeoisie themselves—a possibility denied those who were raised by
non-bourgeois standards.

We have tried to show how the bourgeois family was both an
agent and a conduit of modernization, especially of the latter's components of individuality and rationality. Both these components were
internalized within the consciousness of individuals who passed
through this family's distinctive socialization process. Norbert Elias
has masterfully described the manner in which external constraints
were internalized and became "spontaneous" patterns of conduct.[20] He
called this development one of "civilization." The sexual instinct was
similarly "civilized."[21] To call this "repression" is rather one-sided,
though one may concede that some of the Freudian mechanisms may
well have been a by-product. (The medicalization of sexuality, which
was to come later, was a more recent by-product.) "Civility," as a
general structure of both taste and conduct, was also a bourgeois creation. Thus every class or ethnic group brought into the bourgeois
world had to undergo what John Murray Cuddihy has aptly called
"the ordeal of civility."[22] The more recent developments of "family
planning" and sexual engineering are further outcomes of this pervasive rationalization.

Margaret Mead has argued that life in a "civilized," rationalized
society is also "simpler"[23] in a different sense. The structure of language is simplified. Social forms and manners become less elaborate.
"Modernism" in literature, art, and architecture tends toward simplic-
ity, functionality, and *ipso facto,* at any rate the *semblance* of rationality. Knowledge itself comes to be functional and rational (in
the philosopher Alfred Schutz's term, "recipe knowledge"). Mead has
further argued that modern Western societies, when looked at in a
comparative cross-cultural perspective, are seen to educate individuals
to make rational choices in the light of adequate information. This
may or may not be seen as "progress"; some have argued (for instance, the German sociologist Arnold Gehlen) that this development
is a form of "primitivization," even a new kind of barbarism.[24] These
are evaluative questions that we would eschew for now. But, whether

this is progress or barbarization, the modern world with its plethora of functional rationality is historically rooted in the well-ordered bourgeois household that we have just discussed. Conversely, the further development of this modern world cannot be dissociated from the fate of the bourgeois family from which it sprang.

Now, one aspect of the classical bourgeois family and its ethos that should be stressed is that of *balance*. The bourgeois family as an institution made it possible to socialize individuals with singularly stable personalities ("strong characters"), who were also ready for innovation and risk-taking in a society undergoing historically unprecedented transformations. This type of family was based on a balance between individualism and social responsibility, between "liberation" and strong communal ties, between acquisitiveness and altruism. Needless to say, such a balance is precarious, in individuals as well as institutionally. Each element in the balance could potentially escalate or be radicalized in such a way as to make the balance impossible. This, we would contend, is precisely what happened in the later period of the bourgeois era. What previously was held in balance now appears as sets of irreconcilable alternatives: rigid stability against mindless innovation, crass egotism against self-abandonment to a community, adventurism without moral restraints (taking *all* risks) against fearful passivity legitimated by an absolutist morality (willing to take *no* risks at all), and so on. With this loss of balance, the enormous civilization-building power of the bourgeoisie is undermined and threatened, and the very notion of a bourgeois society is put in question.

Further, we would once more contend that, in our view of the historical evidence, this balance of the bourgeois ethos was based on religion, especially on the Protestant version of Christianity. Only by accepting a higher force, located outside the individual, the family, and society as a whole, could there be a perceived unity between individual, family, and societal interests. Especially the fine balance between individualism and voluntary cooperation, which was particularly important in America (as Alexis de Tocqueville saw so clearly), required powerful religious underpinnings. We cannot pursue here the development of religion itself in the modern period and the rise of the phenomenon commonly called secularization. Suffice it to say that, as secularization advanced, the religious underpinnings of the bourgeois balancing act weakened and the earlier unity of values came to be polarized into antagonistic alternatives. In an earlier work of ours, we spoke of "counter-modernization" and "demodernization," to designate reactions against modernity.[25] We will shortly describe some contemporary family developments that may be adequately subsumed under these categories. But it also seems to us now that these categories do not fully fit some recent developments. We would, therefore, introduce the term "*hyper-modernity*" (with the subcategories of "hyper-rationality" and "hyper-individualism") to describe the radicalization of modern themes to the point where the earlier fabric of modern bourgeois society can no longer contain them. Curiously (or perhaps not so curiously if one thinks anthropologically), *hyper*-modern developments often show considerable affinity with *counter*-modern ones. *Both* are efforts to resolve the tensions of the old bourgeois balancing act, which to many has become too difficult and demanding.

A common interpretation of the recent changes in the family, as we have seen, is that most people had no intention of giving up the earlier patterns and values of family life but that change was forced on them by external agents (economic, political, and so on). There is, of course, some validity to this. But we would insist that there were also internal causes of the changes of the recent period, transforming the family from within as its latent "contradictions" came to the fore. In this view we are close to the sociological theory of Vilfredo Pareto, who believed that every human society contains within itself the kernels of its disintegration and that furthermore the latter are usually the very factors that originally brought the society into being. In this instance, the ideas and practices that created the bourgeois family in an earlier age, as they perdure over time, are subtly transmuted in such a way as to erode the bourgeois family. More broadly, hyper-modernization is a radicalization of distinctively modern themes, which at a certain point "tilt" over into counter-modern effects.

This can be seen very clearly with regard to that rationality which has been the hallmark of modernity from the beginning. The rationality of science and technology, which was designed to free man from the dominance of blind natural forces, is now extended into every area of human life, including the family, which, even in the heyday of the faith in science, had been immune to the engineering mentality in its more radical forms. Quantification and experiment have always been tools of modern science. They were indeed "liberating" as they were applied to man's natural environment. But as they are applied to man himself and to the most private sphere of his life, they come to be experienced as oppressive, even as dehumanizing. Thus the family itself becomes an object of scientific quantification and experiment. A "good home," "healthy sexuality," "normal childhood," and "good parenting" are defined in terms of quantifiable criteria and become objects of experimentation by supposed experts (*scientific* experts, no less) who claim jurisdiction over these realms of life. The engineering mentality, with its notions of "componentiality," options, and technique, invades family life, including the crucial area of socialization. The "components" of personality development are measured and experimented with, and living individuals are judged (and often enough, coercively controlled) by their adherence to these allegedly scientific standards. The languages of modern psychology and (to a somewhat lesser degree) modern sociology pass from the scientific to the everyday frame of reference. That is, ordinary people now view themselves, their spouses, and their children as if they were participants in an engineering enterprise. This brings about a hyper-rationality that is very hard to bear—and which, for this very reason, is susceptible to "tilting" over into gross irrationalism.

This has enormous consequences. Arnold Gehlen has described it very well: "The penetration of the experimental spirit into arts and sciences of every kind has as a necessary consequence their objects' *loss of naturalness*. The referents of the theory, being generated exclusively by the method one chooses, lend themselves to being analyzed and resynthesized in numerous ways."[26] For one thing, this inevitably introduces an element of instability into every area of life thus affected. By definition, every experiment is *ad hoc*, "until further notice"—or until a better idea comes along. But even more pervasively, the scientific concepts and standards, as they are applied to actual life situations, become *clichés*, mindlessly mouthed as "recipe knowledge" and as criteria of conduct.[27] The immediacy and concreteness of individual experience is threatened by these clichés, and in consequence the most intimate human relationships—between spouses and children, above all—acquire a strange patina of abstraction. Or, put differently, these relationships are experienced as "mechanisms"—a "good relationship," a "good marriage," perhaps now also a "good divorce," and so on—the "goodness" in each case being determined by the allegedly scientific standards proclaimed and administered by the experts. The same hyper-rationalization extends to the body itself—in health cults that become institutionalized hypochondria, in sexual experimentation, in the techniques of birth control and abortion, and perhaps soon in genetic engineering.

This hyper-rationality affects the family both from the outside and from within. On the outside there are the professional empires of experts and advice givers of all sorts, increasingly relying on the state to enforce and subsidize their jurisdictional claims. But obviously these outside forces do not operate by coercion only, or even primarily. Rather, they mostly impinge on people who are all too ready to give credence to and to cooperate with the instrumentalities of control. This is particularly the case in the upper middle class, the most direct offspring of the old bourgeoisie, whose ethos has a strong affinity with the hyper-rationality embodied by the new institutions of scientific therapy and technical management. In the working class there are more unease and resistance but also much less power to stop the "friendly intruders"—a political problem to which we have referred before.

Hyper-rationality is a radicalization of one central theme of modernity; hyper-individualism is another. It entails an increasing emphasis on the individual over against every collective entity, including the family itself, which had been the historical matrix of modern individuation. The recent rise of feminism is particularly important in this connection. The individual woman is now emphasized over against every communal context in which she may find herself—a redefinition of her situation that breaks not only the community between the spouses but (more fundamentally) the mother-child dyad, which, if anthropologists are correct, is the most basic human community of all. Thus the search for individual identity in isolation from all communal definitions becomes a central concern of life. This search, of course, has personal as well as political aspects, so that hyper-individualism becomes both a principle of "engineered" biography and a political platform. On the biographical level, hyper-individualism orders the life-planning of individuals, legitimating what quite frequently are brutal assertions of self against the claims of others (such as: notably, children and spouses). On the political level, hyper-individualism becomes an ideology motivating campaigns for legal and social reforms that would protect the individual against all such claims.

A very interesting aspect of this, which we can only touch upon briefly here, is the role of modern psychology and psychotherapy in legitimating the normative assumptions of hyper-individualism. The latter is based on two basic psychological presuppositions: that the individual self is the *only reality* in the human sphere, and that this reality is the result of a *process* that in principle can be interfered with in a deliberate way. In other words, only the individual is real, as against the pseudo realities of all and any collective entities; and the individual, by himself or with the help of experts, can go about modifying and styling his own self—identity ceases to be a given and becomes a project. Classical psychoanalysis laid the groundwork for these presuppositions, but it is more recent (and almost all indigenous American) developments in psychotherapy that relate much more directly to the new hyper-individualism. The new therapies, which often take on the character of cults or sects, are geared to liberate the individual's authentic self from the allegedly alienating prisons of collective institutions. The psychological approaches of Abraham Maslow and Carl Rogers have become important as theoretical legitimations of what by now has become a personal-liberation industry, loosely subsumable under the heading of the encounter or human-potential movement. Within this movement, of course, there are both sophisticated and popularized expressions. What all have in common is the underlying idea that socialization distorts an originally positive human nature, which can be freed from the unnatural restraints imposed on it by society.[28]

It is hardly surprising that the family appears as the chief villain in this liberating scenario—after all, everyone has learned from Freud how important the family is as the (putatively pathogenic) context of early socialization. But Freud was still a "bourgeois thinker" in the full sense of the word: While he was intent on assuaging the "neurotic" effects of societal "repression," he had no doubt that the latter was necessary; the "healthy" individual of the Freudian scenario has made a successful adjustment to the demands of society. The new psychologies substitute rebellion for adjustment, and indeed Freud has become a primary villain in their interpretations (this has been most virulently so in the case of those feminist writers, who, quite correctly, have interpreted Freud as basically inimical to their understanding of female personality). Other people, and especially members of one's own family, are now seen as repressing the individual's quest for self-realization (the aforementioned identity project) or at least as failing to support it sufficiently. The very important consequence is that the individual becomes free to look for other "support groups—be it in the therapeutic group, or the sisterhood collective, or the political cell, or what-have-you. In other words, the family, at best, is reduced to being one of many freely chosen and freely disposable mechanisms whose purpose is the fostering of the individual's project of self-attainment. One further important element in these new psychologies is the emphasis on spontaneity—in sharp contrast to the bourgeois virtues of discipline and self-restraint. It would be incorrect to say that the value of responsibility is directly challenged, but responsibility toward others (including one's closest family members) tends to be subsumed under the overall project of self-realization.

Modernization, while experienced by many as a great liberation, produces tensions and discontents. These in turn lead to resistances and counter-formations, all of which can be subsumed under the category of counter-modernization. If the above view of the modernizing role of the bourgeois family is correct, then it is only logical that counter-modernizing forces should have chosen the bourgeois family as a particularly favored target of criticisms and attacks. This is precisely what has happened.

The two great themes of modernity that we discussed earlier, rationality and individualism, have been major foci of the counter-modern assault. Science and technology, the twin engines of modern rationality, have been reinterpreted as oppressive, alienating forces, separating man from his "natural" impulses and ways of life. The machine is the image of this alienation, robbing man of his dignity and enslaving him in mechanical, dehumanizing structures—the "dark satanic mills" of Blake's famous metaphor. The bourgeoisie, and more specifically the bourgeois family, are now seen as the bearers of this alienating rationality. The same animus is directed against bureaucracy, that other important engine of modern rationality. Similarly, modern individualism, especially in its bourgeois form, is reinterpreted as alienating man from his "natural" propensity for collective, communal ways of life. Individualism is supposed to engender egocentricity and avarice, and to stifle true feelings and imagination as well. Again, the bourgeoisie is held accountable for this alleged dehumanization, and the capitalist economic system is identified as an important (for some, the most important) institution embodying this distorted definition of the individual. Counter-modernization implies a message of salvation, and the realities *from which* man is to be saved are, plausibly enough, the central institutions of modern rationality and modern individualism.

Obviously it is not feasible here to go in detail into the history of counter-modernization in Western countries, but a few points must be made to indicate the importance of counter-modern ideas in the contemporary battle over the family. The idea that the bourgeois family institutionalized false values, especially a false rationality repressive of authentic emotions and a false individualism prohibiting true community, is by no means new. It was held by groups who resisted the societal ambitions of the bourgeoisie in the earlier period of the latter's ascendancy, such as the aristocracy and the peasantry. What is very interesting, however, is that the same idea arose, at least by the early-nineteenth century, among dissident circles originating from within the bourgeoisie—traitors to that class, if one wills. The Romantic movement is a clear case of this, in philosophy as well as literature. The same anti-bourgeois animus, however, early found political expression as well, in various radical and populist movements (for example, the Narodniki in Russia). There are important counter-modern themes in Marxism, too, with its strictures against the false rationality and individualism of the bourgeoisie—strictures that often bear a surprising resemblance to what was said about the same bourgeoisie from the right, by spokesmen for the aristocratic values of the *ancien régime*. (We cannot develop this point here, but it must be emphasized that Marxism has very effectively synthesized these counter-modern themes with emphatically modern ones, derived from the Enlightenment and its ideals of rational control; nor can we develop the argument that much of the attraction of Marxism may be explainable by this synthesis of modern and counter-modern themes.) Moreover, the ideologies of various nationalist movements have been suffused with similar themes, the emotive and collective unity of the nation, the *Volk*, being counter-posited against the emotional poverty and the false individualism of bourgeois existence.[29]

An interesting case of counter-modernizing themes arising within the bourgeoisie itself is that of bohemianism in its various forms.[30] There can be found all the major themes outlined above and a particularly vehement antagonism against the bourgeois family and its values. It was bohemian intellectuals (typically of bourgeois background themselves) who developed, as early as the close of the nineteenth century, an *aesthetic* critique of bourgeois existence and morality. Their contempt for the latter has shaped the ideas of self-defined intellectual and aesthetic elites ever since, so that the very term "bourgeois" connotes crudeness, pettiness, greed, and above all, lack of refined feelings. This attitude has been well summarized by Martin Green in his study of bohemianism in the pre-World War I period in Europe: "They scoffed at the notion that the higher man should have to make any effort to achieve economic respectability. They scoffed at technical progress, pride in one's work, and sexual morality, because all these values and inhibitions seemed equally incompatible with the free expression of the creative mind. . . . They exalted the creativity of the pagan-cosmic principle, which they saw as opposed to the life-hostile Judeo-Christian principle. Feeling and instinct were spurred on to attack and triumph over reason and clarity of understanding."[31] While the bohemian animus against the bourgeoisie is primarily aesthetic ("those vulgar philistines!"), it can easily lead to political positions of an anti-bourgeois kind—of the right or of the left. Thus, during the period described by Green, both fascism and communism drew prominent recruits from these circles.

The bohemian antagonism to the bourgeoisie invariably included the family as a prime target of attack. The family is supposed to domesticate and distort the erotic; against this, the bohemian upholds "natural" passion, "free love" outside the bonds of marriage, and the equality of all forms of sexual expression. Marriage, of course, is above all a prison. Bourgeois childhood is the incubator of all the false values. What is interesting here is that counter-modern themes converge with hyper-modern ones: The fully "liberated" individual may be understood in either mode, and hyper-modern individualism seems to move into counter-modern collectivism with the greatest of ease. Perhaps that is only to be expected, once the balance of bourgeois existence is upset.

The counter-culture, whose advent was hailed with so much enthusiasm in the 1960s, was the latest powerful eruption of counter-modernity in American society.[32] It is noteworthy that this was an overwhelmingly middle-class phenomenon—another instance of bourgeois dissidents rebelling against the bourgeois ethos and, with particular vehemence, against the bourgeois family. The counter-culture also affords a particularly clear example of hyper-modern themes becoming radicalized and then, very easily, changing into counter-modern forms. On the one hand, the counter-culture extolled a hyper-modern ideal of individualism: "letting it all hang out," "doing one's own thing," untrammeled by any bourgeois restraints. But then, curiously, people were "doing their thing" *together*, in striking conformity with group norms, and collective solidarity was stressed against the alleged selfishness of middle-class individualism. Cooperation was posited against competitiveness, relaxation against achievement, and collectivistic ideologies (in this instance of the Left, rather than the Right) found many adherents in the counter-cultural milieu: Bourgeois capitalism and the bourgeois family were (quite correctly, one may say) perceived as closely related enemies. The counter-cultural commune was the practical expression of these themes. Among these themes antagonism to "repressive" rationality was prominent. Feeling was extolled against allegedly arid reason, and all "natural life-styles" against the alleged artificiality of modern life. The affinity with nature (or what was understood as such) expressed this attitude as aptly as the sympathy with Third World peasantries, who, supposedly, were not yet poisoned by the diseases of modernity. All these themes continued, albeit in less strident forms, in the ecology and anti-nuclear movements, in various health cults ("natural foods"), and in the more romantic branches of the feminist movement. Significantly, all these tendencies combined anti-capitalist, anti-technological and anti-family orientations; again, one must concede that, however inarticulately, there was sound instinct in this juncture of various key institutions of modern rationality.

If there is a certain logical progression from hyper-modern individualism to counter-modern collectivism (the essence, perhaps, of what Erich Fromm once called "the escape from freedom" and of the profound seductiveness of totalitarian ideologies), there is a built-in logical contradiction between the anti-rationalism of the counter-culture and its continued reliance on a modern technological structure. The same people who denounce the dehumanizing effects of life-denying technology are fervently in favor of abortion. The anti-nuclear movement, far from wanting to give up the benefits of energy-rich existence, is placing great hopes in technological innovations of the most sophisticated sort. And one need only mention here the technology of drug-induced changes in consciousness. There is a profound contradiction here, theoretical as well as practical, and this may well be one of the chief reasons why the hoped-for revolution of the Age of Aquarius never went very far. It remained parasitical on the modern technological society and, at best, was successful in revolutionizing the private lives of relatively small numbers of people (although it certainly had an influence on the private lives of larger numbers). Still, the counter-culture continues to be effective in a number of its negative attitudes—and the antagonism against the family, as we saw much earlier, is one of these.

We would stress once again the middle-class/bourgeois roots of the great majority of these counter-modern movements. In that, too, counter-modernity resembles hyper-modernity. Both are disintegrative (one might also say decadent) developments from within the bourgeoisie. Their greatest influence has accordingly been in the upper-middle-class strata of Western societies. As we have seen, because of the great power of these strata as a result of their hold over the "knowledge industry," their values and attitudes have affected other strata as well. Nevertheless, it remains true that the lower classes—notably the lower middle class and, even more so, the working class—have been much less penetrated by the anti-bourgeois rebellion. There is, of course, great irony in this. It is these lower classes that were the objects of the great bourgeois missionary effort in the nineteenth and early-twentieth centuries. The evangelism was very successful. The bourgeois ethos did indeed "trickle down." The bourgeois family and its norms became society-wide. Now a very different ethos, indeed a diametrically opposed ethos, is being propagated by upper-middle-class evangelists among the lower orders of society. It is meeting with strong resistance.

It remains to be seen whether the new evangelism-from-the-top will be as successful as the earlier one. For now, however, Theodore Roszak, one of the apostles of the new ethos, is very perceptive when he complains about the recalcitrance of his social inferiors: "The working class, which provided the traditional following for radical ideology, now neither leads nor follows, but sits tight and plays safe: the stoutest prop of the established order."[33] Shades of Major Barbara, who had very similar complaints! But, of late, this working class has

been somewhat less inert, has even shown some readiness to be ideologically radicalized—though not quite in the way that Roszak and
his fellow missionaries would wish! The demise of modernity, like the
demise of the modern family, has been announced somewhat prematurely.

# EXCURSUS

# Are
# We
# Decadent?

Doctors used to talk to each other in Latin, so that patients would remain ignorant of the true (and putatively fatal) nature of their condition. It is plausible that even patients who knew some Latin found it more tolerable to tell themselves that they were suffering from an elegantly named affliction than to acknowledge in plain English that they had had it. Could it be that sociologists are performing a similar charade today? So we have been going on about modernizing consciousness, about hyper-modernity and counter-modernity. Could it be that what we are really saying is that our society is permeated with decadence? Have we had it? Are we decadent? If so, then all we are doing in this book is describing one particular zone of infection. Given the importance of the family as a social institution, it is arguable that its decadence is particularly interesting. But if the crisis of the family is but one specific symptom of a disease that is already well on the way to consuming the whole body of society, then our analysis has little practical value and is, at best, an entertainment for professional pathologists.

Conservatives are especially fond of speaking in terms of decadence. This is consonant with the pronounced conservative tendency (analyzed very well by Karl Mannheim) to view society as an organism—"healthy" or "sick," as the case may be. If, by contrast, one looks at society as a process (the more favored viewpoint of liberals and radicals), the notion of decadence is less plausible: An organism may be sick, but what would be a sick process? Decadence, in the organic perspective, is more than just sickness, though; it is a special kind of sickness, the one brought on by aging. The organismic view of society sees it as going through stages very similar to those of the individual life cycle: childhood, youth, maturity, and old age. These stages, as in the lives of individuals, are inevitable and predictable. A decadent society, then, is one embarked on the decline of old age; decadence is the societal equivalent of senile debility. Since conservatives are also very fond of saying that the family is the basic institution of society (the procreative apparatus at the center of the organism), decadence in the family is readily seen as a major symptom of society-wide disease. There is perhaps a certain inconsistency if the same people then propose this or that cure for the disease. How can one cure senility? Should one not, rather, plan for a decent funeral? In any case, those who tell us that the contemporary family is decadent or diseased tend to view society as an organic or at least organism-like entity, even if their projects of surgical intervention do not follow all too logically from their diagnosis of the condition.

We have serious problems with this type of thinking. Whatever else it is, society is *not* an organism. Consequently, viewing social change through the metaphor of the individual life cycle is distortive. If decadence, then, depends on such a quasi-biological perspective, the concept must be rejected. Also, those who talk about a decadent present typically labor under all sorts of illusions about the allegedly non-decadent past. It is a safe guess that most of the people who criticize the "sickness" of contemporary Western societies would not wish to stay even briefly if a time machine could deposit them back in a "healthier" period. Further, if one were to designate contemporary Western societies as decadent, one would have somewhat of a problem as to which other societies are *not* decadent. The poorest candidates for this status are certainly the societies of the Soviet sphere; if *we* are decadent, *they* must be in an advanced state of senile dementia. Presumably the "healthy" societies must be somewhere in the Third World; trying to locate them amid the less than inspiring countries of those regions of the world is not very easy. Decadence theorists must always be on the lookout for barbarians. As C. P. Cavafy put it well in one of his best-known poems: "And now what will become of us without Barbarians?—Those people were some sort of a solution." Unfortunately, locating the "true barbarians" is as difficult a task for decadence theorists as locating "true socialism" is for the theoreticians of the Left.

We have said enough to indicate that we have problems with the concept of decadence. Still, with proper care, the concept does have a certain usefulness. Let us discard the quasi-biological and quasi-medical associations of the concept. Instead, let us apply it to two empirically available phenomena: Decadence is a situation in which the central symbols of an institution, or of society as a whole, have become "empty" or "hollow"—that is, have lost an earlier power of providing meaning and identity. Further, decadence in this sense has the consequence of creating a disparity between actual conduct and the legitimations of this conduct that continue to be ceremoniously (and in terms of individual meanings, hypocritically) reiterated. In other words, the symbols, which once corresponded to the actual motives of human actions, now become a ritual in which no one really believes and which may even appear as objects of humor. Unless new symbols appear around which people can rally, such a hollowing-out process must result in a paralysis of action at least in those areas of social life to which the hollowed-out symbols refer. As Émile Durkheim has brilliantly shown, societal solidarity depends on a moral consensus, in the name of which individuals are prepared to undertake risks and sacrifices. Who would take a risk in the name of an empty symbol? How can one sacrifice one's comfort or security for what, when all is said and done, one takes as a joke? A decadent situation is one in which everyone plays safe.

If one defines decadence in such terms, it is indeed plausible to look on various developments in Western societies, especially in their elite and upper-strata groups, as manifestations of decadence. This is analytically useful to the extent that it illuminates the disjuncture of legitimations and motives as well as the resultant inhibition of self-assured action. The institutions affected by decadence are then no longer plausible in the terms in which they are publicly legitimated. Consequently, the motives of individuals have little relation to the "official" purpose of these institutions, and the actions of individuals are characterized by social disruptiveness, lack of self-assurance, guilt, of a combination of these. To some extent at least, such a configuration does correspond to the classical picture of decadence. By contrast, "barbarians" (if we may so designate *non*-decadent groups) sincerely believe in their "tribal" symbols and rituals, are motivated by the latter in their actual conduct, have a high degree of collective solidarity, and act with self-confidence and without guilt.

In this sense, then, it is possible to apply the concept of decadence to the bourgeois family in contemporary Western societies. Indeed, hyper-modernity and counter-modernity may then be seen as kindred phenomena, both characterized by the "hollowing out" of the old symbols by which the family was legitimated and sustained in the actual lives of individuals. The disjuncture of symbols and motives comes out most sharply on certain ceremonial occasions when the former are solemnly exhibited. For example, take a couple, he on his third and she on her second marriage, going through a ceremony in which they promise to stay with each other "till death do us part." Or, for another example, imagine a progressive, multiply psychoanalyzed, and thoroughly "non-repressive" individual playing the role of parental authority toward his or her adolescent child just arrested for a drug offense. One may say that these scenes "won't play," and it is easy to see why: The disjuncture between symbolic role and actual conduct is too great; indeed, because of this disjuncture, there is a very real threat of comic disintegration—it is difficult for any of the participants in these scenes to keep a straight face. And *that* is about as good a rule of thumb as any for the detection of decadence.

As the old symbols of the bourgeois family become "hollow" and the rituals affirming them become "empty," individuals are free (one may say, in existentialist language that applies here with great precision, they are *condemned* to be free) to substitute their own idiosyncratic and self-constructed meanings for the traditional ones. The family ceases to be an objective given and becomes a locale where miscellaneous subjective motives intersect. Put differently, the family ceases to be an institution in the full sense of the word; instead, it becomes a project of individuals, thus always susceptible of redefinition, reconstruction—and obviously, termination. Being part of a family is replaced by participating in a personal life-style. The unpredictability and instability of the latter definition of the situation is built-in, intrinsic. It becomes virtually impossible to act with self-assurance under these circumstances. Everything—including, finally, "gender roles," sexuality, and child rearing—is uncertain, open to revision—in social philosopher Alfred Schutz's phrase, "until further notice." For

EXCURSUS — ARE WE DECADENT? 133

those with any degree of moral sensitivity, guilt is also an unavoidable feature of this situation.

We are being descriptive here. The description does not in itself imply a negative moral judgment. There are aspects of this constellation that we, for our part, are unable simply to condemn. Most important among these is the aspect of freedom. It is difficult to deny that those to whom the above description applies are freer than people who take their family institutions for granted and are typically incapable of even conceiving alternative possibilities. We regard freedom as having great value, and we cannot be very sympathetic to conservative theoreticians who idealize a traditional situation in which people view the family as an immutable destiny, sovereignly independent of the will and the actions of individuals. But freedom has costs. These costs must be weighed, especially when they are disproportionally borne by the weakest members of society, who are its young children. Also, it is possible to argue that there is such a thing as excessive freedom—excessive because it is based on a denial of certain givens in the human condition itself. As we have tried to show in the preceding chapter, such excessive freedom tends to become radicalized and, in this process, falls over into the opposite of freedom: An ideal of total freedom all too often results in a practice of extreme unfreedom, the "liberated" individual seeking solace and solidarity in the most totalistic collectivism.

It is our view, which we will spell out in greater detail in the remaining chapters of this book, that one of the foremost human achievements of the bourgeois family has been the balance it provided between freedom and restraint, between individual self-realization and social responsibility. This achievement has been of immense personal and political significance. Conversely, the disturbance of the balance institutionalized in the bourgeois family has led to both personal and political costs, which, as we see it, have outstripped the gains of individual "liberation." But even more basically, the bourgeois family has provided a stable context that has enabled individuals to act responsibly in a rapidly changing world and thus allowed them to undergo the process of modernization without succumbing to its tensions. We are *not* conservatives in the sense of believing that this particular, historically relative family type is the only "natural," God-given, or immutable one. If for no other reason, such a belief would be very difficult for sociologists. But we *are* conservatives in that we have reached the conclusion that there is no viable alternative to the bourgeois family in the contemporary world. The values of this institution are among the great human achievements of our civilization, and as such they are worthy not only of respect but of a concerted practical defense.

There are givens of the human condition that one denies at great peril. One of those givens is that human beings, if they are to take risks, must be supported by firm, reliable institutions. This is so with regard to all sorts of risks, including economic, political, and (last but not least) military ones. Aaron Wildavsky has made the point that an aversion to risk-taking is one of the hallmarks of contemporary Western society, at least in its elite or upper strata. This manifests itself in an antagonism to capitalist enterprise (risk-taking is the condition *sine qua non* of entrepreneurship), in uncertainty about democracy (a very risky polity indeed), and in a tendency toward pacifism (war is the ultimate risk). This is not the place to spell out the implications of this pervasive quest for total security among wide segments of Western societies or to develop the argument that, as Wildavsky argued, those who take no risks end up risking the most—thus the quest for total social security risks bankruptcy, the effort to reduce the risks of democracy by overregulation and excessive controls may undermine the very survival of this type of polity, and unilateral pacifism greatly increases the risk of war. What is interesting in the present context, though, is that the same strata who are so intent on risk reduction in the public sphere are also the most hesitant to shoulder the risks of bourgeois family life. In *that* sense, once again, the category of decadence would seem to be pertinent.

Anthropologically, one of the greatest risks that human beings can undertake is the founding of a family. This has always been so, from the earliest bonding of a male and a female for the purpose of building a home for their offspring. Modern technology has indeed reduced some of these risks, such as the horrendous risks of childbirth and infant mortality. But the very high personal expectations that modern individuals now invest in marriage and parenthood have *increased* the risks of this undertaking. To marry and to have children thus is and remains one of the great risk-taking ventures of human life. The bourgeois family, as we have seen, greatly changed the meaning of this venture. It did *not* change its risk-taking quality; indeed, it underlined this quality by its stress on personal discipline and responsibility. Those who would do away with the bourgeois family would like, if at all possible, to do away with *all* risks. This fantasy of a risk-free existence expresses itself in some of its central causes: the ideal of the "swinging single," with no ties on his or her project of endless self-realization; the idealization of abortion, once and for all eliminating the vestigial risk of pregnancy in sexual relations; the insistence that a "gay life-style" is as socially legitimate as heterosexual marriage, thereby putting on the same level a relatively risk-free (since childless) relationship with the most risky relationship of all. All these themes can be subsumed under the category of "anti-natalism." They can then be seen in a perfectly logical configuration with other ideological themes prevalent in the same strata: political leftism, zero-growth and zero-population theories, anti-nuclear and more generally anti-technological sentiments, pacifism and a benignly nonaggressive posture in international relations, a deep suspicion of patriotism (which always has an at least potentially military dimension), and a generally negative attitude to the values of discipline, achievement, and competitiveness. In the aggregate, this is indeed a constellation of decadence. A society dominated by these themes has rather poor prospects in the real world, which is mostly inhabited by people with very contrary norms and habits.

We recognize the likelihood that some readers will be offended by the above paragraphs; we certainly do not expect to persuade anyone by such a sketchy argument. We only make it here to indicate that the fate of the bourgeois family is linked, in our opinion, with much broader questions of the survival chances of contemporary Western societies. In any case, our defense of the bourgeois family does not necessarily depend on agreement concerning these wider issues. But there is one more point that should be stressed if one places this topic in the framework of decadence: That is the point that the decadent syndrome is not distributed uniformly throughout our societies. Both in North America and in Western Europe it is concentrated in those strata that we have described as the new "knowledge class," though it radiates into other strata from this epicenter. There are other classes (notably the lower-middle and working classes) and large, relatively unassimilated ethnic groups that are much less marked by this syndrome and, in some instances, not touched at all by it. The fate of the bourgeois family (and, we believe, the future survivability of these societies) thus hinges on the future development of these groups. This is why we cannot feel outraged by some of the resistance against the wisdom of the *nouvelle bourgeoisie* that has of late appeared in these groups. Put in terms of classical decadence theory, the "health" of a society often depends on the vitality of its "internal barbarians." They are the ones who take up the old symbolic banners cast aside contemptuously by the decadent elite.

In this perspective, American society may well depend for its survival on the continuing influx of immigrants (legal or illegal) with a sturdy sense of family, work, and ambition. If one is concerned for the future of America, one might willingly exchange the entire membership of the American Sociological Association (or, for that matter, the combined faculties of all the Ivy League universities) for the people who cross the Rio Grande in any given year. A parallel argument may be made about the "guest workers" of Western Europe (though the decadence of the latter region may have reached the point where even the Turks and the Algerians will not be able to reverse the trend). In any case, if one rejects the organismic fatalism of classical decadence theory, one will look for possibilities of revitalization in the *less* decadent groups within the population. And then there is always the possibility that decadence is reversed even in groups that have been subject to it for a while. If we did not believe in this possibility, we would not be writing this book.

# III

# THE FAMILY
## A Reasonable Defense

# 6

# Assumptions
# of a
# Reasonable
# Defense

In the preceding chapters, we have tried to provide a perspective on the contemporary condition of the family in modern society. The purpose of this, however, has not been to provide yet another diagnosis. Rather, it has from the beginning been our purpose to provide this perspective as an aid to what we consider to be a reasonable defense of the family, and specifically of the so-called bourgeois family. The adjective "reasonable" has two implications in the present context. First, of course, it implies a non-doctrinaire, mediating approach. Second, it means that a defense of the family must take cognizance of the findings of the historical and social sciences, that is, must not neglect the empirical evidence that in now available; in this intention we certainly reflect our viewpoint as sociologists, but it is not at all necessary to be a sociologist (or, for that matter, any other species of scientist) in order to appreciate or share the approach we recommend. In any case, in this last section of the book we shift the emphasis from analysis to advocacy. Clearly, this shift implies that we cast aside the cloak of scientific detachment and argue the *values* of the family as we see them. These will be clear enough in what follows.

However, we must also clarify our *theoretical assumptions*, the "map of the world" that serves to orient our views of this particular issue. To do this is the purpose of the present chapter.

In terms of values, it is very significant that most of those who have become influential in defining the condition of the family in the modern world have been, explicitly or implicitly, suspicious or downright hostile with regard to that institution. It should not be surprising that this anti-family animus has colored their theoretical assumptions as well, as we have already seen in some of the preceding chapters. This trend goes back to quite early times: Erasmus, Bacon, Rousseau, Marx. It continues today. Even those who have of late rediscovered the staying power of the family continue to stress its discontinuities and loss of functions and to prognosticate a variety of impending disasters—not without a good deal of satisfaction, one surmises.

There is a very important point where our values as human beings and our theoretical assumptions as sociologists come together —and that is the conviction that, in any assessment of a social phenomenon, one must take with utmost respect the values of those who participate in that phenomenon. We consider this a basic moral value, expressing respect for other human beings and for their right to shape their own lives with the greatest possible freedom; the same value, needless to say, is also basic to democracy. But we also consider it to be a basic methodological principle of the social sciences that society is constituted by the meanings of those who live in it (in sociology, this makes us disciples of Max Weber and of the phenomenological tradition). In consequence, it is very important indeed that large segments of the population of Western societies, in all likelihood a substantial majority, continue to be attached to the family both in practice and as an ideal. More specifically, this attachment pertains to that type of family that has been called the bourgeois family, more or less in the historical form that we have delineated. This attachment continues despite all sorts of tensions and difficulties, and it even takes on a vehemently defensive quality, as we have seen.

To be sure, there are class differences in this attachment, as we have also seen. Thus in upper-income, upper-middle-class, college-educated strata in America there is much less certainty than elsewhere in the society about the meanings and values of family life. On elite campuses, where the next generation of Americans is preparing (or not preparing) for life, the desire for a family has become some-

what shamefaced—almost a "dirty little secret," looked at as irrational, uninformed, or plain reactionary. It seems to us that the time has
come to remove this shame from one of the most fundamental aspirations of human life. In view of the great power wielded by the cultural elite in a modern society, it is important to change attitudes in
this stratum even if one does not grant its rather exaggerated sense of
self-importance. (This is certainly a necessary assumption of anyone
writing a book on the subject, since very few people outside that stratum are likely to read it!)

What, then, are some of our assumptions?

Let us first spell out what they are *not*. This book is not an exercise in nostalgia or reactionary romanticism. We are aware of the
complexities of historical research and we are not positing an idealized past over against the realities of the present. We have made it
quite clear that there are many aspects of the contemporary situation
that we find problematic, negative, even decadent. But there is no
comfort to be found in the past, as some conservative thinkers like to
imagine, in a historically naïve way. On the other hand, though, we
do not find much hope in the various "alternatives" that have been
suggested by "progressive" thinkers, nor are we persuaded by those
who claim moral superiority for utopian projects yet to be realized.
We assume that history has always been full of ambiguities and always will be. There was no perfect family in the past, and there will
be none in the future (at least not in this world, or this side of the establishment of the Kingdom of God). Reasonable people will try to
grasp the values in what has historically developed, to reduce the
costs of this development, and to eschew illusions of either the back-
ward-looking or the forward-looking variety.

Implied in the above is that we do not share the Enlightenment
faith in "progress," in this or any other area of human life. That is, we
do not believe in "progress" in the singular, as it were. We do believe
in the plural version of the idea, in "progresses." Thus a society without slavery has achieved *a* progress over one with slaves; in the same
sense, the reduction of infant mortality, the abolition of judicial torture, and the legal recognition of equal rights for women are distinctive progresses of the modern age. (Speaking of progress in the plural, rather than in the metaphysical singular, also implies that any one
progress can be lost again—and therefore must be ongoingly defended and institutionalized.) In this understanding, we emphatically

believe that the bourgeois family achieved a progress in human values over its predecessors in Western societies, and we further believe that these human values continue to be valid today. The slanted interpretations of the family have done a great disservice by obscuring these values. To quote Fontenelle: "We sometimes find the truth concerning problems of considerable importance. But the misfortune is that we never know we have found it." It seems to us that the family is a good case in point for Fontenelle's observation.

These assumptions of ours have led us into a skeptical and at least partially dissenting stance with regard to much of the contemporary literature on the family. Modern historians and anthropologists have taken great delight in showing the seemingly endless variety of family forms. We share that delight up to a point, in that it discloses the vast richness of human culture and thus liberates one from narrow ethnocentrism. We are not delighted, though, by the recurring theme of moral relativism that has accompanied much of this enterprise. We cannot be human without making moral judgments, and while morality must take cognizance of history and its relativities, history is not a night in which all cats (morally speaking) are gray. It is one thing to delight in the rich variety of cuisine and the wealth of imagination this variety testifies to; it is fine if, as a result, one can appreciate meals such as Mother never used to make; it is quite another thing to accept cannibalism as a morally neutral fact. In the present context, the relativities of historical and anthropological data must not blind us to the moral achievements of our own culture.

Our problem with psychologists is of a different kind. Their approach (perhaps inevitably) emphasizes how socialization shapes the adult personality. Since the family continues to be the main locale of socialization, there is the tendency to view it primarily in terms of this particular function. This has led psychologists to search for the "good home"—"good" as being conducive to whatever socialization patterns a particular school of psychologists regards as desirable. The notion of a "good home," however, tends toward absolutism, and thus toward insensitivity to the sociocultural relativity of family types. In a sense, one could argue, psychologists have made the opposite mistake from that of historians and anthropologists; in a curious way, the allegedly scientific evidence on personality development has made psychologists (and others whose approach is primarily psychological) vulnerable to a new sort of ethnocentrism. As to our fellow sociologists, depending on their theoretical orientation they have fallen prey to both of the aforementioned aberrations. We have seen, in the first part of the book, how these various findings and approaches from the human sciences have come to be utilized as weapons in the current ideological controversies—mostly, of course, on the side of ideologies critical of the bourgeois family.

The social-scientific literature on the family has stressed how the loss of earlier functions (economic, political, educational, and so on) has shifted the emphasis to more-personal functions (procreation, psychological rewards, and the like). Yet it is precisely these more-personal functions that have now come under attack. Thus one can acknowledge the continuing attachment of many people to the family and still predict its eventual doom. Even Mary Jo Bane, who in her earlier book *Here to Stay*[1] reported on the continuing strength of the American family, in her later work, with George Masnick, *The Nation's Families, 1960–1990*[2] projects discontinuities becoming more pronounced as the century moves toward its end. These discontinuities are all centered in the most personal functions of the family: high divorce rates, low birth rates, low remarriage rates, psychological disengagements from familial relationships, and a concomitant shift of personal satisfactions to work and career. We cannot enter here, once again, into the social-scientific argument over these matters. But there are indeed some important questions that must be raised in this connection.

Could it be that there is so little left of the psychic substance of the bourgeois family that its prospects must be deemed gloomy, however much one may regret such a prognosis? If so, given that there will continue some human needs that this type of family satisfied, is it not reasonable to think of viable alternatives? In that case, our defense of the bourgeois family would be an exercise, if not in nostalgia, then of a sort of historical rehabilitation without relevance for the future—as if, say, someone wrote a book arguing that feudalism, however obsolete today, had some good points that previous analysts overlooked.

Obviously, we do not think so. We think that the loss of functions has been greatly exaggerated. We will argue in the next chapter that the significance of the family (and the bourgeois family, to boot) continues unabated for the individual. And in the chapter after that we will take the position that the family continues to have important functions for the public sphere as well. Before we do this, though, there are some other assumptions of our approach that ought to be clarified.

Our approach, by its very nature, tends toward proscription, rather than prescription. That is, we can say with some assurance what social processes and public policies have been harmful to the family; we are much less prepared to prescribe specific cures. This, of course, follows from the aforementioned view (ethical as well as methodological) to the effect that the values of people in any situation must be respected—which implies that they, rather than outside experts, must decide what actions to take in order to realize these values. Thus the social scientist, strictly speaking, should never give prescriptive advice; rather, his contribution should be of the "if/then" type: "*If* you want to obtain these goals, *then* these are the practical options before you." And: "*If* you decide upon this option, *then* these are likely consequences." In other words, the contribution of the social sciences lies in the clarification of options and trade-offs, *not* in telling people what they ought to do. Within these limits, we will indeed have a few things to say about policies in the last chapter of this book. But we deliberately step away from the usual practice of first determining what a "good home" is (or, for that matter, a "good" alternative to what used to be considered as such) and then recommending a "good" policy.

What, more specifically, are our assumptions *qua* sociologists?

There are, of course, various schools of sociology. The quarrels between them cannot be dealt with here. All we can do is spell out, without defending or elaborating, the basic assumptions of the sort of sociology to which we are committed—derived from Max Weber's concept of an "interpretative sociology," as modified by the approaches of phenomenology and the sociology of knowledge.

In this perspective, society is not "a system," and while there may be some heuristic use in looking at it as if it were for this or that intellectual purpose, "systemic" thinking about social phenomena always distorts the empirical reality. Rather, society is a construction of living human beings, and an ongoing construction at that. Any social situation is the "coming together" of many individual meanings and motives, and the situation cannot be understood except "from within"— that is, by understanding what the situation means to those who are in it. Thus the experience of the individual is paramount for the sociologist who seeks to interpret the situation. In the situation at issue, no amount of analysis of the family in terms of this or that "systemic" functionality will be helpful unless it takes cognizance of what individuals mean and intend by their actions in this particular area of their lives—and it is a safe bet that these individuals do not see themselves as operating units of a social system. (If they do, it is likely that they have taken too many sociology courses! An interesting area of research would be the lives of individuals who actually act in accordance with the assumptions of sociological systems theory. But, unfortunately, this particular field of personal pathology must remain outside our purview here.)

But, while society is ongoingly constructed by the meanings and motives of living individuals, it is not reinvented every moment. Rather, the meanings of individuals, past and present, become fixed in patterns that endure in time and can be transmitted from one generation to the next. There are differing terms for describing this process: "objectivation," "sedimentation," and others. The simplest way of putting this is to say that human beings create *institutions*, which embody and carry on particular meanings, which to that extent depend upon continuing acceptance and consent but nevertheless are experienced by individuals as having an independent existence outside their own consciousness. Thus, if a man and a woman marry, their marriage is indeed their own construction, yet the institution of marriage was not invented by them, and it determines, at the very least, the parameters of their individual modifications of the pattern.

Human beings could not survive without institutions. In this they differ decisively from other animals. (The work of human biologists, and its application to sociology by Arnold Gehlen, have taught us this point.) Unlike other animals, human beings do not have the sort of instincts that provide them with reliable guides for most actions. Therefore, human beings have to create their own guidance, and this is what institutions provide. If it were not for institutions, the world would have to be reinvented every day—an impossible idea. This is as true of the family as of every other institution. If a man and a woman, mutually attracted to each other, had no institutional patterns to have recourse to in their efforts to act on the basis of the attraction, they would have before them a vast number of thinkable options. To be sure, this would give them a great deal of freedom and could be very exciting for a while. As a permanent state of affairs, it would be impossible: It would take all their time and energies, leaving neither time nor energy for anything else. To imagine the whole human race existing in this fashion would be to imagine a very short-lived species: Who would take care of the economy (to take but the most important case) while all this marital experimentation was going on? Also very important, even if two individuals could spend their lives reinventing the world on a daily basis, it would be well-nigh impossible to socialize children in such a situation: Children need *a world* to grow into. It follows that any program of radical deinstitutionalization is futile in this as in any other area of social life. The meaningful question is not *whether* there will be an institution of the family in the future but, rather, *what kind* of institution is likely or desirable.

Not all institutions provide a sense of community or belonging for individuals (the modern economy is an example of that, for most people at least). There is no problem with this, as long as there is "guidance" in the area of life covered by the institution—and as long as individuals can find community elsewhere. But human beings cannot live without community any more than they can live without institutions. Indeed (George Herbert Mead has taught us this), socialization is impossible without a strong sense of belonging existing between the child and one or more "significant" adults. Minimally, therefore, every human society must provide community in the social locale where children are reared. This, of course, has been a major task of the family for thousands of years. If, as some argue, the family can no longer do this or must share the community-giving function with other institutions, the alternative communities suggested must be scrutinized very carefully indeed, especially in their likely effect on children.

All these assumptions are cross-historical and cross-cultural in scope. But there are other assumptions that pertain more specifically to modern society. As we have seen, one of the very important developments of modernization has been individuation—the emergence of high-profile individuals with a sense of identity that, at least in principle, allows them to stand out over against the community in which they were reared. This type of individual, of course, has been both a personal ideal (aspired to in much of modern education) and a presupposition of the political ideal of democracy. If one wishes to hold on to this ideal, then one must ask what institutional structures are conducive to producing (that is, socializing) and supporting this type of individual.

Put differently, identity is not something an individual is born with; rather, it emerges from specific social processes. The child develops his specific identity in interaction with others, in the way he learns to relate to his own body and to physical objects in his environment, and in the process of acquiring a world of meanings and motives. In this, fundamental sense, the locale of socialization mediates a world. Insofar as any human world is shaped by ideas, these are of great importance: They live in us, as we live in them. Consequently, the ideas, values, and norms operative in a society are crucial factors in the socialization process; they determine what kinds of human beings inherit the future of the society. Also, identity is not acquired once and for all; it must be supported, reaffirmed, "nurtured" in interaction with others. This "nurture" of identity, of course, need not (and, in a modern society, typically does not) occur in the same locale in which an individual was originally socialized. It so happens that the family, through most of history, has provided the locale for *both* the formation *and* the nurture of identity. If these two functions are now widely dissociated, it is all the more important to inquire in what institutional settings they are now best satisfied. In other words, the problem of the modern family is not only that of children but of adults—at all stages of the individual life cycle!

Identity is very closely related to the overall framework of meaning within which the individual can make sense of his life. Modernity has let loose a variety of processes that weaken or undermine such frameworks of meaning—mostly by relativizing them. The weakening of religious meanings commonly called secularization has very probably been the most serious of these, but in an extended sense there has also been "secularization" of all other frameworks of meaning in society. The weakening of firm moral meanings has clearly had far-reaching and unsettling effects. We have learned from sociology (Émile Durkheim has been the most important teacher of this) that a society cannot survive without a widely shared moral consensus. Thus it is crucial to ask which institutions in modern society are capable of providing a shared and plausible morality. If not the family, then who? The church? The state? Or (heaven help us) the educational system? Or perhaps institutions that are still in the making, still not

fully visible? In any case, for every individual, the questions of identity, meaning, and morality are closely interwoven: "Who am I?"
"What is the world?" "How should I live?" Once again, the problem
of the family in modern society involves all three questions for most
individuals.

These, then, are the assumptions that underlie our considerations
in the final portion of this book. They inform both our analysis and
our advocacy of the bourgeois family. This does not mean that only
those who share the same assumptions can agree with us. But it is
only right that our assumptions be on the table, ready for inspection
both by those who may agree and by those who may disagree with our
position.

# 7

# The Family
# and the
# Individual

When a child is born into this world, he seems to enter into it in a natural, effortless fashion. This process of growth is a source of never-ending excitement to the child and of joy to his or her parents. Selma Fraiberg, in her by now classic book *The Magic Years*, has written evocatively about these experiences from the viewpoint of modern psychology.[1] The wonder of these experiences is universal, shared by every conceivable group of human beings in the past or the present, and no amount of psychological and social-scientific analysis can detract from it for those who participate in it. However, what modern tools of analysis have done is to make us much more aware of the intricacies and problems involved in this process and thus have made us more aware, more deliberate, in this crucial area of human life than probably any other generation in history. It is futile to argue whether this is good or bad; knowledge, once available, cannot be wished away, and there is no point in waxing nostalgic about the unreflected, spontaneous relation to the miracles of birth and growth of earlier, less sophisticated ages.

One insight that the modern study of childhood has sharpened in great detail concerns the manner in which the infant, later the growing child, is shaped, molded by those who are in charge of him. We now know a good deal about the way in which infancy and early childhood serves as the matrix (a singularly apt word, in this instance) for everything the particular individual will be and think in later life. In these early years of life, to put it simply, both personality (or identity) and consciousness are formed. Later modifications of each are possible, of course, but never again does the human individual have the same malleability and readiness to respond positively to the actions of others toward him. And that, of course, is why the institutional setting of this process is of such great importance.

While we know much more about this than was known, say, fifty years ago, large areas of controversy remain. We certainly have much more certain knowledge now about the physical requirements of healthy infancy and early childhood—in terms of prenatal and postnatal health care, hygiene, nutrition, and the like. Child psychologists have also acquired very reliable knowledge about the details of the developmental process—such as the amazing variety of communications between infant and adults (smiles, "eye language," the acquisition of symbolic communication, the stages of language learning). Child psychologists have also come to understand the manner in which the infant establishes "bonding," first with one individual, then with others. And perhaps surprisingly, our rational and experimentally inclined science of child psychology has rediscovered what human beings have taken for granted for many thousands of years: the overriding importance of love for the healthy development and even the sheer survival of children.[2] Still, much has not been clearly established.

There is a far-reaching controversy between those (like Margaret Mead and Philippe Ariès) who see modernity as having imposed peculiar strains and conflicts upon childhood and those (mostly influenced by psychoanalysis) who insist that childhood has *always* been stressful and conflict-laden.[3] In recent years there has been a particularly sharp controversy over the question of the existence or nonexistence of a "maternal instinct"—a controversy of special interest, of course, to feminists.[4] The question here, broadly put, is whether the "bonding" between mother and infant is biologically grounded and because of this unique, or whether comparable powerful bonds can be established between the infant and other adults (perhaps of either sex). Controversy has also raged around various child-rearing patterns, notably "permissive" as against more-"structured" (termed "authoritarian" by opponents) patterns.[5]

It is important to note that, on all sides of these debates, positions have been taken in the name of science—a weighty legitimation in an age of great respect for anything that can pass itself off as science. Thus parents have invested great amounts of energy and faith in this or that "scientifically correct" style of child rearing. As Midge Decter put it well: "We were told, and we told ourselves, that the years of unprecedented watchfulness over our children—attending to every cry, responding to every threat of unhappiness, preemptively offering our anxious assistance at every suggestion of difficulty—had paid off. We were told, and we told ourselves, that somehow, with the aid of new scientific insights . . . we had managed to create a new breed of offspring."[6] If the results fell short of these expectations, or if the allegedly scientific assumptions of these procedures were questioned (and questioned by people with scientific credentials), there ensued, very understandably, a great deal of anxiety and even anger. The vehemence and intolerance of differing "camps" of child-rearing advocates express both the anxiety and the anger.

In this book, at least, we cannot possibly arbitrate or decide among the various sides in these controversies. Nor is this necessary to make our point. What we can do, however, is to relate both our general assumptions about human society and our specific knowledge of modern developments to the one issue that concerns us here: the ability of the bourgeois family, as against other available or imaginable alternatives, to satisfy the basic needs of the early stages of individual life. Knowing the "plasticity" of human nature, we also know that the institutional setting of early socialization will have very far-reaching consequences. We can then propose the kind of "if/then" options that we described in the preceding chapter. Despite all cultural relativism, most childhood analysts today agree in certain minimal imperatives, without which a reasonably healthy and happy childhood is very unlikely.[7]

There are, of course, basic physical requirements: protection against outside dangers, feeding, treatment of illness (with whatever means are available), and encouragement of physical learning (including opportunities for motor development). In addition to these, which are obvious, there is broad agreement that there are four further minimal imperatives so that a healthy, alert, and emotionally content infant may develop: a stable structure, physical as well as social; in this structure (and thus stably present), care and love by adults; a fair amount of interaction, communication, and stimulation between the infant and adults; and consistency and predictability in the relations with the important adults in the infant's environment. While these four imperatives can be analyzed discretely, they are closely related. Indeed, two words summarize all of them quite well: *stability* and *love*. Child experts differ on a lot of matters, but there is overwhelming consensus to the effect that here we have the irreducible minimum of a viable socialization context. This consensus, minimal though it may be, has far-reaching implications.

The biological presuppositions for these imperatives are known and need no elaboration here; they refer not only to the helplessness of the human infant in a dangerous physical environment, but to his "unfinished" quality at birth, which means that essential steps in the physical and (even more) the psychic and social growth of the individual take place in the "extrauterine" phase—that is, in the course of socialization. This, it appears, must entail intensive interaction between the infant and a caring adult, as the studies of infant death and of development in orphanages suggest.[8] It seems that without the presence of caring adults an infant is much less likely even to physically survive, let alone develop emotionally. One may say that, in reaching these conclusions, modern child psychologists have simply reinvented the wheel; after all, human beings have always known this, perhaps even known it instinctively. Still, the findings are important by way of confirmation.

By far, in most societies, it is the parents who are in charge of the infant's care and socialization. Father and mother live together in a structured relationship known as the family—though, of course, there is a seemingly endless variety of structural forms. The anthropological evidence strongly suggests that the precise form does not matter for the infant, *as long as* the minimal imperatives are not violated—most important, as long as the structure is stable and allows for the expression of love toward the infant. The evidence also suggests that it is not essential that both parents have the same intensive interaction with the child; it also suggests, though, that initial interaction is tied to the mother or, in her absence, another female, whom, *faute de mieux*, we will have to call a "mother figure." This evidence can be accepted, regardless of whether one agrees or fails to agree with the notion that there is a "maternal instinct" in the human species. The evidence also leaves open the theoretical possibility that a male could play the role of "mother figure," though this is not too likely and for a simple reason: If such an arrangement were viable for the development of healthy infants, the vast variety of family arrangements in differing cultures would make one expect that it would have been successfully tried somewhere!

In any case, it is possible to talk about an innate tendency toward *individualized ties*—that is, the infant is "bonded" with individual adults, in small numbers, and not with a large, anonymous collectivity. It should be noted that this does not, as yet, imply modern-style "individualism"; the individualized ties are found in societies all over the world, many of which (indeed, most of which) are strongly "collectivistic" in other matters, if compared with our own. The psychologist J. Bowlby has coined the term "monotropy" for the phenomenon of the child seeking contact with only one person in the early stages of infancy.[9] Bowlby also argues that the infant cannot form this sort of attachment indiscriminately and that, once formed, the attachment leads to strong possessiveness on the part of the infant. It also appears that "monotropy" is even stronger in children afflicted with any kind of handicap, physical or mental.

Given the cross-cultural presence of these imperatives, one cannot use them in defense of the bourgeois family *tout court;* clearly, other forms of the family have been able to satisfy them adequately. The question, though, is what other forms are *available today* for this purpose. We should recall again what has been one of the most salient characteristics of the bourgeois family: its balance between communal and individual requirements, and more specifically, its balance between authority and love. The bourgeois family, from the beginning, was "child-centered," lavishing care and affection on its children. But, *at the same time,* it provided stability, "authority," predictability. What exists today by way of suggested alternatives is not reassuring on these counts. This is as true of the various utopian experiments, which often emphasized love but have been singularly lacking in stability, as of the more professionally conducted child-care facilities, which very commonly supplied *neither* love *nor* stability. Erik Erikson has emphasized the importance of *trust* in the development of a healthy personality: The child must be able to trust the love of the adults who care for him—and he must also trust in the fact that they will *continue to be around* in the future.[10] None of the available alternatives to the bourgeois family provide a basis for either kind of trust; for that reason alone, they are not viable alternatives.

This is not to deny that the bourgeois family itself, having been weakened by some of the disintegrative processes we looked at in earlier chapters, often fails to provide the necessary structure for healthy child development. A good case can be made that the inconsistencies and the lack of authority in the contemporary middle-class family, even in its "intact" condition, have produced anomic and emotionally unstable children; this effect is probably magnified as the number of "intact" families shrinks as a result of divorce. It seems evident, though, that the remedy for this cannot be dispensing with this type of family in favor of even riskier arrangements.

In this context, the various camps assaulting the family today, as we discussed them in the first chapter of this book, must be looked at again. The bourgeois family, as the primary locale of socialization in the full meaning just described, is threatened by several outside forces as well as by disintegrative forces from within. Divorce, most of all, but also other destabilizing developments, will undermine the stable structure on which children depend. One destabilizing development, which originates in (mostly economic) tensions within the family but then creates powerful outside forces, is the much larger participation of mothers in the labor force. In recent years, this shift has particularly affected women with preschool children—that is, mothers who, in an earlier period, would have stayed at home if at all possible. (It is arguable how much of this shift was caused by simple economic necessity: women who would have preferred to stay at home being forced to work outside to increase the family income; and how much by the influence of feminism: women desiring to escape the "domestic prison" for reasons other than economic. In all likelihood, both factors were present and reinforced each other.) This change has meant, quite simply, that even very young children have come to have less intensive interaction with their mothers. Neither is there any indication that in this new situation fathers are able and willing to take over this function. If the above-listed imperatives are valid, this is a serious development. It is interesting to see how it has been dealt with.

Some analysts, especially those close to the feminist movement, have denied the imperative. Others, especially professionals, have coped by arguing that the role of the mother is not unique and can be replaced (partially or *in toto*) by other caring adults, or by insisting that the quality, rather than the quantity, of mother/child interaction is what counts. The professional interest in all of this, of course, has been to advocate large-scale (and professionally managed) day-care facilities to receive the children of working mothers.[11] From the point of view of the individual child, the shift has meant ever earlier and ever longer separation from intimate family contacts. We are not persuaded of the harmlessness of this. Let us assume (which is hardly warranted, in the light of past performance) that the new day-care arrangements will indeed be humane and efficient. A persistent feature of all such facilities is a high personnel turnover. Again from the point of view of the child, this is a very negative feature indeed. A long procession of strangers (no matter how humane or how highly trained) pass by the child, and the necessary emotional bonding with one or two adults is either impossible (there simply being no time for it) or (even worse emotionally) each attachment is soon followed by a painful loss. One psychologist has described the effects of this sort of situation on young children as follows (the setting was a hospital, but the same observations would apply to any facility): "The child becomes self-centered and more interested in material objects. A change of nurses no longer makes any difference to him. Even a visit from his parents in the hospital does not mean a great deal to the child. He will appear cheerful and adapt to his unusual situation and apparently be easy and unafraid of anyone. But his sociability is superficial; he appears no longer to care for anyone."[12]

One of the most dramatic pieces of evidence in this area comes from a study, by René Spitz, of the differential development of young children in a foundling home and in a prison.[13] In the latter, inmates who were mothers (mostly minors themselves) were allowed to keep and look after their children. Spitz could show, by his measurements, that the foundling-home children were superior, in various indicators, to the prison children right after birth. By the end of the first year the foundling-home children had fallen dramatically below their initial level, while the children of the jailed mothers had improved dramatically. This also happened in the second year. The foundling-home children were extraordinarily late in all the development phases (toilet training, walking, speech, and so on). This was in marked contrast to the prison children, who, cared for by their own mothers even in this (by definition) stressful environment, developed normally and happily. Spitz's findings on the negative effects of institutionalization and separation from the mother are buttressed by other evidence.[14] This does *not* mean that all institutions caring for children are bad, or that humane and beneficial day care is impossible. It *does* mean that the burden of proof rests on all proposals to deprive children of the intensive interaction with their mothers that for good reason, has been the norm throughout history. By the same token, one should view with great skepticism any claims that the stable structure of the family, as we have come to know it, can be weakened without serious effects on children.

As children grow older, the imperative of direct and intensive care begins to be less acute. Gradually the child is able to adapt himself to strangers and to develop wider relationships outside the family, both with peers and with new adults. This development differs, from child to child, in various details, but there is general agreement among child psychologists that it is a necessary one and, indeed, that restricting a child to the family alone at this stage may be detrimental. There continue to be controversies about various aspects of this development stage; again, it is not our task to take positions on these. The one point that we would insist upon is this: There are no cookbook recipes for child rearing at this or at any other stage, and because of this, parents are usually the best judges of what their child needs; only they, in most cases, know the child fully and can appreciate the individualized needs of the child; by contrast, the knowledge of outsiders tends to be partial (derived, for instance, only from the child's behavior in school or in a psychologist's office) and abstract ("this type of child" . . .). That is an issue to which we will return when we discuss the policy implications of our approach. For now, though, another point is important: For the infant and the young child, the key imperative is the development of personality—or, if one prefers, of the self; we have argued that, under contemporary conditions, there appear to be no viable rivals to the bourgeois family as the best matrix for this development. For the older child, the issue shifts to *the kind of self* that will develop; this issue includes the question of the *development of values*. And here, once again, we believe that the bourgeois family has distinctive positive features that no other available setting is likely to provide.

We have seen how, in an earlier period of history, the bourgeois family socialized the kind of individuals who could both succeed, and survive emotionally, in a social environment of acute competition and rapid change. Put simply, the bourgeois family socialized individuals with personalities and values conducive to entrepreneurial capitalism on the one hand and democracy on the other. David Riesman has given the by now classic term "inner-directed" to this type of individual. Precisely this type of personality and value system has been criticized—by some as being obsolete, by others as being inherently wrong even when it was not obsolete. Thus it has been argued that the new "permissive" style of child rearing, as it has developed in middle-class families in America and other Western countries, is more appropriate to a "welfare-bureaucratic" society, as the older, more "authoritarian," style was appropriate to an "individuated-entre-preneurial" society.[15] In Riesman's terminology, this would constitute the shift from "inner-directed" to "other-directed" types of individuals—that is, from personalities and values belonging to autonomous, independent-minded individuals, to personalities and values of people who make their way by means of complex and nuanced interpersonal relationships. We find this analysis persuasive. The question we must ask, however, is whether we really want to foster the personality patterns and values of "other-direction," as against the old ideal of the autonomous individual. If not, then the bourgeois family remains the one great barrier against an all-embracing bureaucratization of life! Put simply, the question is, Do we continue to believe in the autonomous individual as an ideal in our society?

One curious aspect of this, previously discussed by us, is that the old bourgeois ideal is today safer in working-class than in middle-class layers of our society. Working-class parents, more than middle-class parents, today want their children to be independent, ambitious, competitive, and risk-taking. This suggests that, perhaps paradoxically, the working class may eventually be inheriting the entrepreneurial positions that many in the middle class find uncongenial. The data on this matter are quite inconclusive.[16] But the existing alternatives to the bourgeois family that show most clearly the qualities of the latter's socialization are those experiments that were started in conscious rebellion against the bourgeois ethos. The contrast with the bourgeois patterns is sharply illuminating here.

Very interesting evidence comes from studies of the Israeli kibbutzim, where there is a consciously collectivistic and anti-bourgeois policy of child rearing.[17] Of course, Israel is a very distinctive society and the kibbutz is a very distinctive institution, so that conclusions from these studies cannot be directly applied to situations in America or other Western countries. But the kibbutz is interesting because, as all observers agree, enormous care is bestowed on children and, within the limits of its collectivism, the kibbutz can actually be described as a child-centered community. In other words, by every professional or commonsensical criterion, this is very good child care indeed. And as one might expect, kibbutz children are healthy, emotionally stable, and better than average in their intellectual development. There is nothing wrong, if you will, with their personalities. The question is, once again: What kind of personality develops in this setting and what kind of values are internalized by these children? The answer is quite clear: Both personality and value system are emphatically collectivistic and conformist. These are individuals who find it extraordinarily difficult to stand up against their group, who find it difficult to develop an inner life outside the sphere of collective activity, and who very often find it hard to exist in any less-collectivistic situation (such as the rest of Israeli society, outside the kibbutz). The conclusion, of course, can only be put in "if/then" terms: If one deems such conformist individuals admirable, then the kibbutz provides one of the best counter-ideals to the bourgeois family; if not, then the kibbutz only serves to clarify why the bourgeois family continues to be the matrix of individual autonomy.

There now exists also a good deal of evidence about child-rearing in American communes.[18] These are much more varied than the Israeli kibbutz, and one may also say that they developed under much less favorable conditions—as marginal utopian experiments unsupported by the larger culture, as against the honored place of the kibbutz in the political ideology of Israel. The data collected on these experiments are overwhelmingly negative: children subjected to bizarre and frequently damaging experimentation, instability in all the relationships significant to the child, neglect and neurosis, and children suffering from all sorts of physical and emotional deprivations. These findings are all the more weighty in that many of them were conducted by researchers who started out with very positive attitudes to the communes they were studying and who changed their minds only as their research proceeded. Indeed, the damage done to children has been a major reason why many initially sympathetic observers turned against the communes. Without entering into the often fascinating details of these studies, suffice it to say that this is one of the most implausible corners of the society to look for viable alternatives to the bourgeois family.

Childhood and the growth toward adulthood are, of course, universal human phenomena, insofar as they are grounded in the organic makeup of man. Modern society, for reasons that cannot be elaborated here, has "invented" an intermediary phase, that of adolescence, or youth.[19] This phase is the one, as it were, "officially designated" as the period during which the individual is supposed to "find himself." It is also understood that this process will, indeed should, involve a stepping away from the individual's family, a new independence—on the basis of which the individual will then be in a position to marry and start a family of his own. A further assumption is that the individual's socialization and education, within and outside his family, will have prepared him for this emancipation. All these definitions of reality, as we have seen, were developed by the bourgeois family ethos; they strongly survive in contemporary Western societies, as ideals, although they have been challenged both by competing definitions and (more important) by the practical difficulties of a changing society.

One of these difficulties that we have dealt with before in this book is the loss of family functions to the educational complex. This has weakened the capacity of the family to provide emotional support and moral guidance to the individual as he passes through the (aptly named) "adolescent crisis." But this has been accompanied by yet another, equally important, change: the rise of a separate youth culture (separate, that is, from *both* the family *and* the formal educational complex). It may be argued that this happened precisely because the educational institutions have been unable to provide the emotional and moral "services" that the family surrendered to it; in consequence, the young individuals, left to themselves in this bewildering and stressful situation, had no recourse but to turn to each other. Be this as it may, there now exists a new and very powerful socializing force, the young individual's own peers, in many ways arrayed *against* the influences of both the family and the educational system. The effect of this new force (which has actually become an institution in the youth culture) has been studied by many social scientists.[20] Some of the latter have been quite sympathetic, others more critical. But there is very wide consensus on the importance of the phenomenon, especially in America.

The youth culture has been identified in the public imagination with the extravaganza of the 1960s. This is an oversimplification: The youth culture as a general phenomenon is much older than these particular manifestations of it, and it has survived them. Thus one should not focus on these. But whether one is mainly sympathetic or mainly critical will finally depend on how one stands with regard to the bourgeois ethos. By its very nature as a counter-definition, the youth culture has institutionalized a number of anti-bourgeois attitudes and values: rebelliousness, hedonism, a fixation on the here and now, and all this in a strongly collectivistic/conformist mold (peers at this age level are, perhaps instinctively, *a horde*). In moderation, it may be argued, all these features may be benign features of growing up into responsible adulthood. We would argue that the youth culture has tended to go beyond such moderation and has therefore become a socializing influence weakening or undermining the psychological and moral achievements of individual autonomy. To use Riesman's term again, the youth culture has become an important factor in the emergence of the "other-directed" personality and value system. In consequence, it now exerts an influence far beyond the particular biographical stage in which it originated—many people, so to speak, refuse to leave it and remain something like "youth for life." This, we would further argue, is debilitating both for them and for society as a whole.

It seems to us that the individual, finding himself at the center of these competing psychological and moral pressures (from family, school, and peers), is threatened by anomie in a very direct way. The empirical consequences of this are not difficult to discover: juvenile delinquency and (increasingly) serious crime, drugs and alcoholism, suicide, a frenetic preoccupation with sexuality, mental disorders, and the appeal of fanatical cults. It seems to us plausible to ascribe the increase of all these phenomena among young people to the anomic burdens imposed on them by our society. It is also important to note that the majority of young people who do *not* fall victim to these debilitations and who do succeed in passing through this biographical stage without undue harm must expend great effort in doing so, and we are not at all sure that the energies required for this effort could not be better spent on other things. We are not alone in this assessment. Those who agree, quite logically advocate two diverse solutions: one, to reassert the authority of the family; and two, to mobilize outside forces, within the educational and therapeutic complexes, to provide moral guidance to youth.

A recent example of the latter attempt at solution is the moral education movement.[21] It developed in the 1970s as it became increasingly clear that the much-heralded youth culture did not produce the new, liberated individual but, rather, a multitude of new pathologies and anxieties. Led by Lawrence Kohlberg, this movement claims to be based on established psychological insights on human development and seeks to incorporate moral education into the school curriculum. It is impossible here to analyze the presuppositions of the moral education movement in detail. Suffice it to say that we agree with the critics, who have seen the movement as based on a misunderstanding of developmental psychology and as being essentially a program of indoctrination in liberal values elevated to absolute status, with tolerance toward all and anything as the only positive norm.[22] Also, we believe that the movement greatly overestimates the ability of the school as an institution to incorporate this kind of moral guidance—or rather, its ability to do so in a pluralistic and democratic society. In other words, *either* moral education in schools will be an empty rhetorical exercise, *or* it will be effective to the extent that schools become agents of an increasingly conformist and authoritarian society. It should also be stressed that the notions of morality embodied in this program are overwhelmingly those of the college-educated upper middle class (or "new class")—ideologically liberal-to-left and strongly secularized—so that the movement represents yet another missionary project of this class to impose its values on the lower classes. It is thus part and parcel of the cultural class war that we described in an earlier chapter.

The other possible solution is to seek ways to reassert the emotional and moral primacy of the family. Politically, this means to reassert the authority of parents, of whatever class, against both school and youth culture. Movements such as Moral Majority are only the extreme expression of this reassertion. There is a much broader view that parents must regain control over their growing children. It is strong in all classes (even within the "new class," whose children have been very strongly afflicted by all the aforementioned problems), and has been particularly strong among racial and ethnic minorities (where parents have felt impotent in the face of arrogant educational

authorities and a particularly troublesome youth culture). It is this solution, of course, that we would embrace.

We do not endorse the Freudian idea that an individual's "super-
ego" must derive from the father. Rather, it seems to us that the
strongest internalization of moral norms comes about when both father and mother are present in the growing child's immediate environment. In this situation, two individuals, each of paramount
significance for the child or adolescent, reinforce each other in
representing a way of living responsibly in the world. This need not
mean that parents agree on everything; even in debate or conflict they
represent to the child the importance of norms. The phrase "role
model" has become somewhat of a cliché, but it nevertheless refers to
something very real: Father and mother represent to the child the
strongest possible models for the performance of adult roles. Even
when the child, in the process of growing up, struggles with and
against these models, they are indispensable in serving as points of
orientation. In those cases where either or both of the parental figures
are absent, the child's personal and moral development becomes more
difficult—and logically enough, it is made easier to the degree that
substitute parental figures are available in his social milieu. The bourgeois family, with all its weaknesses and problems, continues to provide this essential service to both children and adolescents. That is
why the *ideal* of this type of family continues strongly even among
people who often miss its reality. Research findings bear out these
contentions: Children growing up in this situation have fewer emotional and behavioral problems, do better in school, have higher rates
of achievement, and move more easily from dependence to autonomy.[29]

Inevitably, when looking at the relation of the family to the individual, the focus has to be on the ages of childhood and youth;
procreation and socialization have always been the chief functions of
the family. This does not mean, however, that the family becomes
unimportant to the individual when he or she has moved beyond this
biographical stage and has also outgrown the stage of active parenthood. At least in modern society, the case can be made that the family
continues to be of crucial importance for the individual's values and
identity. This becomes clear when one looks at the character taken on
by marriage in modern society.

In recent decades, marriage has been the subject of violent disputes, and a variety of alternatives have been proposed: singlehood, lesbianism and homosexuality, childless marriage, "serial marriage," "open marriage," and even more-imaginative arrangements.[24] These disputes have had their effects, at least in the college-educated upper middle class, where there is widespread skepticism about the institution (and where one finds college students earnestly discussing divorce even before they consider marriage). People today marry later, divorce is continuing to increase, and expectations of marriage seem to be affected by misgivings. Still, people continue to marry as frequently as they used to, and there has been no lessening of marriage by the divorced (giving continued credence to Dr. Johnson's famous dictum about marriage as the triumph of hope over experience). To say the least, it is premature to declare marriage as obsolete, either as an ideal or as a social reality.

The continuing predominance of marriage is amply borne out by demographic data.[25] In theory, these data would be reconcilable with the notion that the individuals "caught" in that institution (for whatever reasons of adherence to traditional habits or "biographical accidents") are quite miserable. Such a theory does not stand up. On the contrary, data on expressed happiness show the continuing emotional power of marriage.[26] Married people are much more likely to say that they are happy than single people, regardless of what questions researchers asked in various studies—concerning love, sense of recognition, personal growth, even job satisfaction. Women, contrary to feminist assumptions, are even happier than men when married, though there are interesting variations by age in this set of data: Married women under the age of twenty-four are only slightly happier than their unmarried sisters; in higher age brackets, married women stay about as happy as when they were younger, but single women express much less happiness, and single women over forty appear to be the least-happy group in the population. Curiously, it is marriage, rather than parenthood, that seems to be the crucial factor here: Married couples with children are not happier than those without. Nevertheless, large numbers of both men and women continue to want children; the figures on children per family have not changed much since 1960 (the end of the postwar "baby boom"), and only 5–6 percent of young married couples expect to remain childless. Also interestingly, married women who work outside the home appear to be happier than those who do not.

Very recent data on the importance of the family to individuals are even more dramatic.[27] Of adult Americans, 92 percent rate the family as their most important personal value (followed, in descending order by friendship, work, patriotism, and religion); 83 percent would welcome more emphasis on *traditional* family ties; 33 percent said they place more emphasis on family togetherness than their parents did, 55 percent the same amount, and only 12 percent less; 78 percent said they consider the family to be the most meaningful part of their life (as against only 9 percent making this claim for work). Also, while these data show the great majority of the individuals surveyed following very traditional patterns, both as an ideal and in actual practice, they were quite tolerant of others following different patterns. This is an important finding, because it indicates that one should not interpret *tolerance* of deviant life-styles as a *preference* for them. In other words, Americans are on the whole a tolerant people, but this does not change their adherence to conventional patterns in their own lives. One more curious finding should be mentioned: Although married women are considerably happier on all indicators, many complain about being married; this includes women who say that they love their husbands and are happily married. What they complain about is not their husbands, but the constrictions they perceive in married life: inability to pursue outside interests, to develop a career or a distinctive identity; being "pinned down" by family obligations. These women, in all probability, cannot imagine loneliness; they take the community of family life for granted; but they still have an elusive vision of freedom outside the family. Thus, paradoxically, while married women are happier than single ones, many in each group say that they wish to be in the other group!

These data suggest many questions, and interpretations vary. One thing is quite clear, though: Despite misgivings and dissatisfactions of various kinds, marriage continues to be the norm for most men and women in our society. This norm will be redefined by some in innovative ways. This will be especially the case as the growth of the percentage of married women in the labor force continues. But there is no empirical evidence for any large-scale turning away from marriage as such.

In order to understand this fact, we believe, the peculiarly modern functions of marriage must be understood. The male-female couple, bonded together for the procreation and raising of children, has always been at the core of the family, and modernity has not changed this. But the married partners now have an enormously more complex and nuanced relationship with each other, apart from or in addition to their children. George Herbert Mead's category of the "significant others" can be utilized here. In all human societies, socialization (or, as Mead would say, the genesis of the self) takes place in intimate interaction between the developing infant and a few individuals who are of primary significance for the former; we may assume that this fact is rooted in the biological constitution of human beings. For similarly fundamental reasons, we may assume that close, significant relationships are important throughout life for the maintenance of identity and meaning. This is but another way of saying that man is a social animal, both initially and lifelong. In this, modern man is no different from his remotest ancestors. What is peculiar about the modern situation is that the marriage partner has been culturally defined as *the most significant other* in adult life. This cultural definition, of course, has been one of the radical innovations of the bourgeois ethos, and it has been very widely realized in the bourgeois family. This has given to marriage an altogether new weight, which can be seen as a great cultural achievement but which also has created an emotional burden of its own: These are very high expectations, and tensions and dissatisfactions are likely in consequence.[28] As one of us put it in an article some years ago: "Every individual requires the ongoing validation of his world, including crucially the validation of his identity and place in the world, by those few who are his truly significant others. . . . Marriage occupies a privileged status among the significant validation relationships for adults in our society."[29]

This is saying much more than the common notion (quite correct, as far as it goes) that modern marriage is based on the so-called "romantic complex." To be sure, the modern West has developed a distinctive form of "sublimated" sexuality, and it is a cultural expectation that individuals "fall in love" and that this emotional condition is a prerequisite to their marrying. But the definition of the spouse as the most important other for the validation of identity and meaning is a function going far beyond the emotional turbulence commonly associated with "falling in love," and indeed beyond the notion of love in any sense. It is, so to speak, a *cognitive* as much as an emotional function. One of the salient features of a modern society is the tenuousness and fragmentation of the individual's social relationships.

It is only to be expected that, under these conditions, both identity and meaning come to be unstable, unreliable, and therefore full of anxiety. The details of this phenomenon cannot be elaborated here.[30] Suffice it to say that, under these conditions, it is a vital necessity for the individual's sanity and emotional well-being that there be *some* relationships that are stable, reliable, and unfragmented—that is, relationships intended to be lifelong, whose basic presuppositions do not change, and which confirm *all* aspects of the individual's identity (as against this or that aspect that may receive occasional confirmation in the multiplicity of roles performed by the individual). One might say that, if such a relationship did not exist, it would have to be invented. But, in the event, it *was* "invented"; modern marriage is the distinctive institutional invention that is designed to satisfy this need for stable identity affirmation. It, too, of course, has been affected by the destabilizing influences of modernity. The profound need it is designed to meet, though, goes far in explaining why it continues to be aspired to even by those who have been disappointed in their experiences of marriage.

Bourgeois marriage is designed to provide a "haven" of stable identity and meaning in a social situation where these are very scarce commodities. Here there is the norm of mutual concern for all aspects of the individual's life. Further, it is here that two individuals are in a position to construct a "world of their own," again something that is not easy to do elsewhere amid the complexities of modern life. Again, quoting an earlier formulation of this: "It is here that the individual will seek power, intelligibility, and, quite literally, a name—the apparent power to fashion a world, however Lilliputian, that will reflect his own being . . . a world in which, consequently, he is *somebody*."[31] This is not an aspiration that one gives up easily. And thus those who have found it unrealizable in one marriage, in large numbers try again —and if necessary, again once more. In this sense, we would contend, the high divorce rates indicate the opposite of what conventional wisdom holds: People divorce in such numbers *not* because they are turned off marriage but, rather, because their expectations of marriage are so high that they will not settle for unsatisfactory approximations. In other words, divorce is mainly a backhanded compliment to the ideal of modern marriage, as well as a testimony to its difficulties.

Bourgeois marriage, among those who continue to live within its normative boundaries, continues to provide the stable identity and meaning it was originally designed to provide. The data on happiness are the latest evidence for this contention. It further appears that the well-being engendered by marriage extends to the physical aspects of life too. Data indicate that married individuals have less disease and a greater life expectancy than those not married.[32] Some of this is presumably to be explained in terms of the better nutrition and more-regular habits associated with being married. But it is not fanciful to speculate that the psychic stability brought about by marriage will have physical ramifications.

To sum up our argument in this chapter: We are not blind to the tensions and dissatisfactions of the bourgeois family. We are conscious of its sociohistorical relativity, and we do not wish to absolutize it in an ideologically conservative manner. However, we believe that there is no viable alternative to the bourgeois family for the raising of children who will have a good chance of becoming responsible and autonomous individuals, nor do we see alternative arrangements by which adults, from youth to old age, will be given a stable context for the affirmation of themselves and their values. The defense of the bourgeois family, therefore, is not an exercise in romantic nostalgia. It is something to be undertaken in defense of human happiness and human dignity in a difficult time.

# 8

# The Family
# and
# Democracy

As the twentieth century draws to its close, the overriding question is likely to be the capacity of Western-style democracy to survive; for some, especially among intellectuals, it is whether this type of society is even worthy of survival. Put differently, people are asking more frequently just what it is that our kind of society stands for. Clearly, it cannot be our task here to present a comprehensive philosophical defense of Western society in general and of its political heritage in particular. Also, we are, of course, well aware of the fact that there are sharp differences of viewpoint on this matter within Western society (not to speak of its critics elsewhere). All the same, it seems to us that there is a wide consensus, spanning various ideological divides, on the following propositions:

Western society stands for the value of the individual, regardless of race, social background, or physical endowment. Closely related to this is the belief that every individual has the right to freedom from constraints to which he has not assented, and this right includes freedom of beliefs and ways of life. Implied in this, logically, there is an acceptance of a pluralism of beliefs and ways of life, since free individuals will make various choices. Also implied in this is the democratic assumption that freedom is the right of *every* individual—that

is, freedom is not the prerogative of an elite but of the common people as well. These notions of individual freedom and individual rights
must be institutionalized; democracy, as it has developed in Western
society, is precisely the political system in which this body of convictions has been institutionalized. Democracy, then, rests on a number
of basic assumptions about human nature; these assumptions are both
cognitive (in terms of what human beings *are*) and normative (in
terms of the moral demands human beings are entitled to make).

Political philosophers have put these and similar propositions
much more elegantly than we have; the present statement will do for
our purposes. But we must now point to an important aspect of this
matter: While democracy is clearly based on a set of normative beliefs, it is *also* based on the cognitive assumption that these norms are
capable of empirical realization. Thus one may say philosophically
that human beings are entitled to freedom; saying this, however, one
assumes that there are concrete human beings capable of taking advantage of this entitlement. For democracy to exist, there must be
self-reliant and independent-minded individuals capable of making
use of the institutional provisions for freedom and capable of resisting
the manifold social pressures toward conformity. It follows that a vital
question for democracy is that of the psychological and social conditions under which such individuals are likely to emerge. Shortly after
the demise of the Franco regime, when the democratic forces of Spain
were faced with the problem of how to deal politically with the
authoritarian parties of both the right and the left, one liberal politician remarked: "If you want to build a democracy, you must do it
with democrats." This sentence can serve a wider purpose: Democracy will be a meaningless abstraction (and probably a short-lived
one at that) unless there are living human beings who require it,
demand it, and have the ability to make use of its institutional arrangements for their own aspirations toward freedom. *Where are such
people to be found?*

Ever since De Tocqueville, if not earlier, there have been passionate debates over the question whether democracy, despite the
value of the individual that it has always espoused, may not in fact
tend to operate against individual autonomy, pushing people toward
conformity and herdlike existence. Aristocrats, of course, have always
believed this, and in this they are in curious agreement with critics of
"bourgeois democracy" on the left. In recent years this old debate has

taken new forms. There has been much concern over the alleged decline of public virtue (certainly a presupposition of democracy), with
a tendency of large numbers of people to withdraw from political in-
volvement into private, hedonistic, and even narcissistic concerns.
Thus David Riesman saw this shift in the passage from the "inner-
directed" to the "other-directed" character type—the former self-
reliant and autonomous, the latter pliant and conformist to the changing circumstances of the social milieu.[1] Erich Fromm, more on the left
than Riesman, perceived a similar shift as being due to modern capitalism, with individuals acquiring an overall "marketing orientation"
and finally perceiving their own personality as a marketable commodity, with the result that they become alienated from themselves as
well as from others.[2] In recent American sociology (much of it left of
center at least in tendency), C. Wright Mills initiated a whole school
of interpretation whereby contemporary "mass society" is understood
as the very antithesis of the "public" on which democracy was originally based.[3] A large number of other authors could be cited, all
deploring in various ways the decline of the public and with it the impending demise of democracy. Those who view the situation in this
way (ranging ideologically from the democratic Right to democratic
socialists), whatever else may divide them, agree that the danger to
democracy is a negative development not only politically but in terms
of deeply held human values.

As we have seen earlier in this book, the family (at least in its
"bourgeois" form) has been widely accused of being a prime cause of
this decline—promoting selfishness and privatism and thus standing in
opposition to the common good and the civic virtues. In this perspective, true democracy would have to be anti-familistic. The family constitutes the last and most harmful barrier between the individual and
society. And as we have also seen, there has recently been some important change in this perspective on the family. While there continues
to be the notion that the public has been in decline, the family now
tends to be seen as a *victim*, rather than a *cause*, of this process. Thus,
for instance, Richard Sennett sees the family as but another victim of
what he calls "the fall of public man," a paradoxical development
characterized on the one hand by an escape into the private sphere
and, on the other hand, by a fusion between public and private that
is detrimental to both.[4] Even more sharply, Christopher Lasch has
bestowed victim status on the family in his description of the alleged

devastations of private life by modern capitalism.[5] And of course, on the right there are many people deploring the assaults on the family by an imperialistic welfare state and its professional allies.

This is not the place to go over once again our own perceptions on what has happened to the family under the impact of modernization. Suffice it to say again that we completely disagree with those who would blame the family—and especially the bourgeois family—for the social problems of our time. Compared to this anti-familism, we may further say, the recent emphasis on the family as victim is preferable. But this later view also falls far short of what we would consider an adequate view of the situation: It is not so much a matter of seeing the victimization of the family (though such victimization there has certainly been); it is much more important to see that *the family, and specifically the bourgeois family, is the necessary social context for the emergence of the autonomous individuals who are the empirical foundation of political democracy*. This has been so historically. There is every reason to think that it continues to be so today.

It has frequently been pointed out that the treatment of the family in moral philosophy and political theory is a good indicator of the vision of society being propagated. This has always been so, at least in Western thought. There is one tradition, reaching from Plato through Rousseau to Marx, in which the family is viewed as a barrier to the achievement of virtue, justice, and equality in society. There is another tradition, going back to Aristotle and continued by Locke, Hegel, and De Tocqueville, which declares the family to be the cornerstone of social order. Present-day attacks on the bourgeois family have been most influenced by Marx and by the later developments of Marxist theory. Marx and Engels insisted that "civil society" of the bourgeois type and the bourgeois family developed conjointly. Both social formations are organized around private property, and they continue to reinforce each other, forming a breeding ground for the alleged ills of capitalist society. Marx and Engels were sympathetic to some of the ideals of the early bourgeois family—such as mutual love, equality, and shared work—but they maintained that these ideals were necessarily debased under capitalism. These notions were elaborated by Engels in his seminal work on the origins of the family.[6] We have already mentioned the continuation of this perspective in some recent feminist writings. An important linkage between Marxism and contemporary feminism is to be found in the writings of the so-called

Frankfurt School, especially in the works of Max Horkheimer, Theodor Adorno, and Herbert Marcuse.[7]

Special mention should be made here of Adorno's influential work *The Authoritarian Personality*, published in 1950.[8] The argument here is that (right-wing) authoritarianism has its roots in the type of family produced by bourgeois-capitalist society. This type of family is supposedly characterized by lack of affection and the demand for strict conformity to conventional modes of conduct. Individuals raised in this way are supposed to feel fundamentally weak and insecure and are therefore supposed to admire power and toughness, to despise weak out-groups, and to be prone to succumb to strong leaders. It follows that, as long as the bourgeois family lasts, authoritarianism will remain a constant danger. Conversely, real democracy will be frustrated by the authoritarian patterns reproduced by the family. The connection between bourgeois family patterns and authoritarianism (equated here with fascism) is made even more strongly in the works of Wilhelm Reich, another neo-Marxist German writer who came into his own, somewhat belatedly, in the late 1960s in America.[9] It is but one small step from there to the kind of analyses advanced by R. D. Laing, David Cooper, and other recent radical theorists, who look upon the bourgeois family as the major obstacle to healthy and non-repressed individuals, who alone can be the harbingers of a just social order.[10]

This type of thinking has been very influential in the past two decades in the commune movement in America and Western Europe.[11] The commune is to produce a new kind of human being, freed from the egoism deemed to be intrinsic to the bourgeois way of life and ready to live in collective structures of mutual affection and shared responsibility. This movement has been strongly anti-individualistic and (logically enough) has blamed modern individualism on the bourgeois family. Living communally, within a sharing economy, commune members seek to achieve a collective consciousness radically different from that of the old, individualistic values created by the bourgeois family. The anti-democratic propensities of these groups should not surprise us. Indeed, far from creating the non-authoritarian personalities dreamed of by their original proponents, the communes of recent decades have been the context of some of the most rigidly authoritarian and destructive movements of our time. If any phenomenon can, then the communes constitute the most telling empirical falsification of the theory that the destruction of the bourgeois family is the precondition of freedom. The depressing record of the commune movement may also have contributed to the greater readiness today to reconsider the much-maligned bourgeois family and even to ask anew whether this institution may not be a necessary prerequisite for a democratic society.

We have already made it amply clear that our own position is diametrically opposed to the position of those who see the family and freedom as antithetical phenomena. Nor is our position dependent on the sorry record of recent experiments in anti-bourgeois life-styles. We have tried to show how the bourgeois family developed historically in close correlation with the forces that created modern democracy, and we believe that this historical linkage continues to be of great importance. This belief, however, must be spelled out further.

Aristotle's famous view that if children did not love their parents and family members, they would love no one but themselves, is one of the most important statements ever made about the relation between family and society. The family permits an individual to develop love and security—and most important, the capacity to trust others. Such trust is the prerequisite for any larger social bonds. Only in the family are the individual's social tendencies aroused and developed and with these the capacity to take on responsibility for others. A person who has developed no family bonds will have a very hard time developing any larger loyalties in later life. The normal process of such a development begins in the family and then "moves out" to larger social groupings. In the words of the German ethologist Eibl-Eibesfeldt, "The human community is based on love and trust: and both are evolved through the family."[12]

This, of course, has always been true. That is, these are not aspects of human life that are limited to the modern era or to the specific family type developed by the bourgeoisie. Aristotle had *all* social orders in mind. But a society that puts a premium on individual responsibility, as any democracy must, will have to be particularly mindful of the institutions that nurture this personal trait. As we have tried to show, the bourgeois family, more than any other, at least in modern times, provides this nurture. That is why the attack on the bourgeois family *in the name of democratic values* is peculiarly perverse. So is the attack on the basis of the alleged possessiveness of bourgeois family life—the possessiveness which, ever since Marx, has

been ascribed to capitalist notions of private property. Bourgeois education does not emphasize possessiveness but, rather, sharing with
others—as any visit to an American playground or nursery school will
show. Yet, paradoxically, Marx *was* right in a way: Only if the child
has a sense of what is properly his can he share that property with
others; in the absence of private property of any sort, there can be no
deliberate acts of sharing; the child, in other words, has nothing that
he *could* share. By the same token, private property is the precondition of *any* notions of a "private" realm—and finally, of a "private"
self, which can in principle be free of others. This has obvious implications, concerning the relation of private property and democracy,
that we cannot pursue here. But we do want to point once again to
the evidence that children who are deprived of all possessions become
severely frustrated and, in consequence, resentful of others. Human
culture includes the love of things, of objects. There is no culture in
which individuals do not have some things that they can call their
own and for which they have "private" responsibility. Possessing
things is a prerequisite for the development of individuality and of social development. *This* does not pertain to the bourgeois family as
such; what *does* pertain is the value of sharing one's possessions with
others and being responsible for their productive use. In Puritan
terms, the value of "stewardship" expresses this. One may further
argue that such "stewardship" loses plausibility as religious conviction
wanes, which once again brings out the importance of religion for the
moral base of modern society.

In any event, quite apart from the issue of private property, the
bourgeois family has been the single most important context for the
value of individual responsibility. No substitute has emerged. We
would argue that, because of this, this type of family is essential for
the survival of a democratic polity.

More generally, there is the question of the moral foundation of
any human society, and especially of a democratic polity. Émile
Durkheim was one classical social theorist who has argued that, at its
core, every human society is a moral community; conversely, he tried
to show how, in the absence of shared moral values, a society must
begin to disintegrate. This general sociological truth about society is
doubly valid when a society organizes itself politically as a democracy. The reason for this is simple: In the absence of moral consensus, coercion remains the only instrument for the maintenance of

even minimal social integration. Such coercion, however, cannot coexist with democracy. Where, then, are the institutions that instill basic moral values in individuals? Durkheim (in this respect, very much in the tradition of the Enlightenment) thought that education might perform this function; John Dewey, coming from a very different intellectual tradition, represented an American version of the same faith. We would argue that the experiences of this century give little support to this notion. This is not to denigrate the values of education. But the school as an institution appears to be quite ineffective in instilling basic moral values—*unless* it serves to reinforce values already instilled in the individual by his homelife. Very much the same is true of the churches. The law, which in America has arrogated to itself (or, more likely, been saddled with by others) the role of moral source or guide, is also singularly unsuited for this function; it is far too abstract, far too remote from the concrete social contexts in which individuals find meaning and identity. The family, today as always, remains the institution in which at any rate the very great majority of individuals learn whatever they will ever learn about morality. It is very unlikely that this will change. Once again, this means that the family has a political function of the greatest importance, especially in a democracy.

No amount of legislation and court decisions can produce in the individual such basic moral ideas as the inviolability of human rights, the willing assent to legal norms, or the notion that contractual agreements must be respected. What legislatures and courts can do, of course, is to reinforce such moral values and to impose sanctions on the minority that offends against them. But neither the state nor the judiciary can be moral authorities in and of themselves. When they try to do this, they either are ineffective (the usual case in democracies) or they start out on a path at the end of which lies totalitarianism, in which the political order tries to absorb into itself all values and all institutions in the society (in which case democracy must come to an end). We would further argue that the primacy of the family as the empirical fountainhead of morality is endangered by the decline of religion, but this point cannot be pursued here.

It is a truism to say (but thereby no less true) that modern society has had serious problems articulating the moral foundation on which it rests. Secularization and pluralism have greatly contributed to this moral crisis. Today, in Western countries, there appears to be a particular crisis of legitimacy for the political order. Why should one obey the law? Is the political order nothing but a collection of practical arrangements, a compromise between competing vested interests? What are the foundations of patriotism—or, even more basically, for *any* sentiments of collective loyalty? Why should one make sacrifices for society? These questions are very difficult to answer in the absence of religious beliefs in the ultimate accountability of human actions. Yet there must be plausible answers if society is not to degenerate either into tyranny or into a sort of public convenience (in the full pejorative sense of that phrase). The family alone, in the absence of a religious world view giving ultimate legitimacy to moral actions, cannot reestablish the civil virtues presupposed by a democratic polity. The family, however, remains the indispensable mediator of these virtues wherever they still exist. This is why the protest of many parents, in various countries, against the moral arrogations of the state and especially of the state-supported school system is an important political event. This is not to endorse any particular protest. And, to be sure, there are protests grounded in bigotry or other reprehensible sentiments. On balance, though, it is the state, rather than parents, which has been responsible for the worst moral perversions of our era; conversely, the resistance against the moral imperialism of state and school, on balance, has been a force conducive to democracy and to the moral order on which it must rest.

Closely related to the issue of moral order is the issue of stability. Social order is impossible unless the conduct of individuals is predictable. In human beings, predictability of conduct depends on the development of a stable character and of reliable habits. Everything we know about social psychology indicates that both have their origins in family life. And as we tried to show earlier, the bourgeois family has been particularly effective in providing a haven of stability in a rapidly changing society. The tensions of modernization, even under relatively benign circumstances, are trying for the individual; the family is the most important institution in which the child is prepared to withstand these tensions and in which, later on, the adult is given the emotional support to continue withstanding them. While providing this stability, the bourgeois family at the same time cultivates individual independence and initiative—again, personality traits that are particularly important under conditions of rapid social change.

The bourgeois ethos arose historically in opposition to "mere tradition," challenging the latter's authority in the name of reason and of individual freedom. This challenge, as the bourgeoisie won its battles against the old order, was itself institutionalized in structures that were both durable and flexible—among these structures notably those of the democratic polity, itself a curious blend of tradition and innovation, of the authority of the law and of the autonomous rights of individuals. Such political and legal institutions, however well designed, derive their stability from the personal traits of the many individuals who live under them. The "balancing act" of democracy, therefore, is a faithful reproduction of the "balancing act" of the bourgeois family. Historically, the bourgeois family preceded what we now know as democracy. We would also maintain that the bourgeois family, in its essential features, can survive under nondemocratic or even totalitarian polities; indeed, the evidence from the Communist world indicates how the family becomes extremely important for the individual who wishes to retain any sense of personal autonomy or worth in the face of the all-embracing state. But we doubt very much that the reverse is true; that is, we doubt whether democracy could survive the bourgeois family.

We are, of course, well aware of ideas of freedom that are antagonistic to the bourgeois tradition, notably those related to one or another version of the socialist vision. While we can appreciate the humane ideals of this anti-bourgeois tradition, we are highly skeptical of its possibilities for empirical realization. The term "bourgeois democracy" is a favorite term of opprobrium to many in the socialist tradition. The plain fact is that no other democracy exists, except in the imagination, and at least one reason for this (not the only one, we think) is that the downgrading of the bourgeois family is almost certain to lead to consequences that are incompatible with democracy—or, for that matter, with the freedom of the individual.

In recent decades there has been the cultivation in some social milieus of an extreme individualism, consciously posited in opposition to the bourgeois ethos. There have been a plethora of "liberationist" gospels. Seen in our historical perspective, this has been an ideal of freedom *without* the bourgeois "balancing act." We are not surprised, therefore, that this type of "liberation" has proved itself to be transitory at best, often an illusion from the beginning, frequently a prelude to an abject surrender of individual autonomy to this or that collective authoritarianism. Individual freedom pushed to an extreme inevitably changes its initial quality. It becomes self-absorption once it is separated from the moral principles that initially both inspired and restrained it. It brings with it a sense of disorientation and loneliness. The individual in this condition comes to turn against the very ideal of freedom that first motivated him. Freedom itself becomes an oppression. In Erich Fromm's apt phrase, the individual now seeks an "escape from freedom" and in consequence becomes ready for any authority that promises him a feeling of belonging and stability. In other words, the individual becomes ready for totalitarian movements or ideologies, which "repress" him far more effectively and comprehensively than any of the authorities he first experienced as oppressive. This is the basic social-psychological dynamics of the revolt against the bourgeois ethos. It is distressing to see it work itself out in the lives of individuals. It is also distressing politically, if one has a stake in the survival of democracy in the modern world.

Thus the bourgeois family and its distinctive ethos has a political significance far beyond the level of individual biography. To be sure, an intact democratic society can survive any number of individuals or subcultures of an anti-bourgeois character; indeed, such tolerance of deviance and nonconformity has been the pride of democracy. However, when such anti-bourgeois values and life-styles become widespread, and when they gain the status of respectability in elite milieus of the society, the matter ceases to be innocuous. A society can absorb only a certain amount of dissolution of its moral substance; a democratic society, paradoxically perhaps, is even more vulnerable than a nondemocratic one to such moral erosion.

Democracy is, by its very nature, a highly precarious human artifact. It cannot survive too much coercion. It must always seek consensus, balancing conflicts and compromises. It must therefore be composed and ongoingly reconstructed by at least a majority of individuals with the personality traits making such a feat possible. Very probably, such individuals must be particularly strongly represented in its elites. How can a society produce individuals who are capable of this sort of balance—who can successfully resist the only seemingly opposite temptations of extreme individualism and a total surrender of individual autonomy to an authoritarian collectivity? This question is the basic sociopsychological issue for any democracy. The bourgeois family is one centrally important institution that has, for several centuries now, provided an *empirical* answer to the question; that is, it has answered the question not just in theory but in its social reality.

We have said enough throughout this book to make clear that we are fully aware of the deep-rooted structural forces of advanced industrial societies and their effects on the family. Thus, of course, we are not advocating that the bourgeois family today should be what it was in an earlier period (even if, as is obviously not the case, it were capable of being this). There has been mounting uncertainty as to the proper purposes of the various roles in the family and in the biographical stages of the individual; this uncertainty is not just a matter of intellectual confusion, but derives directly from the structural changes in society. The contemporary youth culture can be viewed initially as a spontaneous creation of individuals having to cope with uncertainty at a crucial stage of biography. This would not have occurred (for better or for worse) if the family had not lost much of its authority with regard to children and teenagers. Young individuals came to be deprived of the protection traditionally provided them by the family and thus became an "open" category, in the sense that new definitions of what it means to be young could be made. "Youth," in other words, could be radically redefined.

The fate of the youth culture since its virtually Messianic advent in the 1960s provides a very clear illustration of the cycle of "liberation" and disappointment that appears to be endemic to the rebellions against the bourgeois ethos. The earlier sense of mission of the "youth revolution" was well caught in Bob Dylan's song "The Times They Are A-Changin'":

> Come mothers and fathers
> Throughout the land
> And don't criticize
> What you can't understand
> Your sons and your daughters
> Are beyond your command
> Your old road is
> Rapidly agin'
> Please get out of the new one
> If you can't lend your hand
> For the times they are a-changin'.[13]

Yet the problems involved in the creation of new institutions were little understood (as, of course, is usually the case with "revolutionary" movements). Despite the heady sense of mission, the real alternatives were limited. It did not suffice to be anti-institutional, as many of the experiments discovered. Above all, it was not understood that institutions are culturally produced forms that must give coherence and continuity, and the enthusiastic people embarked on most of these experiments had little coherence and little capacity to create enduring structures. In consequence, the "new road" was a disappointment to very many of those who set out on it. In some cases, it turned out to be not so new at all, a temporary way station for individuals headed for conventional careers, not too different from earlier versions of "sowing wild oats" before settling down to the "serious" obligations of life. In other cases, the "new road" led to segregated subcultures, many of them cultic or half-crazed. In the worst cases, it was a road to political or religious fanaticism. Large-scale social change in the direction of countercultural ideals of communalism, socialism, or mysticism did not occur, either by radical political transformation of society or by the expansion of new, psychedelic lifestyles. It became clear that there are limits to change in the "iron cage" of industrialized/bureaucratized modern society.

But one important change did take place, at least in elite milieus of the society: a far-reaching delegitimation of bourgeois culture, and with this a stripping away of moral authority from various social institutions—not just the family and marriage, but also government, law, business, and organized religion. As one astute observer put it: "The conflict between utilitarian culture and counterculture in the 1960's left *both* sides of the battlefield strewn with expired dreams and ideological wreckage. It resulted in the disillusioned withdrawal of the young and old, hip and straight alike, away from active concern with public institutions and back into the refuge of private life."[14] This could not be a simple "return to normalcy." Delegitimation had gone too far, in both the private and the public spheres. The family did not reassert its moral authority. Education could not fill the gap, but could only serve as a credentialing machine, without the capacity to provide moral guidance. Young people—disillusioned both in their private lives and by the public institutions in the political and economic sector primarily—appear more at bay than ever before in the history of modern Western societies. The extreme cases of this (of which Jonestown has become a terrible symbol) are only the salient angle of the phenomenon. The great majority of young people do not belong to extremist cults, but the disorientation and malaise that provides recruits for these cults are very widespread indeed.

It may well be that Western society no longer has the vitality and the cultural resources to regain its moral self-assurance and its sense of political purpose. But if such a revitalization is possible at all, it will have to be accompanied by a reconstruction of the institutional context in which self-reliant and responsible individuals can develop. This context will have to be very similar to that of the bourgeois family. Paraphrasing Bakunin's reflection upon Voltaire, one might say that if it did not exist, the bourgeois family would have to be invented. It is fortunate that such reinvention is not necessary. As we have seen, the demise of the bourgeois family was proclaimed prematurely. It is still here, despite all the uncertainties about it, and it provides a solid foundation for any enterprise of moral reconstruction.

As Max Weber understood very well, modern society is characterized by a "polytheism" of values. To cope successfully with the modern world requires both an honest recognition of this fact and a degree of assurance about one's own value; that is, it requires a delicate balance of tolerance and moral certainty. This is a requirement both for individual sanity and for the survival of a democratic polity. Very clearly, public institutions, including the state, cannot generate these qualities by themselves. As Daniel Patrick Moynihan put it: "In particular, Government cannot cope with the crisis in values that is sweeping the Western world. It cannot respond to the fact that so many of our young people do not believe what those before them believed, do not accept the authority of institutions and customs, whose authority has heretofore been accepted, do not embrace or even very much like the culture that they inherited."[15]

But the isolated individual cannot cope with this crisis either. Human beings are social by their very nature, and the individual bereft of reliable social ties cannot acquire moral assurance in childhood and will have great difficulty in retaining it as an adult. What is essential, then, to a modern society, and especially to a democracy, is the existence of what have been called *mediating structures*—that is, institutions that stand between and meaningfully link the isolated individual and the mega-institutions of modernity.[16] The family is not the only such institution. In Western societies one may add the church, the neighborhood, the voluntary association, and the institutional formations of racial or ethnic subcultures. In non-Western societies there are yet others: clan, village, tribe, and caste. Some of these mediating structures are old, premodern institutions that acquire new functions under modern conditions; others are new creations of the recent period. This is not the place to go into the details of this. Yet one thing is very clear: The family is the most important of these institutions, everywhere in the world—in Émile Durkheim's phrase, "the key link of the social chain of being."[17] In a democratic society, though, this must be a certain type of family, as we have described it—to wit, the bourgeois family, or such a reasonable facsimile of it as will retain its essential features.

There is one further point that must be taken up here: the place of the bourgeois family in a *pluralistic* society. Democracy in general, and American democracy in particular, is committed to the coexistence of a plurality of world views and values. How, then, can our insistence on one particular family type and its particular ethos be reconciled with our allegiance to democracy? As we have pointed out earlier, the argument can be made (and has been made) that it is inaccurate to speak of "the family" today and that even the "bourgeois family" rarely exists in its ideal form. Empirically, this is correct. There have always been considerable differences in families in terms of class, ethnicity, and race. More recently, attention has focused on single-parent and second-marriage families. While one may point out that very frequently "non-bourgeois" families are a matter of necessity, rather than choice, it still remains true that there are significant differences, both in values and in actual practice.

American society in particular has always been highly heterogeneous, and it has become more so in recent history. It can be argued that while class cleavages—certainly in life-styles—have become less pronounced, racial and ethnic subcultures have become more so. What is more, the old "pockets" of homogeneity, as in small towns and rural areas, have become "invaded" by the national pluralism, with new values and life-styles being accepted, however grudgingly. The coexistence of these very different groups has naturally created tensions and even strife. Yet there is one remarkable fact in all of this: Americans have been ready to accept differences *as long as,* and *only* as long as, the different groups could plausibly be perceived as sharing some common values of the society. In that case, ordinary and initially prejudiced Americans are quite ready to conclude that these different people are "really okay." What are these common values? Mostly, they pertain to interpersonal relations in the private sphere: reliability, honesty, industriousness, respect and concern for others, willingness to take on responsibility. As long as these values are shared by otherwise different groups, there can be a sense of community despite the many differences—in the best sense of E pluribus unum. The copious evidence on how Americans overcome racial, ethnic, or religious prejudice bears out this point. Needless to say, this does not deny the ugly history of prejudice in America—with racism its ugliest aspect—but, despite the imprecations of various social critics, it is remarkable how tolerant Americans can be even in the face of drastically different newcomers in their midst. One may contrast this with the sharp resistance to newcomers who do not exhibit this allegiance to shared values—as has happened in communities where various countercultural or cultic groups have recently tried to establish themselves.

We would contend that these shared values, making possible a sense of community across the pluralistic spectrum of differences, are in fact the basic values of the bourgeois ethos, and in particular of the bourgeois family. This is not only a matter of outsiders' observations. Rather, people living in situations of intergroup contact and tension perceive things in this way: They are really okay: They, too, care for the education of their children; they respect property; they work hard; they try to be helpful to others in the neighborhood. In other words, "they," too, whatever their origins and their continuing differences, can participate in the civil ethos that has been the creation of the bourgeoisie. In this connection it is noteworthy that overcoming prejudices is very often accomplished via children, as concerned parents get together on problems that cut across all their differences. This has even happened in situations of acute racial conflict; in such situations, if there is one line that has a chance of carrying the day, it is the proposition "Let's think of the kids first." Now, let it be stipulated that these are values that are not solely exhibited by the bourgeois family. But, in American society, it has been the bourgeois family that has represented them most clearly in the lives of individuals. The bourgeois family, with its values, continues to be the single most important institution capable of bridging differences between groups and subcultures, and thus of providing a plausible basis for democratic pluralism.

Finally, despite the empirical differences between the many forms of family arrangements in contemporary society, it is important to stress that the *ideals* of family life have changed much less than the practice of it. As we have tried to show, it is only a minority, and a highly class-specific one at that, which has directly challenged the ideals. Most people, even if constrained by necessity to live under other-than-ideal circumstances, regret this fact and continue to uphold the old ideal of parents living together and sharing responsibility for their children and for each other—the old ideal, in short, of the bourgeois family. Even many of those who started out rebelling against the bourgeois family find, after they have children, that they "reinvent" arrangements that are remarkably similar to the family type they originally repudiated. This is very important sociologically. A society must be perceived as much in terms of its ideals as of its actual practice. On this level of ideals, the bourgeois family continues to occupy a very prominent place indeed. This, too, is a political as well as a private matter, for it points to one central value set that permits the maintenance of a democratic consensus.

# EXCURSUS

## Father
## Mother
## Child

A mother cradling her child, bent over it in a posture of loving solicitude: If there is another image that will immediately be recognized
by human beings of any age or culture and arouse in them comparable feelings of identification, we cannot think what it could be. This
image surely is a universal symbol. In the Western imagination, it is
associated with the Madonna, but we find it all over the world and in
vastly different cultural settings. If there is one image that suggests
anthropologist Mary Douglas' category of a "natural symbol," this
surely is a prime candidate. If a woman and her baby were to find
themselves stranded in the jungle, surrounded by a group of threatening savages with whom no verbal communication was possible, assuming this particular posture would be "natural" for the woman in at
least two senses—she would do it immediately and spontaneously;
and, if she thought about the matter even for a moment, she would
speculate that this gesture, if any, would appeal to the savages' compassion. Now, please note: There is no male figure in this icon; the father of the child is absent.

But now imagine a quite different situation: The human race has
made contact with intelligent beings from outer space. Not only is
there no way of communicating with them in any human language,
but there is the added difficulty that these are beings with a totally

different biological constitution. Consequently, it is decided to present the aliens with a series of pictographs to explain to them some basic features of human life on this planet. Would the Madonna icon be included? Presumably not: It might seriously confuse the aliens; it would suggest some sort of parthenogenesis as the human mode of reproduction; in other words, the absence of the father would convey seriously misleading information.

There is a German nursery rhyme that begins with the words "father-mother-child," and its intention is presumably to impress on its hearers that this triad is a very important matter. Not being scholars in the field of comparative nursery studies, we cannot say whether this little litany occurs in other languages, but we are confident that it could easily be translated successfully into languages ranging from Eskimo to Papuan. In coming to the defense of the bourgeois family, one of many family types in which this triad is central, we have clearly aligned ourselves with those who would save it from various theoretical and practical efforts at dismantling it, efforts that have been quite prominent in recent years. Now, our defense has at no point been on the basis of a claim that this and only this type of family is "natural," either in the sense of being dictated by human nature or of being rooted in a divine commandment. Rather, our defense has been on the empirical ground that the bourgeois family, including its father-mother-child triad, is intrinsically linked to certain values that we, along with most people in the Western world, espouse—notably the values of individual autonomy and democratic freedom. Yet at this one point in our argument we would like to speculate briefly about the wider human significance of the traditional triad.

The moral authority of the father-mother-child triad has been challenged mainly on two levels. The first level has been empirical: Data from the social sciences, especially from anthropology, are cited to argue for the relativity of all family types and, therefore, against the idea that any of them are "natural" in the sense of being biologically determined. Again, we must disclaim competence on this level, although we suspect that the relativity of family types has been frequently exaggerated: Let it be stipulated that somewhere there is a tribe in which children are reared by homosexual pairs of maternal uncles. So what? We do know enough about the biological constitution of *homo sapiens* to be able to say that in many areas of behavior it acts as a tendency, rather than a compelling determinant—and there seems little doubt about a tendency toward the centrality of the father-mother-child triad. In other words, the triad *may* be biologically "natural" even though it is not institutionalized in the child-rearing practices of the Mumbumbu tribe, say in New Guinea, and of some lesbian communes in New Hampshire; all that this would then mean is that the Mumbumbu and the lesbian communards, in "going against nature," may have to make an extra effort and perhaps have to pay an emotional or even a physical price.

The triad has more recently been challenged on normative grounds, especially by some feminists. The argument here is that it gives an unwarranted importance to the father figure and obscures the fact that women can take care of this child-rearing business without, thank you, any male assistance! (The more vindictive proponents of this idea are also nurturing the hope that, eventually, science will allow women to dispense with male assistance even in the business of getting pregnant in the first place—or even allow women to hatch children in wondrous extrauterine receptacles—in which case, of course, the parthenogenic pictograph *would* give the alien anthropologists an accurate idea of the human situation.) The triad is here dethroned in favor of the mother-child dyad, which is proclaimed as the normative icon. Some of the more militant feminists proposing this symbolic revolution would quite happily do away with males completely, we fear, or reduce them to docile drones in the new matriarchy, once the few remaining technical and political problems for this utopia are solved. Most dyad proponents are more moderate. They are not interested in doing males in, but in teaching them a lesson, after which properly domesticated and consciousness-raised fathers will be welcomed as auxiliary figures gathered around the Madonna scene. For some reason, feminist theologians seem to gravitate toward the more radically anti-paternal position; Betty Friedan (by all accounts, a rather amiable lady who is even fond of the to-be-dethroned sex) in her recent work appears to take a moderate position with regard to this matter.

On this level, we do not plead incompetence, because we don't know what competence would mean. The question here is not so much "What is natural?" as "What is good?" We are skeptical of experts in the area of goodness. On both levels, then, we would apply the postulate of ignorance, which we have previously invoked in connection with the abortion issue. To admit ignorance, however, seems to us the beginning, not the end, of productive ethical discourse. In this, as in so many other matters, it is very salutary to begin with the insight that absolute certainty is a very rare commodity, that all of us are stumbling around in a haze if not in the dark, and that being human means making moral choices as best one can.

Despite the grandiose claims that have been made for "sociobiology," we are impressed with the degree of ignorance about the biological understructure of human conduct. Is the father-mother-child triad "natural"? Or is the father an artificial (that is, culturally constructed) addition to the "natural" dyad of mother and child? We don't know. We don't think that anybody knows. The Chinese philosopher Mencius (who lived some three centuries B.C.) thought he knew that a sense of compassion was a universal human trait. In a famous illustration, he took the position that even the most hardened criminal, upon seeing a child skipping about in dangerous proximity to a river, would be moved to come to the rescue. Mencius' criminal, we surmise, would be equally moved to solicitude by coming upon a mother-child scene conforming to the Madonna dyad. Perhaps Mencius knew more than we do. Or possibly we know more than he did; our own century has provided enough cases of slaughtered children to make one doubt the inborn impulse to compassion taught by Mencius. Minimally, if there are "instincts" of compassion in human beings, there also seem much uglier "instincts" as well, and in many instances the latter appear to be more compelling than the former.

One could translate the question about the father-mother-child paradigm into the terminology of human biology by asking whether, in these basic patterns of human interaction, there is at work an "ethogram"—that is, a genetically built-in structure of behavior. Konrad Lorenz and his disciples have done pioneering work in the search for "ethograms" in various animal species; the results have been meager in terms of the human species. We certainly know of no biological findings that would allow us to give a scientific answer to the triad/dyad controversy or to decide whether either one of these two paradigms constitutes a "natural symbol" in the literal sense. We can console ourselves about this state of ignorance by reflecting that the moral issue would not really be resolved even if one or the other side in the controversy could claim that biology is on its side. After all, it is just as possible that human biologists may one day demonstrate a built-in killer instinct in our species. If so, incidentally, the anthro-

pological evidence would suggest that the most "natural" way of acting out this instinct would be to kill by biting through the throat of
our adversaries, apparently the favored method of homicide among
our more remote ancestors. (Our twentieth-century teeth and jaws
may not be quite up to this operation, but perhaps oral surgery might
lend nature a hand here.) Suppose such demonstration were made.
We would then be able to say, on the grounds of science, rather than
out of historically based pessimism, that human beings are killers by
nature. It would hardly follow from this proposition that *therefore* all
moral proscriptions of homicide are to be revoked in favor of acting
"naturally." It is good to remind ourselves here that there is a tradition in philosophy that defines true humanity as a transcendence of,
rather than a conformity to, nature.

If we do not know whether triad or dyad is "natural"—and
if it finally doesn't matter all that much which is and which isn't—
how, then, are we to choose between them morally? More specifically,
if we cannot argue for either the bourgeois family or any of its alternatives in terms of human nature, what moral basis can our advocacy
have? There is, of course, the possibility of making a choice on the
ground of religious precepts. This possibility is plausible to many
people, even in this age of secularization. Human beings have thought
of the family, and of specific family types, as imitations of divine
reality since times immemorial. One may just mention here the notion
of the *hieros gamos*, the sacred marriage, in which human sexuality
in all its aspects was perceived as a mimetic reproduction of cosmic
or divine processes. The Judeo-Christian tradition broke with this
world view, but it substituted God's commandments (including commandments that, supposedly, were "written into" human nature) as
a guarantor for specific social arrangements. Thus both Jews and
Christians have always viewed the family as a divinely instituted
structure, and Catholic Christianity has even defined marriage as a
sacrament—one of the seven means by which human beings can gain
access to redeeming grace. For those who have such beliefs, the issue
can in principle be resolved, one way or the other. (Perhaps the
strident radicalism of some of our contemporary feminist theologians
comes out of the necessity, endemic to theological thought, of having
one's own preferences given absolute legitimation by divine commandment: "Thus saith the Lord." Or, more likely in this case: "Thus
saith the Great Mother.") For better or for worse, we do not share

such religious beliefs (ours are in the tradition of liberal Protestantism, mellower and less blessed with certitude). This, then, is not a solution open to us. Since there are very many people in the same situation, at least we don't have to feel lonely when we confess that we are not certain what God's will is in the matter at issue.

There is only one method left for us to follow. It is an inductive method, not in the sense of empirical science, but in the sense of making moral decisions out of our own and others' experiences of being human. This is a method that can never bring us into a state of absolute certainty, but neither does it leave us in a vertigo of relativities in which moral judgments are impossible. And when it comes to these basic structures of human relationships, induction can draw on a wealth of readily accessible experiences. Very often these experiences come closest to certainty when they are negative: We may not know what the best way of raising children is, but we do know that arrangements imposing fear, loneliness, and a sense of worthlessness in children violates our fundamental experience of being human. (Perhaps old Mencius was not all that wrong!) We may not know whether the bourgeois family is more "natural" than available alternatives, or whether it is the will of God, but we do know about the miseries that the destruction of the bourgeois family continues to produce.

Our defense of the bourgeois family has been, in the main, based on two overall values: those of individual autonomy on the one hand, and of freedom both in its personal and political aspects on the other. We have experienced these values in our own lives, and so have millions of other people. On the basis of these experiences, we do dare to say: These are values that enhance the condition of being human. With even greater conviction, we can say: The denial of individual autonomy and of freedom diminishes the human condition. The totalitarianisms of our age are there before our eyes, in their monstrously empirical availability. In the preceding chapter, we proposed that if the bourgeois family did not exist we would have to invent it. Alas, we do not have to invent twentieth-century totalitarianism.

It goes without saying that what we have just said has vast philosophical (and also theological) implications. We cannot pursue these here. Let us just repeat the little litany: Father-mother-child. We know the wealth of human values that this litany alludes to. Could a similar wealth be hidden in the dyadic formula of mother-child? We doubt it very much indeed, if only because the exclusion of half of adult humanity from the central symbol of human love cannot possibly enhance humanity—it so obviously diminishes it. Beyond that, even though we are skeptical about many theories of child psychology, we know too much about children to be sanguine about the degradation of fatherhood. The moral choice is really not all that difficult. There are moments in individual life and in history when one must gamble on the unknown. It is always foolish to gamble that all or even most of human experience up to one's instant in history has been a gigantic mistake. It is reckless to gamble with the moral heritage of an entire civilization. It is immoral to risk the happiness of children.

# 9

# Policy Directions
# Capturing
# the
# Middle Ground

This book is not intended to contribute detailed recommendations for public policy concerning the family. We are not practitioners of "policy science" as this term has come to be understood. However, as will have become obvious by now, we are very much concerned with the relationship between public policy and the family, and we would not feel responsible if we defended the bourgeois family and then simply left it to others to spell out the policy implications of the perspective on which this defense rests. We thus feel constrained to conclude this book with some observations on policy. These observations will deal with broad directions that we believe follow from our perspective.

It will also be obvious by now that we are not (and would not want to be) in the position of offering panaceas for intractable problems that have plagued policy makers in this area. Our perspective inevitably leads to a modest view of the possibilities of public policy with respect to the family, both on normative and on empirical grounds; that is, we believe that public policy *should* have modest goals in this area, and we also believe that public policy will run into increasingly grave difficulties if it sets itself more grandiose goals, as the empirical record to date shows very clearly.

The recent controversies over the family have led to what to us is an unnecessary and unproductive political polarization in terms of "right" and "left," "reactionary" and "radical." To be sure, these labels do pertain to real and distinctive positions, but they also serve to obscure the issues on many points. It will also be evident by now that we cannot fit ourselves comfortably into any of the ideological encampments on the scene today. We do not consider this to be a disadvantage, either intellectually or politically. Intellectually, it seems to us that, in an age of strident ideologies, thoughtful individuals will usually recoil from identifying with any of these. Sometimes this can be a lonely business. In the present situation, however, this is not the case. In America, at any rate, the strident ideologists constitute a noisy but small minority. Politically, therefore, the middle ground is the most promising. The most viable directions for public policy (in this as, indeed, in many other areas) are those designed to capture and hold this middle ground, with which the great majority of Americans almost instinctively identify. We think that this middle ground can be defined in a sufficiently pluralistic manner so as to draw in many who now see themselves as engaged in battle on opposing sides. There will be some whose extremism precludes any compromise. Unless the society changes much more than seems likely at present, it can well tolerate such dissent within the framework of the democratic polity.

A modest view of the potential utility of public policy in this area is reinforced by the lessons of the recent past. We should have learned the lesson, from the many experiments with alternative lifestyles, that it is vain to expect paradise from the substitution of new, unconventional arrangements for the bourgeois family. There is also the broader lesson of the limits of interventionist state policies in *all* areas, a lesson that has had profound impact not only among "neoconservatives" but right across the political spectrum, both in this country and in other democracies. We should also have learned to become suspicious toward all those who claim to discern allegedly inexorable historical trends and who, usually in tones of great certainty, tell us what to do in order not to be crushed by these trends. This lesson is, or should be, particularly telling in the area of family policy, as Gilbert Steiner has most succinctly and persuasively demonstrated.[1] The

American experience has been very clear indeed: Policies that were developed in the 1960s to "target" what then seemed very straightforward problems were revealed in the 1970s to have consequences that the policy makers neither intended nor foresaw, and we are still trying to solve the political muddles resulting from this.

Today there is broad agreement in the debate over a national family policy that, in Mary Jo Bane's felicitous phrase, the family is "here to stay." After more than fifty years of viewing the family as standing on its last legs and of looking for sometimes bizarre alternatives, the family and its virtues have been rediscovered, even by many of its former foes. Very recently indeed, the growing view of the staying power of the family has been empirically reinforced by the findings of Theodore Caplow and his associates on life in Muncie, Indiana, the Mecca of American sociology, made famous as "Middletown" by Robert and Helen Lynd.[2] It appears that the family in that community has changed remarkably little since the 1920s, when the Lynds first descended upon it with their tools of sociological dissection. In a world that seems to become ever more complex and abstract and uncontrollable, Americans continue to look on the family as the most significant and lasting reality in their lives. There is every reason to think that things are not very different at least in other Western societies.

This rediscovery of the family now dominates the public-policy arena. It may be recalled that we began this book with a description of the major alignments in the current battle over the family. We believe that this description is empirically correct. It is important to stress, however, that the more extreme anti-family positions, while still voiced and important in distinctive milieus within the society, have become unimportant within the policy community. Pro-family sentiments are routinely pronounced all over that community, while at the same time there are sharp differences as to what a pro-family policy should look like.

Governmental responses to the real as well as the perceived needs of families have been different in America from those in comparable countries, for a variety of reasons. Above all, governmental actions have been influenced by the realities flowing from the heterogeneity of American society (ethnic, cultural, religious, and regional), making the formulation of a uniform national policy for the family very difficult indeed. The various models of family policy can be located on a continuum between reliance on the state and reliance on private philanthropy. In the statist model, it is assumed that only the state can effectively take over a number of functions traditionally carried out by the family, especially those related to the care of children, the care of the sick and handicapped, and the care of the aged. These functions are now to be taken over by specialized agencies—designed, staffed, administered, and above all financed by the state. In this model, tax funds flow to institutions and programs, rather than to individuals and their families. In the private-philanthropy model, preference is given to the more traditional ways in which families have handled their problems. There is an inclination to rely on altruism and voluntarism, and there is an animus against state interference. Needless to say, these models rarely exist in pure form, but they serve as distinctive points of orientation in policy debates. It is worth pointing out, though, that *both* models frequently share the same assumption: that the family by itself cannot solve its problems and requires the assistance if not the supervision of outside agencies. In other words, social workers and other professionals in the "delivery of human services" tend to think alike, no matter whether they are employed by public or by private institutions.

Public policy concerning the family in recent American history has oscillated along the continuum between these two models. In the best tradition of American politics, concrete policies have often been compromises between them. Still, it is fair to say that the statist model has gained the upper hand in recent decades. With the advent of the Great Society, of the 1960s, there occurred a vast expansion of interventionist programs by the state, as the family-service field became a growth industry clamoring for more public concern for the allegedly urgent problems of the family and as the idea of massive state intervention in previously private areas became generally more respectable in America. At the time, this seemed to be an irreversible trend. All of us, so to speak, appeared to be on the road to a Swedish version of the modern welfare state. History is always full of surprises, especially for those who proclaim irreversible trends. The recent rediscovery of the family has allowed quite different ideas to surface again, ideas based on more traditional or conservative notions about the proper relationship of state and family. There has been a new recognition of the pluralistic character of American society and a political call for returning to families "the means for participating more directly in making decisions about matters directly affecting them, rather than having solutions generated at a more centralized level where sensitivity to the needs of various factions may be dulled by distance and disinterest."[3]

A case could be made that some of the more extreme anti-family positions have actually been absorbed into the statist model and that, in the process of absorption, becoming subjected to the bargaining logic of interest-group politics, these positions were somewhat moderated. The politicking around the White House Conference may be taken as an illustration of this. In any case, recent developments seem to have reestablished more of a balance between reliance on the state and reliance on private initiatives in dealing with family issues. Yet, on looking closer, the situation has not changed all that much. Virtually all parties to the discussion of family policy agree that the family is in a state of acute and deepening crisis, urgently calling out for measures of assistance (though, of course, there is disagreement on what these measures should be). More interestingly, both liberals and conservatives want the government (in particular the federal government) to intervene in the alleged crisis. This is an intriguing commonality. Thus people on all sides of the discussion call for a national family policy, despite the sharp differences as to the content of this policy.

Liberals continue to demand government action (and especially government funds) on a wide array of issues supposedly relevant to the family, from such obvious ones as child care and women's rights to more-elusive ones (elusive, that is, in their bearing on family policy) such as "comparable worth" of female occupations and even issues such as the environment, employment, and disarmament. The liberal insistence on government action to protect and foster abortion is, of course, very strong indeed. But conservatives, too, clamor for government action, sometimes in the precisely opposite direction (such as action to limit or proscribe abortion), sometimes with regard to issues that liberals do not want government to be involved in at all, such as interferences with sexual conduct or supporting prayer in the public schools. In other words, both liberals and conservatives tend to look upon the family as an "endangered species," even if they perceive the dangers in different and often contradictory ways, and both want the government to step in as protector. It is no wonder, then, that "special interests" in this area have rapidly multiplied, each carrying on intense political campaigns to promote its agenda and each prepared to subordinate every other policy issue to the single issue around which it was formed. Observers with quite discrepant political views at least agree that the resulting disarray is a serious problem in itself. Thus veteran liberal Joseph Califano (Secretary of Health, Education, and Welfare in the Carter administration) writes: "What is most pernicious as we enter the 1980's is that we have institutionalized, in law and bureaucracy, single-interest organizations that can accede only in the narrow interest and are incapable of adjudicating in the national interest."[4] And "neoconservative" sociologist Nathan Glazer, who certainly disagrees with Califano on many things, urges us to find a way "for the Government to do good without becoming entangled in a web of interests and passions that prevent it from doing anything at all."[5]

It seems to us that what is required first of all is a narrower (or, if you will, a more modest) understanding of the range of family policy. It is necessary to resist inclusion, under the rubric of family policy, of issues that have only indirect bearing on the family, such as income distribution on the one hand and a reformulation of the relationship of church and state on the other. This is not to say that these issues are necessarily irrelevant or ill-advised, but to include them in the discussion over family policy can have no other effects but polarization and paralysis. *All* possible issues of public policy have *some* bearing on families—not only unemployment and the condition of religion, but the future of energy supplies, the evolution of Third World nations, and the prospects for space exploration. But to include all these issues under the heading of family policy is a perfect formula for political futility. More important, there must be a narrower understanding of family policy based on the hard-won insight that not all human problems can be solved politically. Government cannot meet all human needs, at least not in a democratic society, and the ever-expanding growth of bureaucracy in the service of governmental problem solving is neither economically nor politically tolerable. There is, therefore, a new urgency to the question of the *limits* of government action in this as in other areas of social life.

We do not have ready-made, comprehensive answers to the questions raised here. However, we do want to spell out some broad directions that appear to us to be indicated. We are also prepared to say that these add up to an approach that is distinctive as compared with other approaches being proposed today. This distinctiveness must now be spelled out; much of it, naturally, flows from our analysis of the family in previous chapters.

We have analyzed the family in the process of modernization as both *actor* and *reactor* to that process. This underlying perception puts us at odds with the prevailing view of the relationship between the family and modern society. That view is one-sided, with the family perceived as an almost passive object (or victim) of the powerful social forces surrounding it. Curiously, both liberals and conservatives tend to see the family in this way. To see the family as historical actor, as we do, has policy as well as theoretical implications: If the family is seen as actor as well as reactor, one will be much more prepared to bet on the family's capacity to change or even initiate new social processes. For example, in looking at the (mostly disturbing) data on scholastic achievement among American schoolchildren, one will be encouraged, rather than discouraged, by what these data indicate about the importance of family background. Those who are discouraged, of course, would have liked to see the school or other professionally managed institutions (all supposedly more subject to rational design than the family) be the decisive variable in accounting for scholastic achievement. Being encouraged, rather than discouraged, comes from having confidence in the ability of families to rise to the challenge; the policy implication of this is to provide as much support to families as possible; in education, the voucher concept is the best expression of this policy approach. For another example, one will not be overly impressed by the power of television to shape family life in general and the lives of children in particular. One will, then, have a better understanding of the data from mass-communications research that indicate that the effect of television is almost always "filtered" to the audience by the latter's immediate social context—which, for the great majority of adults and almost all children, is dominated by the family. It is interesting how the Archie Bunker television series, designed as an exposé of working-class life-styles, was perceived as a celebration of these—a perception that very soon influenced the producers of the series. The viewing families were hardly passive reactors in this case; there is good reason to think that the case is typical.

Also, our analytic framework of modernization/counter-modernization gives us a different perspective on the ideological crosscurrents of the contemporary situation. We understand these, at least in part, as efforts to cope intellectually and morally with a very difficult moment in history, rather than as abstract exercises in logic fueled by irrational emotions. This has no direct policy implications, but it allows one to look beyond the polarizing ideological labels and deal at least somewhat more dispassionately with the issues raised, for instance, by the opposing militancies of feminism and religious fundamentalism.

In a similarly broad way, the epistemological differences between us and most analysts dealing with the family are important. Analytic models for policy tend to look on the family as a system of interacting individuals, which system is related to other systems (such as the government). Such a view has many implications: The focus is on individuals facing systems, overlooking the institutional networks that stand and mediate *between* the two—a fatal oversight in the case of the family, which, as we have tried to show, is the most important such institution. The systemic approach, with its mechanistic imagery, has tended to emphasize "needs" and "services" of a functional sort, overlooking the importance of meanings and values in human life— again, a very serious oversight especially in the case of the family, an institution bestowing meaning and value above all. The systemic approach, with its seeming rationality, is naturally congenial to administrators, who employ it to reduce the complex reality with which they have to deal to neat typologies that often violate the self-definitions of the people involved. Such bureaucratic reductionism has much to do with the current malaise of many people concerning the welfare state. Finally, this way of thinking has facilitated the notion that the family as an institution is in deep trouble (that is, is "malfunctioning" within the social system), necessitating outside intervention. In consequence, "normal," or "ordinary," families are as problematic as those with special characteristics, making for the expansion of family policy to include the entire population. This way of thinking is a handicap even to those who are now seriously trying to restore the balance between family and government in policy thinking.

By contrast, our epistemological assumption is that society is not a functioning system, but a meaningful construction. For certain analytic purposes, it may have heuristic value to look at society as if it were a system (we are not at all doctrinaire in our theoretical position in sociology), but even then it is very important to keep in mind that one is applying a conceptual scheme to an empirical reality composed of human beings who try to make sense of their lives. This forces one's attention back to individuals and the way they themselves define their situation. In terms of policy, it leads one to take with utmost seriousness the meanings and values of people, even if one disagrees with some of them. To the extent that people perceive the family as the major source of meaning, value, and identity, *that* is what the family is—no matter what a systemic analysis might have to say about its functioning. We would further contend that this epistemology, while its roots are not political, has a particular affinity to democracy. Thus, for example, we have argued before that the ideal of the bourgeois family continues to be of very great importance, regardless of all the statistics that show how many people actually live in different settings. And, for the same reasons, it is misleading to think of people as isolated individuals when in fact they are constantly striving to be part of larger communities—even if these communities are often elusive or fragile.

Be this as it may, our policy approach cannot be neatly fitted into any of the existing camps. We have agreements as well as disagreements with the major parties in the current debates. We agree with conservatives about the importance of values and of morality in society, about the need to respect pluralism and tradition, and about the limited power of government to solve human problems. We agree with liberals about the necessity for a modern welfare state (though not necessarily about its existing mechanisms) and about the impossibility of returning to some (mostly imaginary) past of self-reliant families. We disagree with conservatives when it comes to their enthusiasm for dismantling every politically possible structure of the modern welfare state; we disagree even more strongly with conservative efforts to impose, by law, an essentially provincial morality on the entire society. We disagree with liberals to the extent that they continue to believe that an endless expansion of government programs, bureaucracy, and professionalism will rescue the family from all its woes; we disagree as strongly with liberal efforts to impose *their* provincial morality on the rest of us (the "provinces" differ, as between the moral ideas of Evangelicals and feminists; the provincialism is very similar). We disagree with all who would include under the heading of family policy all sorts of issues that, however important in themselves, do not properly belong there—be it the place of religion in national life or the future of nuclear weapons.

In the last connection, a word on the abortion issue is in order.

This issue has, on all sides of the debate, been coupled with family policy. This strikes us as absurd. In one excursus, we have indicated our own approach to this issue, again one that cannot easily be fitted into any of the existing encampments. We believe that this is indeed a very important issue, touching on some of the fundamental questions about the human condition, and it is an issue both of private morality and of public policy. But it is hardly a *family* issue, except in the broadest sense, in which *all* questions about the human condition touch on the family. We are not for one moment suggesting that there should be a cessation of public debate on the abortion issue; such debate is absolutely necessary, though we would wish it to be conducted in a different spirit. At the same time, we think that it would be very helpful if that debate were separated from the discussion over family policy. For this reason, we will say no more about abortion here.

Finally, our understanding of the family as a mediating structure makes it impossible to view it either as a purely private matter or as being subject *in toto* to public policy. The family has both a private face and a public one, and both must be taken into account in terms of policy. Those who have wanted to transform the family into a public institution, or at least into an institution guided and controlled by public decisions, have greatly contributed to its erosion. On the other hand, those who have regarded the family as solely a private affair have aided those who would supplant, rather than support, it. Both distortions must be avoided.

In what follows, we will summarize the broad policy principles that, we believe, follow from our overall perspective. To repeat, it is not our purpose here to give detailed recommendations but, rather, to indicate the general direction in which we would like to see family policy moving:

*1. Recognition of the primacy of the family.*

The family, and no other conceivable structure, is the basic institution of society. If we have learned anything from the tumultuous activities surrounding the family in recent decades, it is that there are no alternatives or substitutes, no matter how well intentioned or attractive they may appear at first sight. The prestige of the family must therefore be restored. Now, it is clear that this cannot be primarily a matter of public policy. The democratic state is not and should not be the fountainhead of morality in society, and just about the last thing we would suggest is that government at any level engage in a propaganda campaign to promote family values—a notion as objectionable in theory as, in all likelihood, it would be ridiculous in practice. But the negative side does have policy implications: Public policy must not allow itself to be captured by groups who would want their anti-family positions legitimated if not outrightly enforced by government. Above all, while public policy cannot restore the prestige of the family, it should self-consciously refrain from harming the family and from increasing the problems faced by the family.

Since feminists have been particularly prominent in efforts to utilize public policy for the promotion of "alternative life-styles," a further word about feminism is in order here. Feminists have stood in tension with the family. This need not be so. There is a wide range of feminist issues—that is, issues dealing with women's rights—that command very wide support in Western societies and that would command even wider support if they were not perceived as, intentionally or unintentionally, opposed to the family. It seems to us that the recognition and enhancement of women's rights should be on the agenda of every decent society today. In themselves, these are not family issues. Feminist causes come into conflict with the family as increasing numbers of women seek or are compelled to seek careers outside the home, and when in consequence family obligations come to be perceived as obstacles to self-realization in those careers. Individual women will have to decide on their priorities. Our own hope is that many will come to understand that life is more than a career and that this "more" is above all to be found in the family. But, however individual women decide, they should not expect public policy to underwrite and subsidize their life plans.

It will be amply clear by now that it is the *bourgeois* family, with its historically and empirically distinctive features, whose primacy we want to be recognized. Again, of course, public policy cannot and should not be a propaganda agency for the bourgeois ethos. But neither should it promote the anti-bourgeois values that have become fashionable in relatively small milieus within the society.

Any society must be concerned with its own future. It cannot, therefore, take an attitude of indifference to the social institution in which children are reared. The implication of this is simple but far-reaching: Public policy with regard to the family must focus on *children*. The protection of the family must be a function of the state for this overriding reason. Conversely, it is *not* a function of the state, at least in a democracy, to regulate the arrangements by which "consenting adults" arrange their private lives—*as long as* they are unencumbered by children. And of couse, it *is* a function of the state to assist families in the care of members, children or adult, when this care exceeds the families' resources—a proposition that has been at the root of the modern welfare state.

The most important policy direction suggested by our approach, however, could well be summed up by the line in the Hippocratic oath "First, do no harm!" Public policies of any sort defeat their own purpose if they weaken the family. This includes all policies intended to diminish poverty that have produced family instability as a major consequence. We refer here, of course, to the welter of welfare legislation with the (of course unintended) consequence of weakening the families of the beneficiaries—a problem of particular seriousness in the racial minorities in America, as has often been pointed out. The "do no harm" injunction also has far-reaching implications for tax policy. As has also been pointed out frequently, the heavier tax burden imposed on married couples is a peculiarly perverse feature of the current American tax system, and redress is long overdue.

   *2. The restoration of the private.*

The recent trend of turning private preferences into public issues must be reversed. The private must be restored as an area of life in which politicization is inappropriate. This, of course, refers particularly to the wide range of sexual matters, on which so much attention has been focused recently. Here if anywhere, a public attitude of "benign neglect" would be very helpful. Now, in saying this we would not want to be confused with those liberals who have taken the position that all morality is a private matter and thus of no concern to government. We are convinced that no society can exist without a basic moral consensus; this is particularly so in a democratic society. The tenuousness of the aforementioned liberal idea is quickly revealed if one applies it to, say, race relations: Has the civil rights legislation of recent American history been a big mistake because it tried to use government to impose moral principles? We think not. But the civil rights legislation dealt almost exclusively with behavior in the public sphere—at the polling booth, in schools, in places of public accommodation, and so on. This is a very different matter from trying to use government power to influence or control behavior within the family.

The restoration of the private does not mean, then, that morality is never the business of public policy, law, or government. Rather, it is called for by reflection as to what kind of society we want to have: a totalitarian society, in which political agencies control even the most intimate areas of life, or a democracy, which will have to accept the behavior of individuals and even subcultures that may be morally repugnant to many. While it is the necessary function of the state to protect the family, it is *not* the function of the state, in a democracy, to protect the sexual or other private preferences of adult citizens. Having to live with practices that sometimes offend us morally is one of the prices we have to pay for democracy. It seems to us that it is a rather moderate price. Compare the price we pay by not using totalitarian methods to combat crime—methods that would undoubtedly reduce crime dramatically. If, to protect democratic rights, we have been willing to tolerate crime rates that are inconceivable in a totalitarian society (one can walk the streets of Moscow, perhaps, safely at any hour of the night; the only thing one has to worry about is the police), then surely we can tolerate this or that morally offensive lifestyle in our community.

By the same token, there are other, non-sexual private choices that should not become the concern of the state but have become that because they were pushed as public issues by special-interest groups. For example, it has been proposed that government should take care of the housing needs of divorced families—a clear case, in our view, of private choices becoming inappropriately politicized. It is just this sort of policy that has led to the immense expansion of government interventionism; the crisis of the welfare state to which this has led is unnecessary, could have been avoided, and can still be reversed. There should be very great care taken that no more private matters be "problematized" as public issues. Put differently, a heavy burden of proof should be placed on anyone who proposes policies of this kind.

We have made it sufficiently clear that we consider bourgeois values as essential for democracy, at least in Western societies (we cannot deal here with the important question of democracy in the non-Western world). This, to be sure, is an issue of morality. The nurture of these values, however, must necessarily be the task of individuals and their families. Public policy can protect their freedom to nurture these values, and it can refrain from actions that will hinder them; it cannot itself create such values.

3. *Respect for pluralism.*

Public policy toward the family in America will have to take account of the existing pluralism of family types. Empirically, there are considerable differences in terms of class, ethnicity, race, and religion. In addition to these, new types have gained prominence recently— single-parent, grandparent, and foster families—types that more often than not are the products of necessity, rather than choice. In addition, families differ in terms of values, even within otherwise similar categories. We believe that it is part and parcel of the American democratic creed that this pluralism be respected and protected by public policy. This is a proposition that will rarely be challenged, but its implications may be uncomfortable for some. For it implies that no particular family type should be either elevated or denigrated by public policy. Thus public policy should not impose middle-class standards on non-middle-class people, as it has so often done in the past. But neither should it fall into the opposite trap, more common recently, of being guided universally by what are understood to be the needs of targeted groups, such as poor ethnic or single-parent households; that is, principles derived from the perceived needs of the latter types should not now be imposed on everyone else.

For understandable reasons, public policy in the modern welfare state has been aimed toward those who are weak and in need of help. Commonly, the people who fulfill these criteria are rather few in number, and certainly are a minority of the population. This very limited definition of the scope of public policy clashes with the expansionary tendency of the bureaucratic and professional empires spawned by the welfare state. Quite logically, the latter tended to inflate the definitions both of weakness and of need. Ever more families were added to the category of those too weak to cope by themselves, and new needs were invented. Thus, in America, the definition of the family was changed to "families," all of these were supposed to be in "crisis," and at the same time the real needs of certain types of families were magnified and distorted. Much of this was done in the name of pluralism, yet with purposes quite different from respect for the human diversity and richness of American society.

This development should be arrested. Public policy with regard to the family should primarily be concerned with the family's capacity to take care of its children, its sick and handicapped, and its aged. The basic principle here should be that, whenever possible, these needs are best taken care of *within* the family—*any* family (barring a very few families to whom one would not entrust those who are weak or in need), regardless of social or cultural type. This means that the overriding concern of public policy should be to provide support for the family to discharge these caring tasks, rather than to relieve the family of these tasks. The family should be recognized as the most stable and effective structure, not only for taking care of children but for meeting the needs of the sick and the handicapped and the aged. To be sure, there are families who are either unable or unwilling to perform these tasks. In such instances, which are remarkably few, other arrangements must, of course, be provided. But even here the evidence indicates that arrangements work best that resemble the family as much as possible.

A policy implication of this perspective is to favor some variety of child allowance, and of special allowances for the care of sick, handicapped, and aged family members. There are various problems connected with this idea that cannot be pursued here. The basic principle should be, though, that families should not be forced to delegate the care of their weaker members to outside agencies merely on the ground of financial incapacity. It further follows that professional staffs and services should be understood as much as possible as backup, rather than as substitutes for the family.

Is there a contradiction here between our calling for respect for pluralism and our declared preference for the bourgeois family? We do not think so. Our preference is very strong indeed, and it has a strong moral dimension, but this does not necessarily mean that we want it to become a governmental agenda. What is more, we are convinced that the great majority of people in Western societies share this preference. Therefore, if one wants to foster the bourgeois family, the best course to take is to give people freedom of choice. Most of them will choose bourgeois values and bourgeois life-styles—especially people in the "targeted" groups of the poor and disadvantaged.

*4. Autonomy and empowerment.*

The chief issue in the current crisis of the welfare state (apart from the one of its economic costs) is the widespread feeling that the state is encroaching more and more on people's lives. This is also the chief issue with regard to the welfare state's family policies. We believe that this feeling is quite justified and that its political expressions are to be taken very seriously as much more than irrational or reactionary eruptions. We would also stress that this is not just a "neoconservative" position. At least in America, it can now be heard voiced pretty much all across the political spectrum, and while obviously there are differences as to what the response should be to this malaise about the welfare state, very few commentators have suggested that the malaise is unjustified or that it should be ignored.

In terms of family policy, it seems to us that high on the agenda should be measures to arrest the rampant interventionism by the state and to restore the autonomy of the family. This entails measures to empower families to take control of their own problems. It should be strongly emphasized that such measures are particularly important for the poor. More-affluent families, in most cases, already have considerable control over their lives. One does not have to be a Marxist to understand that money empowers, as does status. An upper-middle-class family, faced with the crises of sickness or old age, may also be vexed by the insensitivity or inefficiency of the professionals and bureaucrats who are supposed to help in such situations, but such a family will have various resources and responses. Most important, when it comes to professionals, such a family will have the option of switching from one to another, and this option will always be in the forefront of everyone's consciousness, including the professionals' in the case: If I don't like doctor A, I'll switch to doctor B. And when it comes to bureaucrats, whom one usually cannot switch, middle-class people have access to political resources usually unavailable to the poor. It is, therefore, a very big misjudgment to think that the value of autonomy is an upper-middle-class luxury. On the contrary, it is an urgent concern of the poor, much more than of those who already have a lot of autonomy.

The area of education brings this out most clearly. The formal educational system is the principal agency to which the family has surrendered important functions; it is in most countries a principally governmental system, endowed with monopolistic and coercive powers. In America, where there exists an established and extensive private school system, upper-income parents can escape this monopoly and in consequence establish a good measure of autonomous control over the education of their children: We didn't like the program at school A and so we switched little Johnny to school B. Lower-income parents, of course, are deprived of this option and are stuck with the monopolistic public system, to which (despite public-relations gimmicks like PTA) they remain in a basically passive relationship. Incidentally, no amount of "participation" of parents is likely to change that situation very much: There is no participatory voice likely to match in clout the ability to take one's child, and one's money, out of a particular school.

It was in the context of debates over education in America that the concept of the voucher emerged.[6] There are by now differing versions of this concept and it cannot be our purpose here to go into the details. But the basic idea is quite simple: Instead of channeling all public funds for education to *institutions* (that is, into the public school system), funds will be channeled to *individuals* (that is, to individual children—in effect, to their parents), who will then have the right to expend these funds within a range of publicly approved schools. In terms of American social legislation, the important precedent for such a policy was the GI Bill, after World War II, under which each veteran also received a "voucher" to expend as he wished within a range (in this case, a very broad range) of approved educational programs. Such a policy mechanism does a number of things: It introduces market forces into a previously monopolistic situation, forcing recipient institutions to compete with each other. As in most situations of demonopolization, costs go down as a result. But the most important thing that a voucher mechanism does is to empower individuals to make choices and exercise control. It changes clients into consumers. Not surprisingly, this is fiercely resisted by those who have a vested interest in the erstwhile monopoly—in this instance, by the teachers' unions and by other organizations of professional educators.

Because of this resistance, educational vouchers have not gone very far beyond a few experiments in this country (or, for that matter, anywhere else). Even in a period of widespread and intense disappointment with public schools, the political prospects for the concept remain uncertain. We are nonetheless convinced that the voucher concept, or some version of it, represents the most promising policy direction to restore autonomy to people, especially to lower-income people. We are also convinced that the concept is applicable not only to education but to a wide array of other social services. Indeed, the concept may be more viable politically in other areas, where vested interests in a monopolistic *status quo* are less developed and organized. Indeed, we would contend that the most important priority in social policy in this country should be the systematic exploration of *all* the areas in which the voucher concept could be plausibly applied. Family policy would, we think, be a particularly fertile field for such exploration.

5. *Restoration of parental rights.*

To some extent, this idea is already implicit in the foregoing propositions on autonomy and empowerment, but it is so important that it should be dealt with discretely. The chief issue here is the extent to which parents are to be trusted to make decisions on the affairs of their children. In practice, this issue is one between parents on one side and miscellaneous professionals on the other side. Education, of course, is the area in which the issue arises most frequently, though there are other areas as well. The professionals' argument is always that parents lack the expertise to make the necessary decisions and that children must be protected against being harmed by their parents' ignorance.

Of course it must be stipulated that there is expertise that most parents lack. But the issue touches the very heart of the democratic creed. An interesting exercise is to listen to the arguments of professionals as to how parents lack the expertise to make intelligent decisions on their children's education—and then to apply the same arguments to, say, foreign policy. It is safe to say that the arguments will be even more persuasive there: If we are unable to trust ordinary people with the education of their children, how can we trust ordinary people to vote intelligently on issues of war and peace in faraway countries, or on the complexities of weapons policy, not to mention the intricacies of economic policy that even the best economists cannot agree upon? The seemingly inevitable conclusion is antidemocratic: Let foreign policy be in the hands of (one hopes) the best experts available, without the irrational distractions of an uninformed and volatile electorate. The Achilles' heel of this argument is in the parentheses of the preceding sentence: What grounds does one have to hope that the experts know what they are doing? The empirical record of the American foreign-policy establishment in recent decades induces very healthy skepticism. We would contend that the educational establishment is no more impressive. Indeed, we would make an *a fortiori* argument: If ordinary people can be trusted to reflect responsibly on issues of foreign or economic policy, which often seem far away from their actual lives, they can be trusted much, much more to make intelligent choices concerning their own children's welfare, which for most of them will be their highest and most immediate concern. The policy imperative is to provide choices to *all* people.

We believe that, in the great majority of cases, the common sense of parents can be trusted. Where expertise is needed, parents will seek it, and they will seek it intelligently. To be sure, there are always exceptions, as there is a small minority of parents who don't care about their children. It is complete folly, however, to base policy on this small minority. It is particularly odious, and empirically nonsensical, to think that poorer and less educated parents are to be trusted less in these matters. On the contrary, we incline to the view that lower-income parents will invest *greater* care in such questions, precisely because of the disadvantages they know their children must face.

As we observed above, education is an area in which the issues of family autonomy tend to focus, and this is *ipso facto* the case with parental rights. The recent eruption of parental protest movements against textbooks perceived by them to violate their religious beliefs is a good example of this. And incidentally, a voucher system in education would quickly make this and similar controversies quite obsolete. But there are important issues involving parental rights outside the area of education. The current movement for so-called children's rights is a case in point; since small children, however their rights may be defined, are not in a position to exercise them legally, the issue is really one between parents and various professionals who claim to represent the interests of children. Another case in point is the debate over parental authority in matters of teenage sexuality and pregnancy. It will be clear from the above that we feel strongly that parental rights should normally take precedence—*not* over children's rights, which are usually not the real issue—but over the claims of various professionals to represent the best interests of children. Our general maxim here remains: In general, trust parents over against experts; the burden of proof against individual parents should be very strong indeed before the opposite choice is made.

A particularly poignant area involving parental rights is that of custody—that is, all those cases in which public authorities place chil-

dren in situations outside their natural families. This may be in consequence of alleged neglect or mistreatment of children by parents, as
in cases of child abuse. Or it may be the result of circumstances
unrelated to parental conduct. In both cases, there is a serious problem of professionals employing upper-middle-class criteria to people
operating under quite different standards—a matter of special concern to blacks, who have long had an informal family and community
system of taking care of children in need, a system that is commonly
not even perceived by the professionals in question.[7] This, though,
leads over into our final point, that of the maintenance of community.

6. *Maintenance of community.*

Most families, especially those of the lower-middle-class and
working-class strata, are embedded in larger communities—of ethnic
or racial subculture, neighborhood, church, and voluntary association.
All of these, taken together, constitute a network of mediating structures that is of crucial importance both in giving meaning to private
life and in providing linkage with the large public institutions, as we
have argued in a previous chapter. We believe that many of the problems of the modern welfare state would be greatly mitigated if not
eliminated if public policy would favor and even utilize these mediating structures more, instead of ignoring or even running over them, as
has been the tendency to date. This is particularly important for family policy.

A general direction of public policy should be to turn to *other*
mediating structures, if individual families are no longer able to cope,
*before* there is recourse to professional or bureaucratic agencies of
"service delivery." Clearly, this cannot be done in all cases, but it can
and should be done in many cases. There are two reasons for this that
are directly related to the preceding discussion (the reason that
mediating structures are generally more cost-effective cannot occupy
us here): One, where an individual family is still extant and able to
take responsibility for its needy members, these communal institutions
are much closer and much more likely to respond to the values and
desires of the family. Two, where such a family is no longer "available," experience has shown that the most effective institutions in
many areas of social service are those that *resemble* natural families
as much as possible—for reasons that probably do not have to be
spelled out. These considerations have far-reaching implications for
policies of child care, for the treatment of troubled adolescents, for

the care of the aged, and for a substantial array of health services.[8] One of the most interesting experiments along these lines, utilizing spontaneous and indigenous community institutions to deal with delinquent adolescents, is that of the House of Umoja, a project in a black section of Philadelphia that has been studied by Robert Woodson.[9] We believe that the Umoja model is applicable to many other areas of concern besides youth crime; we also believe that much of its success can be ascribed to the conscious effort to create a new kind of family for young people whose natural families, for one reason or another, were no longer there as supports. We further believe that the nonprofessional, nonbureaucratic character of Umoja has been equally important to its success.

Two final comments under this heading are important: First, we want to emphasize that nothing said here is intended to express an overall anti-professionalism. We have no doubt that professionals are useful and important in many areas, including education, social work, health, and so on. The point is *not* that professionals should be dispensed with. Rather, the point is that professionals should serve people, not dominate them. The ideal professional relationship in Western societies has been the fee-for-service relationship common in the middle classes with regard to doctors, lawyers, accountants, and other professionals. Such a relationship in no way detracts from the professional status of the one party, but it also does not violate the autonomy of the other party. Public policy should seek to empower non-middle-class people to have the same sort of relationships with the professionals needed by them.

A final comment pertains to religious institutions: For many Americans, especially in the lower-middle and working classes, churches are centrally important mediating structures. Public policies favoring mediating structures therefore quickly run into legal and political difficulties stemming from the principle of the separation of church and state. Once again, we cannot enter here into the complex issues raised by this fact.[10] We certainly believe in the separation of church and state. However, we think it very foolish to leave unused the vast capacity of churches to perform societally important services because of a narrow, indeed sectarian (the sect being secularism) interpretation of the First Amendment. If one respects the communities in which people live and from which they derive meaning, then one must also respect the fact that many of these communities are religious. Public policies that do not do this are not only exceedingly abstract and remote from social reality, they will inevitably (and, we think, needlessly) offend and polarize people.

We are fully aware of the fact that the policy directions outlined in this chapter are very general. Much work will be required to fill in the details. This, though, cannot be our task here. We have sketched the outline of what, in our view, a reasonable family policy should look like. It is not a revolutionary view. Yet it would require substantial rethinking of many issues and, eventually, substantial revamping of many programs.

What are its political prospects? That is, of course, very difficult to predict. We have a measure of optimism. Our general approach to the family is based on the conviction that the middle ground between the existing ideological extremes is the only position that makes sense both intellectually and morally. We are not prophets in the wilderness in thinking this. There is a very broad consensus, at least in America, that something like this middle ground is where one ought to stand. As long as America remains a democracy, such consensus will push toward political expression, even if strong vested interests resist this. The further advantage of this centrist consensus is that it is not dependent on either the conservative or the liberal camp's gaining ascendancy in the political arena, for either camp (and certainly either major political party) could accommodate itself to this consensus. What is most necessary, though, is that this consensus be voiced and spelled out. Toward this end, we hope, the present book constitutes a modest beginning.

# NOTES

## CHAPTER 1

1. Philippe Ariès, *Centuries of Childhood—Social History of Family Life* (New York: Knopf, 1962).

2. Frank Musgrove, *Youth and the Social Order* (Bloomington: Indiana University Press, 1964).

3. The dramatic change in attitudes toward the family ushered in by the Enlightenment vision of life is well reflected in such influential writings as: Thomas Hobbes, *Leviathan* (first published in 1690) (New York: Dutton, Everyman's Library, 1934). See in particular Ch. XX.

John Locke, *Civil Government* (first published in 1690), in *Essays in the Law* (New York: Dutton, Everyman's Library, 1924). See in particular Ch. VI of the second treatise.

Jean Jacques Rousseau, *Social Contract* (New York: Dutton, Everyman's Library, 1950). However, compare also Rousseau's *Émile* (New York: Dutton, 1950), where his general inconsistency with regard to matters of the family becomes clearly evident.

For general reference: An interesting and detailed summary of changing attitudes toward the family in history up to the mid-twentieth century in terms of a cyclical understanding of ideas and social practices is presented by the late Harvard sociologist Carle C. Zimmerman in *Family and Civilization* (New York: Harper, 1947).

4. Diane Ravitch, *The Great School Wars* (New York: Basic Bks., 1974), renders a fascinating account of the peculiar American dynamics of an immigrant society in the nineteenth century.

The flavor of the nineteenth-century discussion is well caught in such writings as:

Florence Kelley, *Some Ethical Gains Through Legislation* (New York: Macmillan, 1905).

Ellen H. Richards, *Euthenics: The Science of Controllable Environment* (Boston: Whitcomber & Barrows, 1910).

Richard Hofstadter, *The Progressive Movement* (Englewood Cliffs, N.J.: Prentice-Hall, 1963), which supplies a general background against which this modern trend unfolds.

Similar processes can be observed in other societies as well:

H. C. Barnard, *A Short History of English Education* (London: Cambridge University Press, 1947);

Jacques Donzelot, *The Policing of Families* (New York: Pantheon, 1979);
Willy Moog, *Geschichte der Pädagogik*, 3 vols. (Stuttgart: Henn Verlag,
1967)—with special reference to nineteenth-century developments in Germany; see Vol. 3.

5. E. A. Wrigley, ed., *Nineteenth-century Society* (London: Cambridge
University Press, 1976).
Jean-Francois Bergier, *The Industrial Bourgeoisie and the Rise of the
Working Class, 1700–1914* (London: Cambridge University Press, 1971).

In this fascinating book, Bergier describes the rise and the ultimate
dominance of the industrial bourgeoisie in England from the reform movement of 1832 until the First World War and places special attention on
"the development of an ethos, a culture peculiar to industrial bourgeoisie"
(p. 23).
J. H. Plumb, "The Great Change in Children," *Horizon*, Winter 1971.
Donzelot, op. cit.
Edward Shorter, *The Making of the Modern Family* (New York: Basic
Books, 1975). Although Shorter primarily traces the history of the family
prior to that of the rising of the bourgeois model, he nonetheless demonstrates the dramatic shift in the structure of mind with which the middle
classes approach individuals, families, and social life.
Musgrove, op. cit., Chs. 3 and 4.

6. Charlotte Perkins Gilman, *Women and Economics*, originally published
in 1898 (New York: Harper, 1966).
Alice Freeman Palmer, *Why Go to College?* (New York: Crowell, 1897).
Thomas Woody, *History of Women's Education in the United States*, Vol. I
(New York: Science Press, 1929).

7. Ann Douglas, *The Feminization of American Culture* (New York:
Avon, 1977).

8. Norman MacKenzie and Jeanne MacKenzie, *The Fabians* (New York:
Oxford University Press, Touchstone Books, 1977).

9. Herbert Spencer, *Principles of Sociology* (New York: Appleton, 1896),
Vol. I, Pt. III, Ch. IX, "The Family." Although his critics claim that
Spencer's treatment of the family shows him at his weakest, he paid
considerable attention to the place and role of the family in his evolutionary
schemes for interpreting the whole of history and destiny of the human race.
For Spencer, progress in society and the family are coextent features of
general evolutionary trends.

10. Friedrich Engels, *The Origin of the Family, Private Property and the
State* (New York: International Publishers, 1972).
August Bebel, *Women Under Socialism* (New York: New York Labor
News Co., 1904).

For a more contemporary interpretation of this vision, see:
Eli Zaretsky, *Capitalism, the Family, and Personal Life* (New York:
Harper, 1976).

11. From the large number of publications emanating from the Chicago

School that have a bearing on the influence of urbanism on family structure and life, the following deserve to be singled out:

Ernest W. Burgess and Harvey Locke, *The Family: From Institution to Companionship* (New York: American Book Co., 1945).

Ernest R. Mowrer, *The Family: Its Organization and Disorganization* (Chicago: University of Chicago Press, 1932).

William F. Ogburn, *Social Characteristics of Cities* (Chicago: International City Managers' Association, 1937); see in particular Ch. 3, "Family Life."

Louis Wirth, "Urbanism as a Way of Life," in *On Cities and Social Life* (Chicago: University of Chicago Press, 1964).

12. W. I. Thomas and F. Znaniecki, *The Polish Peasant in Europe and America*, 5 vols. (Boston: R. G. Badger, 1918–20).

13. Burgess and Locke, op. cit., p. 7.

14. Ogburn, op. cit.

15. Talcott Parsons, Robert Bales et al., *Family, Socialization and Interaction Process* (Glencoe, Ill.: Free Press, 1955).

16. S. de Grazia, *Of Time, Work and Leisure* (New York: Twentieth Century Fund, 1962).

William J. Goode, *The Family* (Englewood Cliffs, N.J.: Prentice-Hall, 1964).

S. Greer, *The Emerging City: Myth and Reality* (Glencoe, Ill.: Free Press, 1962).

Betty Friedan, *The Feminine Mystique* (New York: Norton, 1963).

17. William H. Whyte, *The Organization Man* (Garden City, N.Y.: Doubleday, 1957).

J. R. Seeley, R. A. Sim, and E. W. Loosley, *Crestwood Heights* (New York: Basic Bks., 1956).

18. Friedan, op. cit.

19. Barrington Moore, Jr. "Thoughts on the Future of the Family." In John Edwards, ed., *The Family and Change* (New York: Knopf, 1969).

20. Shulamith Firestone, *The Dialectic of Sex: The Case for Feminist Revolution* (New York: William Morrow, 1970).

Juliet Mitchell, *Woman's Estate* (New York: Pantheon, 1971).

———, *Psychoanalysis and Feminism* (New York: Pantheon, 1974).

R. D. Laing, *The Divided Self* (Chicago: Quadrangle, 1960).

David Cooper, *The Death of the Family* (New York: Random House, 1971).

21. For an excellent account and summary of the new "family policy," see: Gilbert Steiner, *The Futility of Family Policy* (Washington, D.C.: Brookings, 1981).

22. Kenneth Keniston and the Carnegie Council on Children, *All Our Children* (New York: Harcourt Brace Jovanovich, 1977).

23. As a general reference to the pro-family-movement vision, see the quar-

terly publication *The Human Life Review*, published since 1975 by The Human Life Foundation, New York.

All through the 1970s, a number of critical individual voices from a conservative, as well as neo-conservative point of view preceded the emergence of an organized pro-family movement. From these relatively rarely formulated thoughts, the following deserve special mention:

Midge Decter, *The Chastity and Other Arguments Against Woman's Liberation* (New York: Coward, McCann & Geoghegan, 1972).

George Gilder, *Sexual Suicide* (New York: Quadrangle Bks., 1973).

Steven Goldberg, *The Inevitability of Patriarchy* (New York: Morrow, 1973).

## CHAPTER 2

1. Maren Lockwood Carden, *The New Feminist Movement* (New York: Russell Sage, 1974).
Sheila Rothman, *Woman's Proper Place* (New York: Basic Bks., 1978).
Jo Freeman, *The Politics of Women's Liberation* (New York: McKay, 1975).

2. Juliet Mitchell, *Woman's Estate, supra.*
——, *Psychoanalysis and Feminism, supra.*

3. Kate Millett, *Sexual Politics* (Garden City, N.Y.: Doubleday, 1970).
Shulamith Firestone, *The Dialectic of Sex, supra.*
Yoko Ono is quoted in Benjamin R. Barber, *Liberating Feminism* (New York: Seabury Press-Continuum, 1975), p. 29.

4. Betty Friedan, "Feminism's Next Step," New York *Times Magazine*, July 5, 1981.

5. "Humanist" as a term used in this connection was adopted by NOW in the early 1970s to indicate positive values that are "sex-neutral," i.e., "human," rather than "masculine" or "feminine."

During the organization meeting of the National Women's Political Caucus, in July 1971, a number of speakers insisted that it fell upon women to "humanize" society. *Vide* Gloria Steinem: ". . . we can humanize the machinery of politics to make a better society"; Betty Walker Smith: "Let's humanize America and save her"; Bella Abzug: "We have the capacity to build a humanistic society. I hope we will get down to decide how to do this. . . . What is good for women will turn out to be good for the country." Quoted by Carden, op. cit., p. 169. For a recent thoughtful exposition of this view from a psychological frame-of-reference: Jean Baker Miller, *Towards a New Psychology of Women* (Boston: Beacon, 1979).

6. A much flaunted popularization of the neo-traditionalistic position is that of Marabel Morgan in *Total Woman* (Old Tappan, N.J.: Revell, 1973).

The political formulation of pervasive traditionalistic sentiments is well reflected in Connaught Marshner, ed. *Family Protection Report* (Arlington, Va.: Arlington Publishing House, 1979).

Ellen Wilson, a regular contributor to *The Human Life Review*, catches better than anyone else I am aware of the neo-traditionalistic thought on matters pertaining to the family, in her well-argued essays in the journal. Her book *An Even Dozen* is due out in 1982.

7. For general reference, see also Jo Ann Gasper, editor of *The Right Woman*.

8. As quoted by Allan C. Carlson, "Radicals, Liberals, Illiberal Families," *The American Spectator*, Apr. 1981, p. 19.

9. Robert M. Moroney, *Families, Social Services, and Social Policy: The Issue of Shared Responsibility* (Rockville, Md.: U. S. Department of Health and Human Services, 1980).
Sheila B. Kamerman, *Parenting in an Unresponsive Society* (New York: Free Press, 1981).
H. Wilensky and C. Lebraux, *Industrial Society and Social Welfare* (New York: Free Press, 1965).

10. Mid-America Institute on Violence in Families, ed., *Violence in Families: Report to the White House Conference on Families* (Little Rock, Ark.: Graduate School of Social Work, 1980).
*Domestic Violence*, Hearings before the Subcommittee on Select Education of the House Committee on Education and Labor, 95th Cong., 2nd sess. (Washington: Government Printing Office, 1978).
Eunice Corfman, ed., *Families Today—A Research Sample on Families and Children*, NIMH, Science Monograph, Vol. II (Rockville, Md.: U. S. Dept. of Health, Education, and Welfare, 1979)—with special reference to Part V, Families in Distress, chapters by Murray Straus and Richard Gelles on "Physical Violence in Families"; and Julius Segal on "Child Abuse: A Review of Research."
An excellent overview of the family-violence discussion is offered by Gilbert Y. Steiner and P. H. Milius, *The Children's Cause* (Washington, D.C.: Brookings, 1976).
And an illuminating discussion on the uses of domestic abuse in public policy is summarized in Gilbert Steiner, *The Futility of Family Policy*, *supra*.

11. Carole Joffe, *Friendly Intruders: Childcare Professionals and Family Life* (Berkeley: University of California Press, 1977), p. 2.

12. Mary Jo Bane, *Here to Stay: American Families in the Twentieth Century* (New York: Basic Bks., 1978).

13. Kenneth Keniston and the Carnegie Council on Children, *All Our Children: The American Family under Pressure* (New York: Harcourt Brace Jovanovich, 1977).
Richard H. de Lone, *Small Futures: Children, Inequality, and the Limits of Liberal Reform* (New York: Harcourt Brace Jovanovich, 1977).
Alfred Kahn and Sheila B. Kamerman, *Child Care, Family Benefits, and Working Parents* (New York: Columbia University Press, 1981).

14. Cf. Brigitte Berger, "The Family as a Mediating Structure," in Michael

222 NOTES

Novak, ed., *Democracy and Mediating Structures* (Washington, D.C.: American Enterprise Institute for Public Policy Research, 1980).

15. Brigitte Berger, "The Family and Mediating Structures as Agents for Child Care," in B. Berger and S. Callahan, *Child Care and Mediating Structures* (Washington, D.C.: American Enterprise Institute for Public Policy Research, 1979).
Robert Mnookin, "Foster Care: In Whose Best Interest?" *Harvard Educational Review*, Nov. 1973.
Michael H. Phillips et al., *Factors Associated with Placement Decisions in Child Welfare* (New York: Child Welfare League of America, 1971).
See also Gilbert Steiner, *The Futility of Family Policy, supra.*

16. See B. Bruce-Briggs, ed., *The New Class?* (New Brunswick, N.J.: Transaction Books, 1979).
Alvin Gouldner, *The Future of Intellectuals and the Rise of the New Class* (New York: Seabury Press, 1979).

17. Irving Kristol, *Two Cheers for Capitalism* (New York: Basic Bks., 1978).

CHAPTER 3

1. Recent writings on gender and sex roles are voluminous; most are written from a feminist perspective. Only a few are mentioned here:
Vivian Gornick and Barbara Moran, eds., *Women in Sexist Society* (New York: Basic Bks., 1971).
Joan Huber, ed., *Changing Women in a Changing Society* (Chicago: University of Chicago Press, 1971).
Robin Morgan, ed., *Sisterhood Is Powerful* (New York: Random House, 1970).
Judith Hole and Ellen Levine, *Rebirth of Feminism* (New York: Quadrangle Bks., 1971).
Cynthia F. Epstein, *Woman's Place* (Berkeley: University of California Press, 1970).

2. Two very different books offer summaries of the various attempts in American society to come to terms with sexual (i.e., gender) differentiation in the modern world. Though both attempt to develop typologies for this purpose, the one used in this chapter is somewhat different.
H. Carleton Marlow and Harrison M. Davis, *The American Search for Woman* (Santa Barbara, Calif.: ABC-CLIO, 1976).
Lynda M. Glennon, *Women and Dualism* (New York: Longman Group, 1979).

3. Steven Goldberg, *The Inevitability of Patriarchy, supra.*
Alice Rossi, "A Biosocial Perspective on Parenting," *Daedalus*, Spring 1977. This important essay contains up-to-date references.

4. Curt Stern, *Principles of Human Genetics*, rev. ed. (San Francisco: Freeman, 1973).

Hugo B. Bergel, ed., *Advances in Sex Research* (New York: Harper, 1963).
M. Diamond, "A Critical Evaluation of the Ontogeny of Human Sexual Behavior," *Quarterly Review of Biology*, 40, 1965, pp. 147–73.
Natalie Shainess, " 'New' Views of Female Sexuality" (a book review of J. Chasseguet-Smirgel et al., *Female Sexuality: New Psychoanalytic Views*), *Psychiatry and Social Science Review*, 5:4, 1971.
E. H. Erikson, "Inner and Outer Space: Reflections on Womanhood," *Daedalus*, Spring 1964.
Lionel Tiger, *Men in Groups* (New York: Random House, 1969).
—— and Joseph Shepher, *Women in the Kibbutz* (New York: Harcourt Brace Jovanovich, 1975).
See also, for various aspects of gender difference, the voluminous research by Lewis L. Terman.
5. See for instance:
A. Bandura, "Social-Learning Theory and Identificatory Processes," in D. A. Goslin, ed., *Handbook of Socialization Theory and Research* (Chicago: Rand McNally, 1969).
Margaret Mead, *Male and Female* (New York: Morrow, 1949).
L. Kohlberg, "A Cognitive-developmental Analysis of Children's Sex-role Concepts and Attitudes," in Eleanor E. Maccoby, ed., *The Development of Sex Differences* (Stanford, Calif.: Stanford University Press, 1966).
An interesting review of the literature on early sex-typing can be found in Lois Hoffman, "Early Childhood Experiences and Women's Achievement Motives," *Journal of Social Issues*, 28:2, pp. 129–55, 1973) and Arlene R. Hochschild, *A Review of Sex Role Research, American Journal of Sociology*, 78:4, 1973, pp. 1011–29.
6. Recent popular media and professional literature are full of essays and arguments on ERA; just a few titles that provide an overview of the women's movement are given here:
Carden, *The New Feminist Movement, supra.*
Barbara Deckard, *The Women's Movement* (New York: Harper, 1975).
Freeman, *The Politics of Women's Liberation, supra.*
William O'Neill, *The Woman Movement: Feminism in the United States and England* (New York: Barnes Noble, 1969).
Sheila Rowbotham, *Women, Resistance and Revolution* (New York: Vintage, 1974).
7. A wealth of sources for the "superior" woman position can be found in some of the current liberationist journals, such as:
*Tooth and Nail*, Berkeley, California;
*Redstockings*, New York;
*Everywoman*, New York.
See also:
Morgan, op. cit., as well as the writings of Kate Millett, Sophy Burnham, T. C. Lethbridge ("Witches"), etc.
8. Marlow and Davis, op. cit., present a well-reasoned argument for this position.

9. The definition of the family has been a problem for some time in anthropology and sociology. Most recently, consensus seems to be emerging that it no longer makes sense to speak about "the" American family, but about American "families." See:
Bert N. Adams, *The Family: A Sociological Interpretation* (Chicago: Rand McNally, 1975).
Ira L. Reiss, *Family Systems in America* (Hinsdale, Ill.: Dryden, 1976).
    Politically, the definition of the family reached its most recent peak of "official" influence through the monumental efforts of researchers and activities preparing for the 1980 White House Conference on Families. The interested reader can acquaint himself with this problematic issue by perusing the materials developed in behalf of the National Council on Family Relations (publisher of various journals on marriage and the family) in preparation for the White House Conference on Families. The report on the White House Conference on Families, *Listening to America's Families, Action for the '80's*, Oct. 1980, can be obtained from the White House Conference on Families, 330 Independence Avenue, S.W., Washington, D.C.

10. Ira L. Reiss, "The Universality of the Family: A Conceptual Analysis," *Journal of Marriage and the Family*, Nov. 1965, p. 449.

11. Quoted by Allan Carlson, "A Problem of Definition," *The Human Life Review*, VI, 4, Fall 1980, p. 46.

12. Ira Hutchinson, "The American Family," working paper prepared under the sponsorship of the National Council on Family Relations in preparation for the 1980 White House Conference on Families.

13. Quoted in Richard A. Viguerie, *The New Right* (Falls Church, Va.: The Viguerie Company, 1981), p. 155.

14. Carlson, op. cit.

15. Daniel Callahan, *Abortion: Law, Choice, and Morality* (New York: Macmillan, 1970).
L. W. Summer, *Abortion and Moral Theory* (Princeton, N.J.: Princeton University Press, 1981).
Edward Manier, William Liu, and David Salom, eds., *Abortion: New Directions for Policy Studies* (Notre Dame, Ind.: University of Notre Dame Press, 1977).

16. Peter Berger, Brigitte Berger, and Hansfried Kellner, *The Homeless Mind: Modernization and Consciousness* (New York: Random House, 1973).

17. Steiner and Milius, *The Children's Cause, supra.*

18. Joseph Goldstein, Anna Freud, and Albert J. Solnit, *Beyond the Best Interest of the Child* (New York: Free Press, 1973).
Ronald Gross and Beatrice Gross, *Children's Rights Movement; Overcoming the Oppression of Young People* (Garden City, N.Y.: Doubleday, 1977).

19. George Gerbner, Charles J. Ross, and Edward Zigler, eds., *Child Abuse: An Agenda for Action* (New York: Oxford University Press, 1980):

the important dissenting essay by Rena Uviller, "Save Them from Their Saviors: The Constitutional Rights of the Family."

20. See the important essay by Peter Skerry "Christian Schools versus the IRS," *The Public Interest*, 61, Fall 1980.

Gordon Spykman et al., *Society, State and Schools* (Grand Rapids, Mich.: Eerdmans, 1980).

### CHAPTER 4

1. William J. Goode, *After Divorce* (New York: Free Press, 1956).

2. *Daedalus,* Journal of the American Academy of Arts and Sciences, Spring 1977 issue, *The Family*, contains a number of essays that reflect the use and the implications of the new historical data on early history of the family in Europe and America.

Peter Laslett, *The World We Have Lost*, 2nd ed. (New York: Scribner, 1971), first pub. 1965.

——, *Family Life and Illicit Love in Earlier Generations* (New York: Cambridge University Press, 1977).

——, ed., *Household and Family in Past Time* (New York: Cambridge University Press, 1972).

William J. Goode, *World Revolution and Family Patterns* (New York: Free Press, 1963).

Jean-Louis Flandrin, *Families in Former Times: Kinship, Household and Sexuality* (New York: Cambridge University Press, 1979).

Lawrence Stone, *The Family, Sex and Marriage in England 1500–1800*, abridged ed. (New York: Harper, 1979).

D. V. Glass and D. E. C. Eversley (eds.), *Population in History* (London: Edward Arnold, 1965).

3. Emmanuel Ladurie, *Montaillou* (New York: Vintage, 1979).

4. See Laslett's extensive footnote on the Great Russian pattern, p. 14 of his *Family Life and Illicit Love in Earlier Generations, supra,* and there in particular the entire chapter on "Characteristics of the Western Family."

5. See Laslett, *Family Life and Illicit Love in Earlier Generations, supra,* but also the contradictory materials and arguments presented by Lutz K. Berkner, "Recent Research on the History of the Family in Western Europe," *Journal of Marriage and the Family*, Vol. 35, Aug. 1973, pp. 395–445, as well as by Andrejs Plakan, "Seigneurial Authority and Peasant Family Life: The Baltic Area in the Eighteenth Century," *Journal of Interdisciplinary History*, Vol. 4, Spring 1975, pp. 629–54.

Robert Wheaton, "Family and Kinship in Western Europe: The Problem of the Joint Household," *Journal of Interdisciplinary History*, Vol. 4, Spring 1975, pp. 601–28.

6. William J. Goode, *World Revolution and Family Patterns, supra.*

7. See the convincing argument made by Tamara K. Hareven, "Family Time and Historical Time," *Daedalus*, Spring 1977 issue: *The Family*.

8. Nathan Glazer and Daniel P. Moynihan, *Beyond the Melting Pot* (Cambridge, Mass.: M.I.T. Press, 1963).
L. Grebler et al., *The Mexican-American People* (New York: Free Press, 1970).
Herbert G. Gutman, *The Black Family in Slavery and Freedom* (New York: Pantheon, 1976).
Charles H. Mindel and Robert W. Habenstein, eds., *Ethnic Families in America* (New York: Elsevier, 1976).

9. We (with Hansfried Kellner) have discussed this problem, and the phenomenon of carry-over from one social world to another, in our book *The Homeless Mind, supra.* We still stand by the main features of this analysis, but we are now inclined to think that we, too, may have over-emphasized the negative aspect of "homelessness" as against the creative possibility of being "at home" in more than one world.

10. William J. Goode, *World Revolution and Family Patterns, supra,* and Alex Inkeles, *Modernization and Family Patterns: A Test of Convergence Theory,* unpublished MS.

11. Cf., e.g., R. P. Dore, *City Life in Japan* (Berkeley: University of California Press, 1965), and Hiroshi Wagatsuma, "Some Aspects of the Japanese Family," *Daedalus,* Spring 1977, pp. 171–210, as well as Tsuneo Yamane, "The Nuclear Family Within the Three-Generational Household in Modern Japan," in Lois Lenero-Otero, ed., *Beyond the Nuclear Family Model: Cross-Cultural Perspectives* (Beverly Hills, Calif.: Sage Publications, 1977).

12. This argument is well documented by Mary Jo Bane in *Here to Stay, supra,* as well as in the Preface to the *Daedalus* issue on *The Family, supra.*

13. E. Anthony Wrigley, "Reflections on the History of the Family," *Daedalus,* Spring 1977.

14. The best-known representatives of the structural-functional perspective on the family are Talcott Parsons and Robert F. Bales, who spelled out this approach in their *Family Socialization and Interaction Process, supra.* This perspective has greatly influenced contemporary sociology and has become very much a building block in the majority of recent studies on the family.

The Marxist approach to the family was first spelled out by Friedrich Engels, *The Origins of the Family, Private Property, and the State* (1884) (New York: International Publishers, 1972). A contemporary up-date of this approach can be found in Eli Zaretsky, *Capitalism, the Family and Personal Life, supra,* and a quasi-Marxian approach in Christopher Lasch, *Haven in a Heartless World* (New York: Basic Bks., 1977).

15. William J. Goode et. al., *Social Systems and Family Patterns* (New York: Irvington Publishers, 1971).

16. For a general statement of this approach, cf. Peter Berger and Thomas Luckmann, *The Social Construction of Reality* (Garden City, N.Y.: Doubleday, 1966).

Our aforementioned book *The Homeless Mind* is an attempt to apply this approach to the special problem of modern consciousness.

17. For a dynamic case study of this, in a village in Tunisia, cf. Jean Duvignaud, *Change at Shebika* (New York: Pantheon, 1970).

18. Wrigley, op. cit., makes a similarly intriguing argument making the useful distinction between modernization and industrialization, whereby the first has to precede the second.

19. Cf. Ariès, *Centuries of Childhood, supra*.

20. In very different contexts and for very different purposes, similar expositions of available historical data have been made by such diverse scholars as Max Weber, "Household, Enterprise and Oikos," in *Economy and Society* (New York: Bedminster Press, 1968), and in particular his "Zur Geschichte der Handelsgesellschaften im Mittelalter," in Max Weber, *Gesammelte Aufsätze zur Sozial- und Wirtschaftsgeschichte* (Tübingen: Morh & Siebecke, 1924), pp. 353 ff.; Max Horkheimer, "Allgemeiner Teil" to "Theoretische Entwürfe über Autorität und Familie," in *Autorität und Familie: Studien aus den Institut für Sozialforschung* (Paris: Librairie Félix Alcan, 1936); Arnold Gehlen, *Man in the Age of Technology* (New York: Columbia University Press, 1980); Edward Shorter, *The Making of the Modern Family, supra*; E. P. Thompson, *The Making of the English Working Class* (London: Gollancz, 1963); Laslett's various writings cited earlier; Jean-Louis Flandrin, *Familles: parenté, maison, sexualité dans l'ancienne société* (Paris: 1976); Donzelot, *The Policing of Families, supra*.

21. Ariès, op. cit., p. 414.

22. Norbert Elias, *The Civilizing Process* (New York: Urizen Bks., 1977).

23. Ian Bradley, *The Call to Seriousness: The Evangelical Impact on the Victorians* (London: Macmillan, 1976).

24. Bergier, *The Industrial Bourgeoisie, supra*.

25. Bradley, op. cit.

26. Sheila Rothman, *Woman's Proper Place, supra*.

27. Edward Shorter, op. cit., makes a plausible argument along these lines in his *The Making of the Modern Family*, in the chapter "The Rise of the Nuclear Family."

28. Ivan Illich, *Shadow Work* (London: Boyars, 1981).

29. Both Donzelot, in *The Policing of Families, supra*, and Douglas, in *The Feminization of American Culture, supra*, have made this argument the central theme of their books.

30. John M. Cuddihy, in his *The Ordeal of Civility* (New York: Basic Bks., 1975), has made an interesting argument, in a somewhat different context, along these lines.

31. Robert B. Hill, among others, has made a strong counterargument to the pathological view of the black family in his *Strengths of Black Families* (New York: Emerson Hall, 1973).

CHAPTER 5

1. Peter Berger and Thomas Luckmann, *The Social Construction of Reality* (Garden City, N.Y.: Doubleday, 1966).

2. Karl Marx in the *Neue Rheinische Zeitung*, 15 Dec. 1948, quoted in C. H. George, "The Making of the English Bourgeoisie, 1500–1750," *Science and Society*, Winter 1971, p. 385.

3. Max Weber, *The Protestant Ethic and the Spirit of Capitalism* (London: Allen & Unwin, 1948), p. 154.

4. David Riesman et al., *The Lonely Crowd* (Garden City, N.Y.: Doubleday, 1953), p. 278.

5. Samuel Smiles was a prolific writer. He is best known for a series of books eloquently entitled Self-Help (Chicago: Belford, Clarke, 1881), originally published in England in 1859; see also his books *Thrift, Character,* and *Duty* (London: John Murray, 1875). Asa Briggs, in his *Victorian People* (London: Odhams Press, 1954), presents an intriguing discussion of the role and function of Smiles in nineteenth-century England.

6. Smiles, *Thrift, supra,* pp. 30–64.

7. Ibid., p. 290. It is intriguing to note that in this book Smiles makes the argument that successful men are not great because they are rich, but rich because they are great.

8. Horatio Alger stories for America.
Friedrich D. E. Schleiermacher, *Pädagogische Schriften*, Vol. 28, R. Wicker, ed. (Langensalza: Klassiker der Pädagogik, 1912), and Friedrich Froebel, *Gesammelte Pädagogische Schriften*, Vols. 29–30 (Langensalza: Päd. Klassiker, 1912–13)—both social philosophers and strong influences upon German thinking about family, education, social reality, and in Schleiermacher's case, the balancing power of religion.

9. Theodor Fontane, *Romane und Gedichte* (Munich: Droemersche Verlagsanstalt, 1952), p. 1118.

10. F. Musgrove, *Youth and the Social Order, supra,* has an interesting and challenging discussion of the effects of population changes and the status of the young in the England of the eighteenth and nineteenth centuries. In this he takes up Ariès's suggestions (in *Centuries of Childhood, supra*) on the importance of declining infant mortality rates in the emergence of the concept of childhood. Our position here is influenced by that of Ariès as well as that of Musgrove.

11. We do not wish to enter here into the argument that preoccupies psychohistorians such as L. de Mause as well as a good number of ethnographers of childhood who have argued against the universality of parental love of children. We are, however, of the opinion that careful and less ethnocentric studies of methods of child rearing will reveal more the presence of parental love than its absence.

12. The expression is thought to have originated with John Locke, *Some Thoughts Concerning Education*, 2nd ed. (London: Cambridge University Press, 1884). However, Locke still speaks of "innate" differences in talent and temperament, while, at the same time, emphasizing the role of environment. By the end of the nineteenth century, bourgeois thinkers and educators, particularly in the United States, give an almost blanket endorsement to environmentalism. The dominance of environmentalism in the United States is in itself a fascinating question, one that can perhaps be explained in terms of the peculiar role of the middle classes in American history.

13. Daniel Defoe, *The Complete English Tradesman* (London: Charles Rivington, 1726).

14. Charlotte Mason, *Parents and Children* (London: printed for J. Walter, 1786), for instance, saw Rousseau as the principal inspiration for the bourgeoisie's concern with the socialization and education of their own children. Perhaps her arguments and inferences are a bit simplistic, nevertheless her references to cases of the "new" parenthood are substantial.

15. M. Edgeworth and R. L. Edgeworth, *Memoirs* (Boston: Wells and Lilly, 1820–22), Ch. 8.

16. William Cobbett (1768–1835), *Advice to Young Men, and (Incidentally) Young Women* (London: Hills, Jowett & Miles, 1830), pp. 288–89.

17. Berger, Berger, and Kellner, *The Homeless Mind, supra,* Ch. 3, "Pluralization of Life-Worlds," demonstrates the interconnectedness between rationalization and the concept of a life plan.

18. This to our mind apt term was coined by Donzelot, *The Policing of Families, supra.*

19. See Donzelot, op. cit., p. xxi.

20. Norbert Elias, *The Process of Civilization, supra.*

21. Adolphe Pinard, as quoted by Donzelot, op. cit., p. 186.

22. John Murray Cuddihy, *The Ordeal of Civility, supra.*

23. This argument has been made by many anthropologists, most prominently, though, by Evans-Pritchard, Lévi-Strauss, and Mead, who take care to demonstrate the enormous complexities of more "primitive" societies.

24. Gehlen, *Man in the Age of Technology, supra.*

25. Berger, Berger, and Kellner, op. cit.

26. Gehlen, op. cit., p. 38.

27. Cf. here Anton C. Zijerveld's fascinating and important exposition in his *On Clichés* (London: Routledge & Paul, 1979).

28. This shift in emphasis can be traced in the psychology of Abraham Maslow and Carl Rogers and the development of the encounter movement initiated by them as well as in the very middle-class human-potential movement, particularly dramatically expressed in the writings and therapies of the English "anti-psychiatrists" R. D. Laing and David Cooper.

29. We have tried to analyze the interconnectedness of these seemingly very contradictory themes in counter-modernization and quasi-Marxist movements in our *The Homeless Mind, supra,* Pt. 3.

30. Martin Green. *The von Richtofen Sisters* (New York: Basic Bks., 1974), attempts an analysis of the anti-bourgeois sentiments of the bohemian intellectuals of pre-World War I Germany revolving around such personalities as D. H. Lawrence, Ludwig Klages ("The Mind as the Enemy of the Soul"), Stefan George, Karl Wolfskehl, Alfred Schuler, and other members of the "Cosmic Circle." Of particular relevance to our argument is their Nietzchen-inspired repulsion against the petit-bourgeois world of taste, life-style, and morality (Nietzsche's "morality of shopkeepers"). Green in this book compiles some of the arguments that have been made on the connection between this type of world view and its influence upon the Nazis in their antipathy against the "dried-up rationalists of the bourgeois order."

31. Green, op. cit., p. 80; who quotes Marianne Weber, writing in 1938 about the influence of this group on the political, cultural and life of Germany, and its consequences.

32. From the mass of literature on the counter-culture movement of the 1960s in America, two publications seem to be particularly representative: Charles Reich, *The Greening of America* (New York: Random House, 1970), and Theodore Roszak, *The Making of a Counter-Culture* (New York: Doubleday, 1969).

33. Roszak, op. cit., p. 35.

## CHAPTER 6

1. Mary Jo Bane, op. cit.

2. George Masnick and Mary Jo Bane, *The Nation's Families, 1960–1990* (Cambridge, Mass.: Joint Center for Urban Studies of MIT and Harvard, 1980).

## CHAPTER 7

1. Selma Fraiberg, *The Magic Years* (New York: Scribner, 1959).

2. ———, *Every Child's Birthright: In Defense of Mothering* (New York: Basic Bks., 1977), makes an eloquent case for the importance of love in "bonding."

3. David Hunt, *Parents and Children in History: The Psychology of Family Life in Early Modern France* (New York: Basic Bks., 1970), gives an insightful presentation of this controversy.

Of Margaret Mead's many writings, the following deserve to be singled out within the present context: *Coming of Age in Samoa* (New York: Morrow, 1928); *Sex and Temperament in Three Primitive Societies* (New York: Morrow, 1935); "The Implications of Culture Change for Personality Development," *American Journal of Orthopsychiatry,* 17, 1947, pp. 633 ff.

4. Elisabeth Badinter, *Mother Love: Myth and Reality*, London and New York, Macmillan, 1981.

5. A fascinating discussion of this controversy and its possible consequences for American society can be found in Christopher Lasch's two recent books *Haven in a Heartless World, supra*, and *The Culture of Narcissism* (New York: Norton, 1978). It can also be found in the various writings of Midge Decter.

6. Midge Decter, "The New Sterility," *The Human Life Review*, Vol. VI, No. 4, Fall 1980, p. 18.

7. See, e.g., Jerome Kagan, "The Psychological Requirements for Human Development," in Nathan B. Talbot, M.D., ed., *Raising Children in Modern America: Problems and Prospective Solutions* (Boston: Little, Brown, 1976), and Uri Bronfenbrenner, "On Making Human Beings Human," *Character*, Vol. II, No. 2, 1980.

8. R. A. Spitz, "Hospitalism: An Inquiry into the Genesis of Psychiatric Conditions in Early Childhood," *Psychoanalytic Study of the Child*, 1, 1945, pp. 57–74.
S. Provence and R. Lipton, *Infants in Institutions* (New York: International Universities Press, 1962).

9. John Bowlby has dedicated three volumes of his "attachment research" to this question. The series, Attachment and Loss comprises Vol. I, *Attachment;* Vol. II, *Separation,* and Vol. III, *Loss* (New York: Basic Bks., 1969–80). To some contemporary readers, these books may appear conspicuously conservative and embarrassingly out of date. Yet it may be well to bear in mind that the pendulum of family politics swings with extraordinary swiftness.
The term "monotropy" is explained in Vol. I, p. 308.

10. Erik Erikson, *Identity and the Life Cycle: Selected Papers*, Ch. II, "The Healthy Personality" (New York: 1959), and *Childhood and Society*, 2nd ed. (New York: Norton, 1963).

11. From the wealth of materials on child care, only a few will be mentioned here:
Alison Clarke-Stewart, *Child Care in the Family: A Review of Research and Some Propositions for Policy* (New York: a Carnegie Council on Children monograph, 1977).
Sheila B. Kamerman, *Parenting in an Unresponsive Society* (New York: Free Press, 1980).
——, and Alfred J. Kahn, *Child Care, Family Benefits, and Working Parents* (New York: Columbia University Press, 1981).
Selma Fraiberg, *Every Child's Birthright, supra*.
Barry Bruce-Briggs, "Day-Care: The Fiscal Time Bomb," *The Public Interest,* Fall 1977.

12. John Bowlby, op. cit., Vol. II, p. 28.

13. Spitz, op. cit.

Barbara Wootton, *Social Science and Social Pathology* (New York: Macmillan, 1959).

14. See, e.g., Provence and Lipton, op. cit.

15. Daniel Miller and Guy Swanson, *The Changing American Parent* (New York: Wiley, 1958).

16. Data on the "trickle-down" effect of the bourgeois morality are as of now inconclusive, yet highly suggestive. In particular, Melvin L. Kohn in his various research projects has tried to establish this factor (cf. his "Social Class and Parental Values: Another Confirmation of the Relationship," *American Sociological Review*, Vol. 41, June 1976, pp. 538–44). Yet today it can be said in general that the old bourgeois vision of life is mainly to be found in those classes which were more "missionized" by the bourgeoisie: the working classes. In the words of Theodore Roszak (*The Making of a Counter-Culture, supra,* p. 55): "The working class, which provided the traditional following for radical ideology, now neither leads nor follows, but sits tight and plays safe, the stoutest prop of the established order."

17. Melford E. Spiro, *Kibbutz,* augmented ed. (New York: Schocken Books, 1970).

Bruno Bettelheim, *Children of the Dream* (New York: Macmillan, 1969).

Melford E. Spiro, *Children of the Kibbutz* (Cambridge, Mass.: Harvard University Press, 1958).

18. Rosabeth M. Kanter, *Commitment and Community: Communes and Utopias in Sociological Perspective* (Cambridge, Mass.: Harvard University Press, 1972).

John Rothchild and Susan Berns Wolf, *The Children of the Counter Culture* (Garden City, N.Y.: Doubleday, 1976).

Elia Katz, *Armed Love* (New York: Holt, 1971).

B. Berger, B. M. Hacket, and R. M. Millar, "Child-rearing Practice in the Communal Family," unpublished progress report to National Institute of Mental Health, 1972.

19. We have argued elsewhere (Berger and Berger, *Sociology: A Biographical Approach* [New York: Basic Bks., 1975]) how the social category of "youth" evolved in Western society, once the category of "childhood" had been established.

See also Frank Musgrove, *Youth and the Social Order, supra.*

Erik H. Erikson, *Identity: Youth and Crisis* (New York: Norton, 1968).

20. David Riesman et al., *The Lonely Crowd* (Garden City, N.Y.: Doubleday, 1953).

James Colemen, *The Adolescent Society* (Glencoe, Ill.: Free Press, 1961).

Roszak, op. cit.

Lewis S. Feuer, *The Conflict of Generations* (New York: Basic Bks., 1969).

E. Z. Friedenberg, *Coming of Age in America* (New York: Random House-Vintage, 1963).

F. H. Tenbruck, *Jugend und Gesellschaft* (Freiburg, Germany: Rombach, 1962).

21. The best-known proponents of the "moral education" teaching are Lawrence Kohlberg, of the Harvard Center for Moral Education, who has worked up an elaborate stage system of "cognitive moral development," and Sidney Siman, of the School of Education of the University of Massachusetts, who advocates a widely followed "values clarification" approach.

22. F. E. Trainer, "A Critical Analysis of Kohlberg's Contribution to the Study of Moral Thought," *Journal for the Theory of Social Behavior*, Vol. 7, 1977.
William J. Bennett and Edwin J. Delattre, "Moral Education in the Schools," *The Public Interest*, No. 50, Winter 1978.

23. Edward M. Levine, "The Declining Educational Achievement of Middle Class Students, the Deterioration of Educational and Social Standards, and Parents' Negligence," *Sociological Spectrum*, 1980, pp. 17–34.
Uri Bronfenbrenner, op. cit., for instance, makes no bones about the importance of a "dyadic" (i.e., two adults) setting for the development of the child, drawing upon the findings of investigations conducted primarily over the past two decades.

24. The October 1975 issue of *The Family Coordinator* was devoted to the exploration of "Variant Family Forms and Life Styles"; a number of informative essays can be found there.
From the large number of recent publications on alternatives to the "conjugal" family, a few only are singled out here:
Nena and George O'Neill, *Open Marriage* (New York: Avon, 1973) (first published in 1972).
Carl R. Rogers, *Becoming Partners: Marriage and Its Alternatives* (New York: Delacorte Press, 1972).
Gordon Clanton and Chris Downing, *Face to Face* (New York: Dutton, 1975).
Peter Stein, *Single* (Englewood Cliffs, N.J.: Prentice-Hall, 1976).
Gerhard Neubeck, ed., *Extra-Marital Relations* (Englewood Cliffs, N.J.: Prentice-Hall, 1969).
Michael Gordon, ed., *The American Family in Crisis: The Search for an Alternative* (New York: Harper, 1969).
Janet Zollinger Giele, "Changing Sex Roles and the Future of Marriage," in Henry Gruenbaum and Jacob Christ, eds., *Contemporary Marriage: Structure, Dynamics and Therapy* (Boston: Little, Brown, 1975).

25. Evelyn M. Kitagawa, "New Life-styles: Marriage Patterns, Living Arrangements, and Fertility Outside of Marriage," *The Analysis of the American Academy of Political and Social Science*, No. 453, Jan. 1981.
Ruth Clark and Greg Martire, "Americans, Still in a Family Way," *Public Opinion*, Oct./Nov. 1979.
Andrew M. Greeley et al., "A Profile of the American Catholic Family," *America*, Sept. 27, 1980.

26. Summarizing major studies on this topic conducted through *Good Housekeeping* magazine (over 40,000 responses from women), *Psychology Today* in conjunction with Columbia University (over 50,000 responses), Yankelovich, Skelly and White (national random sample of 9,562 people), and a variety of studies done at the University of Michigan Institute for Social Research, Jonathan L. Freedman in his article "Love and Marriage = Happiness (Still)," *Public Opinion*, Nov./Dec. 1978, presents the convincing yet troublesome situation of American marriage at the beginning of the 1980s.
See also:
Freedman, *Happy People: What Happiness Is, Who Has It, and Why* (New York: Harcourt Brace Jovanovich, 1978).
The presentation of our argument relies heavily upon these studies.

27. See the above-mentioned summary of studies in Jonathan Freedman's essay "Love and Marriage = Happiness (Still)," *supra.*

28. Walter R. Grove and Carolyn Briggs Style (both of Vanderbilt University) have written an as yet unpublished paper, "The Function of Marriage for the Individual: A Theoretical Discussion and Empirical Evaluation," on this topic.

29. Peter Berger and Hansfried Kellner, "Marriage and The Construction of Reality," *Diogenes*, Summer 1964.

30. We have tried to sketch the contours of modern identity in our *The Homeless Mind, supra.*

31. Berger and Kellner, op. cit.

32. W. R. Grove and Carolyn Briggs Style, op. cit., summarize, to our minds convincingly, the significance of marriage for well-being, physically, and mentally.

## CHAPTER 8

1. David Riesman et al., *The Lonely Crowd* (New Haven: Yale University Press, 1950).

2. Erich Fromm, *The Sane Society* (New York: Holt, 1956).

3. C. Wright Mills, *White Collar: The American Middle Classes* (New York: Oxford University Press, 1951).
——, *The Power Elite* (New York: Oxford University Press, 1958).

4. Richard Sennett, *The Fall of Public Man* (New York: Random House, 1974). For the argument presented here, see his essay "Destructive Gemeinschaft," in Norman Birnbaum, ed., *Beyond the Crisis* (New York: Oxford University Press, 1977).

5. Christopher Lasch, *Haven in a Heartless World, supra,* and *The Culture of Narcissism, supra.*

6. Friedrich Engels, *The Origin of the Family, Private Property and the State, supra.*

7. See here in particular the early publication of the Frankfurt Institute for Social Research under Max Horkheimer's editorship *Autorität und Familie, supra.* In this lengthy volume are contained the first formulations of such prominent writers as Max Horkheimer, Theodor Adorno, Erich Fromm, Herbert Marcuse, and Karl Wittfogel that contain the peculiar "mix" of the Frankfurt School that characterized their later writings: personality, culture, and thought viewed through a critical, normative perspective.

8. Theodor Adorno et al., *The Authoritarian Personality* (New York: Harper, 1950).

9. Wilhelm Reich, *The Mass Psychology of Fascism* (New York: Farrar, Strauss & Giroux, 1970).

10. R. D. Laing, *The Politics of the Family* (New York: Random House, 1971); and David Cooper, *The Death of the Family* (New York: Vintage, 1970).

11. Herbert Otto, "Communes: The Alternative Life-Style," *Saturday Review,* Apr. 24, 1971).
Rasa Gustaitis, *Turning On* (New York: Macmillan, 1969).
Rosabeth Moss Kanter, *Commitment and Community: Communes and Utopias in Sociological Perspective* (Cambridge, Mass.: Harvard University Press, 1972).

12. Irenaeus Eibl-Eibesfeldt, *Love and Hate* (New York: Holt, 1971).

13. Bob Dylan, "The Times They Are A-Changin'," Columbia Records 8908, 1964.

14. Steven M. Tipton, *Getting Saved from the Sixties* (Berkeley: University of California Press, 1982), p. 29.

15. Daniel Patrick Moynihan, "The Politics and Economics of Regional Growth," *The Public Interest,* No. 51, Spring 1978, p. 14.

16. The mediating-structures concept has been spelled out by Peter L. Berger and Richard Neuhaus, *To Empower People* (Washington, D.C.: American Enterprise Institute, 1977).

17. Robert Nisbet, *Twilight of Authority* (New York: Oxford University Press, 1975), p. 260.

CHAPTER 9

1. Steiner, *The Futility of Family Policy, supra,* p. 124.

2. Theodore Caplow et al., *Middletown Families: Fifty Years of Change and Continuity* (St. Paul: University of Minnesota Press, 1982).

3. Mary C. Blehar, "Families and Public Policy," in Eunice Corfman, ed., *Families Today—A Research Sample on Families and Children,* Vol. II, *supra.*

4. Joseph Califano, *Governing America* (New York: Simon & Schuster, 1981).

5. Nathan Glazer in concluding his review of Califano's book in the New York *Times Book Review,* June 14, 1981.

6. John E. Coons and Stephen D. Sugarman, *Education by Choice: The Case for Family Control* (Berkeley: University of California Press, 1978).

7. Cf. Hill, *Strengths of Black Families, supra.*

8. On child care, cf. Berger and Callahan, eds., *Child Care and Mediating Structures, supra.*
On health services, cf. Lowell Levin and Ellen Idler, *The Hidden Health System* (Cambridge, Mass.: Bellinger, 1981).

9. Robert Woodson, *A Summons to Life* (Cambridge, Mass.: Bellinger, 1981).

10. Cf. Jay Mechling, ed., *Church, State and Public Policy* (Washington, D.C.: American Enterprise Institute, 1978).

# INDEX

Abortion, 19, 25, 26, 65–68,
    73–82, 120
  black families and, 67
  Catholicism and, 29, 67
  the cognitive issue of, 65–66
  critical camp and, 27
  feminist movement and, 66
  general world trend toward
      legal status of, 66
  knowledge class and, 68
  language and, 65–66
  the law and, 77–78
  Medicaid funds and, 67–68
  men and, 66
  moral consensus on, 73–78
  mystery of birth and, 78–79
  neo-traditionalist camp and,
      28–29, 30, 67
  postulate of ignorance and,
      79–82
  rate of performance (1975), 29
  as sole responsibility of pregnant
      women, 82
  in the United States, 20–21, 66,
      76–77
  U.S. Supreme Court on, 29,
      66–67, 77, 80, 81
Adolescence, 5–6, 159
  House of Umoja project and,
      215
  moral education movement, 161
  parents as role models, 162, 213
  problems of, 33
  psychological and moral
      pressures on, 160–61
  rights of, 69–70
  youth culture and, 159–60
Adorno, Theodor, 173

Affirmative action, 56
Age of Aquarius, 5, 46, 126
Aid to Dependent Children, 33
Alcoholism, 160
Alternative life-styles, 26–27, 205
American Sociological Association,
    136
Amish, 70
Anthropology, 12
  empirical challenge to
      father-mother-child triad
      by, 188
  on family forms, 61, 142
  sex roles in, 54
Antiabortion movement, 20–21,
    29, 65, 67–68
  as a moral denomination, 75–78
  mystery of birth and, 79–80
  postulate of ignorance and,
      80–81
Antinatalism, 135
Antinuclear movement, 125–26,
    135
Antiorganic view of the family,
    34–35
Anti-Semitism, 74
Antitechnological movement, 135
Ariès, Philippe, 5, 92, 97–98, 150
Aristocracy, 108, 115
  upbringing versus endowment
      and, 113–14
Aristotle, 174
Artisan families, 95, 98
Arts, appreciation of, 7
Asceticism, inner-worldly, 109
Austria, 94
Authoritarianism, 173

*Authoritarian Personality, The*
    (Adorno), 173
Autonomous individuals, 109–10
Autonomy of the family, 209–12

Bachofen, 58
Bakunin, Mikhail, 182
Bane, Mary Jo, 143, 197
Barbarians, 130–31, 132, 136
Bebel, August, 9
Bellah, Robert, 75
Benedict, Ruth, 61
Berger, Peter, 79
Berkeley student rebellion, 42
Bible, the, 48
Biedermeier family (Germany), 7
Birdwhistell, R., 62
Birth
    abortion and, 78–79
    wonder of, 149
Birth control, 15, 66, 89, 120
Birth-control clinics, 29
Black cultural self-consciousness,
    17
Black families, 12, 104
    abortion and, 67
    children and, 71, 214
    resentment toward professional
        camp, 36, 38
Blake, William, 122
Bohemianism, 123–24
Bonding, 150, 153, 155, 174
Boston Women's Health Book
    Collective, 66
Bourgeois, clarification of the
    term, 107, 108
Bourgeois democracy, 178
Bourgeois evangelism, 8
Bourgeois families
    attitude toward economic
        success, 96–97, 111–12
    attitude toward risk-taking,
        134–35
    authoritarianism and, 173
    balance between authority and
        love in, 117–18, 133, 153

balance of public and private
    spheres in, 99
bohemianism and, 123–24
children and, 13–14, 96, 97,
    101, 112–13, 114–15, 153
commune movement and,
    158–59, 173–74
counter-culture of the 1960s
    and, 16–18, 37, 124–25
counter-modernization and, 118,
    122–27
decadence and, 132–33
dissent and, 99–100
education and, 97–101, 114–15
in England, 7–8, 94, 98
father-mother-child triad as
    central to, 188
feminist movement and, 26, 37
forces threatening the stability
    of, 154–55
formation and nurture of,
    147–48
in France, 94, 98
in Germany, 7, 94, 98, 112
Goshtalk and, 46
health care and, 115
history of, 3–21
    child-raising ideas, 5
    education and liberation, 6–7
    the Enlightenment and
        problematization of the
        family, 6–7
    the family as a national
        problem, 18–20
    the industrial revolution and,
        100
    Marxist view of the family,
        9–10
    medieval social order and, 95
    missionary activities of, 7–8,
        37–38, 100
    modernization of society and,
        11
    in the nineteenth century,
        7–10
    rise of, 94–95

sociological theories about, 10–15
Spencer and, 9
husband/father role in, 102
hyperindividualism and, 120–22, 124
hyperrationality and, 118–20
importance in United States of, 114, 164, 197
individualism fostered by, 109–11, 116, 117, 122–23, 156–57
infant mortality rates of, 112–13
as an institution, 145–46
Israeli kibbutzim and, 157–58
knowledge class and, 38–39, 46, 185
liberation and domestication of, 97
marriage as stable identity in, 166–67
as a mediating structure in democracy, 183, 204
morality of, 108–11, 117–18
in the Netherlands, 94
ordeal of civility in, 116–17
parents as role models in, 162
personal discipline of, 134
philosophical attacks on, 172
place in a pluralistic society of, 183–85
private property and, 98
progress in human values achieved by, 142
Protestantism and, 7–8, 99
rationalization and, 109, 116, 122
religion and, 98, 99
renascence of U.S. family in the 1950s, 14–15, 37
responsibility and, 135
rise of secularization and, 117–18
in Scotland, 94
sexual instinct and, 116
transformation of the household of, 100–1

as victim of decline in democracy, 171–72, 174–75
virtues of, 99–100
wife/mother role in, 101–3
women as major role in development of, 7–8, 102–3
working-class families and, 8–9, 37, 103–4, 115–16, 157
Bourgeois-Protestant morality, 110–12
Bourgeois revolution, 106–7, 108
Bowdlerism, 41, 42, 45, 50, 51
Bowlby, J., 153
Broken families, 60
Bryant, Anita, 30
Bureaucracy, 62, 109
countermodernization and, 122–23
welfare state and, 202
Burgess, Ernest, 12, 13, 15
Busing of schoolchildren, opposition to, 30

Calculus of pain, 80, 81, 82
Califano, Joseph, 200
California syndrome, 16, 27
Callahan, Daniel, 82
Calvinism, 98, 109
Capitalism, 93, 96, 97, 108
inner-directed individuals and, 157
Protestantism and, 97, 108
rationalization and, 109
working women and, 58
Caplow, Theodore, 197
Carnegie Council on Children, 18–19, 35
Carter administration, 200
family as a national problem and, 18–19
professional camp and, 32
Catholicism, 74, 109
abortion and, 29, 67
beginning of human life and, 80–81
sacrament of marriage, 191

Cavafy, C. P., 130–31
Chicago, University of, 10, 12
Chicago School (of sociology),
        10–12, 61
Child abuse, 33, 34
    parental rights and, 214
Child allowance, 209
Child day-care facilities, 27, 33,
        34, 153, 155–56
Childless couples, 60, 163
Child-rearing establishment, 14,
        32
Children, 5, 53
    Aristotle on, 174
    black families and, 71, 214
    bourgeois families and, 5,
            13–14, 96, 97, 101, 112–13,
            114–15, 153
    collectivizing child-raising, 62
    in communes, 158–59
    the community and care of, 214
    controversy over child-rearing
            patterns, 150–51
    critical camp as hostile to,
            27–28
    custody of, 213–14
    development of identity, 147
    development of values in, 156
    divorce and, 154
    establishment of bonding and,
            150, 153, 155, 174
    government action on child care,
            58, 199, 205–6
    Hispanic families and, 71
    importance of community-giving
            function to, 146
    importance of
    father-mother-child triad to,
            192–93
    importance of stability and love
            in, 152, 153
    Israeli kibbutzim and, 157–58
    maternal instinct and, 150
    negative effects of
            institutionalization on,
            155–56
    nuclear family and, 92–93

opposition to busing of, 30
overcoming prejudices via,
        184–85
parents as role models, 162
permissive child-rearing, 157
private property and, 175
relationships outside the family,
        156
scholastic achievement in United
        States of, 201
separation from parents by state
        action (annual rate), 71
working-class families and,
        115–16
working mothers and, 154
Children's rights, 68–72
    conflict between parents' rights
            and professional's rights
            over, 70–72, 213–14
    knowledge class and, 71
    neo-traditionalist camp and, 71
    professional camp and, 69
    religion and, 71
    U.S. Supreme Court decision on,
            70
China, 66
Circumlocutions, traditional, 44
Civic ecumenism, 74–75
Civility, ordeal of, 116–17
Civilizing Process, The (Elias), 43
Civil rights, 26, 49, 206–7
Coalition for Better Television, 30
Cobbett, William, 114–15
Commune movement, 26, 173–74,
        181
    child-rearing in, 158–59
Communism
    bohemianism and, 124
    importance of the family, 177
Community
    importance to society of, 146
    maintenance of, 214–15
Compassion, 190
Compulsory education laws, 7
Consciousness raising, 25
Consensus, 76–78

Conservative Protestants, 67
Conservatives. *See*
    Neo-traditionalist camp
Contraceptives, 66–67
Cooper, David, 173
Counseling professionals, 32
Counterculture movement, 16–18,
    24–25, 26, 37
  antirationalism of, 125–26
  disillusionment with, 181
  Third World and, 125
Countermodernization, 118,
    122–27
  hypermodern individualism and,
    124–26
  modernization and, 201–2
Creative schizophrenia, 88–89
*Crestwood Heights* (Seeley), 16
Crime, 31, 160
Critical camp, 23, 24–28
  abortion and, 27
  children and, 27–28
  difficulties for, 27–28
  family institution as perceived
    by, 25, 27, 33
  feminist movement and, 24–27
  ideas and movements reflected
    by, 39
  knowledge class and, 39
  language and, 46
  noninclusive language of, 50–51
  political and psychological goals
    of, 27
  professional camp and, 36
Cuddihy, John Murray, 116
Cults, 16, 75, 120, 125, 160, 182
Cultural institutions, 102–3
Cultural revolution, 62–64

Decadence, 129–36
  barbarians and, 130–31, 132,
    136
  bourgeois families and, 132–33
  decline of the family due to, 85
  freedom and, 133–34
  knowledge class and, 135
  modern society and, 129–32

Defoe, Daniel, 114
Democracy
  antibourgeois values and, 178,
    179
  authoritarianism and, 173
  basic assumptions of, 169–70
  basic sociopsychological issue of,
    179–80
  bourgeois, 178
  bourgeois families and, 183, 204
  decline of public virtue in, 171
  the family as victim of decline
    of, 171–72, 174–75
  freedom and, 169–70
  importance of a moral consensus
    to, 175–76, 179, 206–7
  individualism and, 157, 170,
    178–79
  the law and, 176–77
  mediating structures and,
    182–83, 204
  morally offensive life-styles in,
    207
  as a pluralistic society, 183–84,
    208–9
  primacy of the family and,
    204–6
  requirement for survival of, 182
  restoration of parental rights,
    212
  risk taking and, 134
  socialism and, 178
  stripping away of moral
    authority from social
    institutions in, 181–82
Demodernization, 118
Demythologizing the family,
    86–87
Dependent family members, 34
Dewey, John, 176
Differential-egalitarian viewpoint,
    58, 59
Discrimination, 56
Dissent, 99–100
Divorce, 26, 33, 34, 86, 154
  housing needs of divorced

families, 207
ideal image of marriage as cause
    of, 166
increase in, 143, 163
*Dr. Bowdler's Legacy* (Perrin), 41
Domesticity, cult of, 16
Donzelot, Jacques, 113
Douglas, Mary, 187
Drugs, 126, 160
Durkheim, Émile, 11, 76, 96, 131,
    147, 175, 176, 183
Dylan, Bob, 180

Eastern Europe
    exporting of Western society's
        problems to, 21
    extended family in, 87, 88
Eastern Orthodox Christians, 67
Edgeworth, Maria, 114
Education, 7, 103
    bourgeois families and, 97, 101,
        114–15
    failure of public education, 20
    liberation and, 6–7
    moral values and, 161, 176
    parental rights and, 159, 212–14
    prayer in public schools, 20, 30,
        199
    private and public school
        systems, 210, 211
    propagation of bourgeois values
        by, 6–7, 14
    scholastic achievement of U.S.
        schoolchildren, 201
    state-supported school system,
        177
    stripping away of moral
        authority from, 181–82
Educational vouchers, 211–12,
    213
Eibl-Eibesfeldt, Irenaeus, 174
Elias, Norbert, 43, 116
*Embourgeoisement*, 7
Empowerment of the family,
    209–12
Encounter movement, 27, 39, 121
Endowment versus upbringing,
    113–14

Engels, Friedrich, 9, 58
Engineering profession, gender
    roles and, 56–57
England
    bourgeois families in, 7–8, 94,
        98
    bourgeois-Protestant morality in,
        111–12
    class language and, 42
English language, intimate form of
    address and, 48
Enlightenment, the, 123, 141, 176
    problematization of the family
        and, 6–7
Environmentalism, 35, 114
Episcopalians, 75
Equal employment opportunity,
    56
Equal Rights Amendment (ERA),
    25, 26, 27, 53
    differential-egalitarian
        viewpoint, 58–59
    feminist movement and, 55–58,
        199, 205
    the new matriarchy and, 58
    opposition to, 30, 57
    U.S. Constitution and, 57
Erikson, Erik, 153
Esoteric neologisms, 51
Ethnic groups, 61, 135
    *See also* types of ethnic groups
Ethograms, 190
European sociology, 11
Evangelical Protestant schools, 71
Experimentation, 118–19
Extended family, 10, 87, 88
Extramarital sex, 26, 64
Extremist cults, 182

Fabians, 8
Falwell, Jerry, 30
Families in Action, 29
Family, problems of defining,
    59–65
*Family, Socialization and
    Interaction Process* (Parsons
    et al.), 13
Family advocates, 18, 32

Family experts, 20–21, 23
Family Impact Seminar, 19
Family Planning Act (1972), 29
Family Policy Advisory Board, 30
Family Protection Act, 30, 64
Fanatical cults, 160
Fascism, 49, 124
Father-mother-child triad, 187–93
    as central to bourgeois family,
        188
    mother-child dyad and, 190–93
    Western society values linked to,
        188
Feminine Anti-Feminists, 30
*Feminine Mystique, The*
        (Friedan), 16, 24
Feminist movement, 16, 19,
        24–27, 37, 39, 54–59, 202
    abortion and, 66
    alternate life-styles and, 26–27,
        205
    bourgeois families and, 26, 37
    challenge to father-mother-child
        triad by, 189–90
    civil rights movement and, 49
    critical camp and, 24–27
    differential-egalitarian
        viewpoint, 58–59
    emphasis on self-realization,
        26–27
    ERA aims and, 55–58, 199, 205
    "feminine" occupations and, 56
    Femspeak and, 46–50, 51, 54
    Freud and, 121
    gender roles and, 54–55
    hyperindividualism and, 120,
        121
    lesbianism and, 25
    Marxism and, 172–73
    maternal instinct and, 150
    matriarchy concept of, 58
    membership in major
        organizations (1971–81) of,
        26
    neo-traditionalist camp and, 20,
        31
    public policy (with respect to

        the family) and, 205
    radicalization of, 17, 25
    sexist language, 47, 48, 49
    women as the superior sex, 58
    working mothers and, 154
Femspeak, 46–50, 51, 54
Feudal system, 93
Firestone, Shulamith, 17, 25
Fontane, Theodor, 112
Fontenelle, 142
Foster families, 208
Foundation for Child
        Development, 19
Fraiberg, Selma, 149
France, 11
    bourgeois families in, 94, 98
    rise of the bourgeoisie in, 99
Franco, Francisco, 170
Frankfurt School, 173
Franklin, Benjamin, 107, 110
Freedom, 192
    decadence and, 133–34
    democracy and, 169–70
Free love, 124
Free Speech Movement, 42, 45
French language, intimate form of
        address in, 48
Freud, Sigmund, 121, 162
Freudian sexual repressions, 116
Friedan, Betty, 16, 24, 25, 189
Fromm, Erich, 125, 171, 179

Garfinkel, Harold, 49
Gasper, Jo Ann, 31
Gay liberation movement, 16, 20,
        26, 30, 54, 64, 135, 163
    homosexual couples as "a
        family," 61
Gehlen, Arnold, 116, 119, 145
*Gemeinschaft*, 11
Gender roles, 54–59
Genetic engineering, 120
Germany, 11
    bourgeois families in, 7, 94, 98,
        112
*Gesellschaft*, 11
GI Bill, 211

Glazer, Nathan, 200
Goode, William, 90
Goshtalk, 44–46, 51
Government handbooks,
    censorship of, 50
Great Society, 33, 198
Green, Martin, 124

Handicapped children, monotropy
    and, 153
Happiness of Womanhood
    (HOW), 30
Haute bourgeoisie, 108, 111
Health care, 115
Health cults, 120, 125
Hegel, Friedrich, 107
Herberg, Will, 75
*Here to Stay* (Bane), 143
Heterosexual sex as rape, 58
Hispanic families
    children and, 71
    resentment toward professional
        camp, 36, 38
Homosexuality. *See* Gay liberation
    movement
Horkheimer, Max, 173
House of Umoja project, 215
Human fetus, beginning of human
    life for, 80–82
Human life bill, 68
*Human Life Review, The,* 29
Human-potential movement, 121
Hutchinson, Ira, 63
Hyde Amendment, 67
Hyperindividualism, 118, 120–22,
    124–26
Hypermodernity, 118, 132
Hyperrationality, 118–20

Ideals of family life, 60–61, 62,
    86, 185
Illegitimacy, 33, 34
Illich, Ivan, 102
Immigration, 11–12, 34, 136
Inclusive language, 47
India, 66

Individual, the, 93, 96–97, 145,
    165, 177
    freedom as right of, 169–70
    importance of marriage to
        stability of, 166–67
    moral values and, 176
Individualism, 103, 108, 153
    fostered by bourgeois families,
        109–11, 116, 117, 122–23,
        156–57
    democracy and, 157, 170,
        178–79
    social responsibility and, 117
    tradition and, 110
Individuation, 146–48
Industrialization, 34, 89, 90–93
Industrial revolution, 91, 92, 98,
    100
Infant mortality, 113, 134, 141
Infrastructure, 88
Inner-directed individuals, 157,
    171
Inner-worldly asceticism, 109
Institutionalization, negative
    effects on child
    development of, 155–56
Interpretative sociology, 144
Intimatist movement, 49–50
Israel, kibbutzim of, 157–58
Italian language, intimate form of
    address in, 48–49

Jansenism, 98
Japan, 66, 89
Jews, 74, 191
Johnson, Dr. Samuel, 163
Jonestown, 182
Judeo-Christian tradition, 82, 191
    bohemianism and, 124
    denominationalism and, 74–75
    image of the family as shaped
        by, 60
    religious world view of, 90
Juvenile delinquency, 33, 160
    House of Umoja project, 215

Kelsen, Hans, 77

Kibbutzim, Israeli, 157–58
Knowledge class, 38–39, 53
  abortion and, 68
  alternatives to marriage, 163
  bourgeois families and, 38–39,
    46, 185
  children's rights and, 71
  countermodernization and,
    126–27
  critical camp and, 39
  decadence and, 135
  language and, 44–45, 51
  neo-traditionalist camp and, 39
  new class, 38–39
  professional camp and, 38–39
Kohlberg, Lawrence, 161
Kristol, Irving, 38

Ladurie, Emmanuel, 87
Laing, R. D., 17, 173
Language, 41–52
  abortion issue and, 65–66
  bourgeoisie and refinement of
    speech, 43–44
  bowdlerism, 41, 42, 45, 50, 51
  connotative importance of
    synonyms, 42–43
  Femspeak, 46–50, 51, 54
  free speech, 42
  gender roles and, 54
  generic use of masculine gender,
    47–48
  Goshtalk, 44–46, 51
  intimate forms of address in
    various languages, 48–50
  knowledge class and, 44–45, 51
  neo-traditionalist camp and, 46,
    50
  nonsexist, 25
  obscene language, 41–45, 47
  political use of, 46–47, 49, 50,
    51–52
  professional camp and, 51–52
  of social classes, 42–45
  traditional circumlocutions, 44
  working-class families and, 46
Lasch, Christopher, 171

Law, the, 77–78, 176–77
  stripping away of moral
    authority from, 181–82
Laxalt, Paul, 30, 64
League of Housewives, 30
League of Women Voters, 103
Leftism, 135
Legal positivism, 77
Lesbian liberation movement, 16,
    25, 163
  lesbian couples as "a family," 61
Life-styles, alternative, 26–27, 205
Linguistic degradation ceremony,
    49
Locke, John, 6, 107
Lorenz, Konrad, 190
Loss of naturalness, 119
Lower-income families
  autonomy and, 210–11
  educational vouchers for,
    211–12
  maintenance of community in,
    214–15
  parental rights for, 213
Lower-middle-class families,
    decadence and, 135
Luther, Martin, 110
Lynd, Helen, 197
Lynd, Robert, 197

Machlup, Fritz, 38
Madonna, the, 187, 188
Magic Years, The (Fraiberg), 149
Maine, Henry, 96
Major Barbara (Shaw), 8
Major Barbara complex, 37
Male and Female (Mead), 61
Male work ethic, 28
Mannheim, Karl, 129
Marcuse, Herbert, 173
Marijuana, decriminalization of,
    30
Marriage
  alternatives proposed to, 163
  constrictions of, 164
  disease and, 167

divorce and ideal image of
    marriage, 166
happiness of men and women in,
    163, 164, 167
individual stability and, 166–67
as an institution, 145–46
life expectancy and, 167
modern functions of, 164–65
as sacred, 191
as social norm, 164
stripping away of moral
    authority from, 181–82
Marx, Karl, 9, 98, 106–7, 140
Marxism, 58, 107, 123, 210
    feminist movement and, 172–73
    view of the bourgeois and
        working-class families, 9–10
Maslow, Abraham, 121
Masnick, George, 143
Maternal instinct, 150, 152
Matriarchy, 58
*May* v. *Anderson* (1953), 70
Mead, George Herbert, 146, 165
Mead, Margaret, 61, 116, 150
Media, radical movements and, 18
Mediating structures, 182–83, 204
    the community as, 214
    religious institutions as, 215–16
Medicaid, abortion and, 67–68
*Memoirs* (Saint-Simon), 99
Men
    abortion and, 66
    biological differences between
        the sexes, 55–56
    gender roles and, 55
    institutional patterns for, 145–46
    marital happiness and, 163, 167
    role as husband/father in
        bourgeois families, 102
    as unnecessary to child-rearing
        process, 189–90
Mencius, 190, 192
Mencken, H. L., 44
Mental disorders, 160
Merchant families, 95, 98
Methodism, 98

Middle Ages, changes in family
    life during, 92
Middle American culture, 10
Military service, conscientious
    objection to, 75
Millett, Kate, 25
Mills, C. Wright, 171
Minority families
    emotional and moral primacy of
        parents, 161–62
    welfare state and, 206
    *See also* Black families; Hispanic
        families
Mitchell, Juliet, 17, 25
Modernism, 116
Modernization, 201–2
    the individual and, 177
    nuclear family and, 88–90, 91
Modern society
    decadence and, 129–32
    decline of the family in, 85–86
    family as basic institution of,
        204–6
    importance of moral consensus
        to, 76–78, 206
    mediating structures in, 182,
        204
    as an ongoing construction,
        144–45
    polytheism of values in, 182
    viewed as an organism, 130
Mondale, Walter, 18
Monotropy, 153
Montaillou (fourteenth-century
    French village), 87
Moore, Barrington, 17
Moral consensus, 147–48
    importance to modern society
        of, 76–78, 206
Moral education movement, 161
Moral foundation of society,
    175–76
Moral Majority, 30, 35, 45, 161
Moral philosophy, treatment of
    family in, 172
Moral pluralism, 74
Mormons, 75

Mother-child dyad, 187, 189
    father-mother-child triad and,
        190–93
    hyperindividualism and, 120
Mother figure, 152–53
Moynihan, Daniel Patrick, 182
*Ms.*, 50
Muggeridge, Malcolm, 50
Muncie, Indiana, 197
Musgrove, Frank, 5
Mussolini, Benito, 49
Mysticism, 181
Myth of the ideal family, 86

Narodniki (Russian populist
        movement), 123
National Endowment for the
        Humanities, 45
National family policy, dispute
        over, 199
National Federation for Decency,
        30
Nationalist movements,
        countermodernization and,
        123
National Organization of Women
        (NOW), 24
National Pro-Family Coalition, 30
National Right to Life Committee,
        30
*Nation's Families, 1960–1990, The*
        (Bane and Masnick), 143
Naturalness, loss of, 119
Natural symbol, 187
Needy families, 19
Neologisms, 47, 51
Neo-Malthusianism, 27
Neo-traditionalist camp, 23,
        28–32, 36–37
    abortion and, 28–29, 30, 67
    as a backlash phenomenon,
        28–29
    built-in tensions faced by, 31–32
    children's rights and, 71
    decadence of modern society
        and, 129–30
    "feminine" occupations and, 56

feminist movement and, 20, 31
gender roles and, 58–59
Goshtalk and, 44–46
knowledge class and, 39
language and, 46, 50
national organizations
        representing, 29–30
negative and positive issues
        uniting, 30–31
political strength of, 30
Reagan administration and, 30
redefinition of the family and,
        64–65
women's rights and, 55–56
Netherlands, the, bourgeois
        families in, 94
New Class. *See* Knowledge class
New Deal, 32
New Left, 16, 17–18, 26, 27, 39,
        62
New Politics, 26, 39
Niebuhr, Richard, 74
Noninclusive language, 50–51
Nonrepressive sexuality, 62
Nonsexist language, 25
Northern Ireland, 74
Nouvelle bourgeoisie, 136
Nuclear family, 10, 85
    central idea of, 87–88
    changes in socialization patterns
        in, 92
    childhood and, 92–93
    creative schizophrenia of, 88–89
    declining influence of religion
        and, 93–94
    economic changes in, 92–93
    incubator effect of, 61
    industrialization and, 89, 90–92
    modern consciousness and,
        91–92
    modernization and, 88–90, 91
    myth of, 87
    political changes in, 93
    privatization of, 93
    urbanization and, 89, 90

Obscene language, 41–45, 47
Ogburn, William, 12
One-parent households, 60
Ono, Yoko, 25
Open marriages, 61
Ordeal of civility, 116–17
*Organization Man, The* (Whyte), 16
Orthodox Jews, 67
Other-directed individuals, 157, 171
  youth culture and, 160
*Our Bodies, Ourselves*, 66

Pacifism, 134, 135
Pain, calculus of, 80, 81, 82
Paine, Thomas, 6
Parents
  bonding and, 150, 153
  controversy over child-rearing patterns, 150–51
  development of values in the child and, 156
  emotional and moral primacy of, 161–62
  forces threatening parent-child relationship, 154–55
  importance of stability and love in child rearing, 152, 153
  overcoming prejudices via children, 184–85
  physical requirements for childhood, 151–52
  restoration of rights of, 71, 212–14
  as role models, 152, 162
Pareto, Vilfredo, 118
Parsons, Talcott, 13–15, 21, 62, 93
*Patterns of Culture* (Benedict), 61
Permissive child rearing, 157
Perrin, Noel, 41
Personal self-realization, 16
Persons in need of supervision (PINS), 60–70
Petit bourgeoisie, 108, 111
Phenomenological tradition of sociology, 140

Philadelphia, Pennsylvania, House of Umoja project in, 215
Pietism, 98
Pluralism, 176, 183–84, 208–9
  moral, 74
*Polish Peasant in Europe and America, The* (Thomas and Znaniecki), 11
Political theory, treatment of family in, 172
Populationists, 62
Pornography, 20, 30, 31, 45, 46, 51, 71–72
Prayer in public schools, 20, 30, 199
Pregnancy
  beginning of human life for fetus during, 80–82
  teenage, parental rights and, 213
Premarital sex, 26, 64
Presbyterianism, 75, 98
Prescriptive advice, 144
Primacy of the family, 204–6
Privacy, 96, 97
  restoration of, 206–8
Private-philanthropy model of family policy, 198–99
Private property, 175
Proabortion movement
  language of, 65
  as moral denomination, 75–78
  mystery of birth and, 78–79
  nature of the human person and, 65
Pro-family movement. *See* Antiabortion movement
Professional camp, 23, 32–36
  "anti-organic" view of the family, 34–35
  black families and, 36, 38
  changing attitudes toward women, 37–38
  children's rights and, 69
  critical camp and, 36
  Hispanic families and, 36, 38

ideal relationship to the family, 215
knowledge class and, 38–39
language and, 51–52
parental rights and, 212–13
shift in the conception of the family by, 60–63, 105
working-class families and, 104
Professional educators, educational vouchers and, 211
Prohibition, 75–76
Proscriptive advice, 144
Protestantism, 71, 74, 117–18
bourgeois families and, 7–8, 99
bourgeois world view and, 108
capitalism and, 97, 108
virtues of, 108–11
See also types of Protestantism
Psychoanalysis, 14
Psychologese, 51
Psychology, 14, 51–52, 142–43
hyperindividualism and, 121
negative notions about the family, 61, 62
Psychotherapy, 14
hyperindividualism and, 121
Public housing, 33
Public policy (with respect to the family)
analytic models for, 202
antifamily position of, 197, 199, 205
autonomy and empowerment of the family, 209–12
conservative demands for, 199–200
feminist movement and, 205
goals for the family, 195–96
liberal demands for, 199–200
maintenance of community and, 214–15
potential utility of, 196–97
private sexual activities and, 206–7
recognition of primacy of family, 204–6
respect for pluralism, 208–9

restoration of parental rights, 212–14
restoration of the private, 206–8
statist model versus private-philanthropy model, 98–99
utilization of mediating structures, 214–15
welfare state and, 208–10, 214
Puritanism, 98
Pyramids of Sacrifice (Berger), 79

Quakers, 74

Racist language, 49
Radical feminists, 17, 25
Radical movements. See Counterculture movement
Rape, heterosexual sex as, 58
Rationalism, 91, 108–9, 116
Rationalization, 109, 116, 122
countermodernization and, 122–23
Reagan administration, 30
Recipe knowledge, 116
Reich, Wilhelm, 173
Reiss, Ira, 63
Reliability, 184
Religion, 7
bourgeois families and, 98, 99
children's rights and, 71
the community and, 215–16
declining influence of, 93–94, 181–82
the triad/dyad controversy and, 191–92
Religious cults, 75
Religious fundamentalism, 202
Religious pluralism, 74
Remarried couples, 60, 143
Responsibility, 135, 175
hyperindividualism and, 122
Riesman, David, 109–10, 157, 160, 171
Right Woman, The (Casper), 31
Roe v. Wade (1973), 66–67
Rogers, Carl, 121

Romantic movement, 123
Romein, Jan, 95
Rothman, Sheila, 100
Roszak, Theodore, 126, 127
Rousseau, Jean Jacques, 6, 140
Ruskin, John, 107

Saint-Simon, Duc de (Louis), 99
Schizophrenia, creative, 88–89
Schlafly, Phyllis, 30
Schlesinger, Arthur, 77
Schutz, Alfred, 116, 132
Scotland, bourgeois families in, 94
Second-marriage families, 183
Sects, 121
Secular humanism, 30
Secularization, 20, 94, 117–18,
    147, 176
Seeley, John, 16
Self-absorption, 178–79
Senior citizens, 33, 34
    the community and care of, 215
    special allowances for, 209
Sennett, Richard, 171
Sensitivity cults, 16
Serial marriage, 163
Sexist language, 47, 48, 49
Sex roles, 35, 54
Sexual engineering, 116
Sexual instinct, bourgeois families
    and, 116
Sexual liberation, 16
Shadow work, 102
Shakespeare, William, 48
Shaw, George Bernard, 8
Sick family members, special
    allowances for, 209
Significant others, 165
Single-parent households, 33, 34,
    86, 183, 208
Singles subculture, 26, 60–61, 135
Slavery, 75–76, 141
Small-town culture, 10
Smiles, Samuel, 111–12
Socialism, 178, 181
Social realities of the family,
    60–61, 63

Social responsibility, individualism
    and, 117
Social Security Act (1935), 33
Social services, 5, 32, 198
    the community and, 214–15
    vouchers for, 211–12, 213
Sociologese, 51
Sociology, 51–52
    Chicago School, 10–12, 61
    European, 11
    oscillating approach to the
        family of, 61–62
    structural-functionalism school,
        13–15, 62, 89–90
Sociology of knowledge, 144
Spain, 48, 170
Spencer, Herbert, 9
Spitz, René, 155
Spouse battering, 33, 34
State-supported school system, 177
Statist model of family policy,
    198–99
Steiner, Gilbert, 196
Stewardship, 175
Stop ERA, 30
Structural-functionalism school of
    sociology, 13–15, 62, 89–90
Suffrage, 93
Suicide, 160
Sweden, 198
Symbolic knowledge, 38
Sympathetic individuality, 62
Synonyms, 42–43

Tax system, 205
Technologization, 62, 109
Television, 201
Temperance movement, 8
Textbooks, censorship of, 50
Third World, 66, 79, 80, 88
    counterculture and, 125
    decadence and, 130
    exporting of Western society's
        problems to, 21
    infant mortality rates in, 113
    neo-traditionalist movement in,
        20

Thomas, W. I., 11
"Times They Are A-Changin',
    The" (Dylan), 180
Tocqueville, Alexis de, 107, 117,
    170
Tönnies, Ferdinand, 11, 96
Totalitarianism, 192
Trading associations, 96
Tradition, individualism and, 110
Traditional circumlocutions, 44
Triad/dyad controversy, 190–93
Tribes, 183
Trust, 153

Umoja, House of, project, 215
Union of Soviet Socialist Republics
    (U.S.S.R.), 66, 120
United States
    abortion and, 20–21, 66, 76–77
    bourgeois family's importance
        in, 114, 164, 197
    bourgeois-Protestant morality in,
        112
    centrist consensus toward the
        family in, 216
    commune movement in, 26,
        173–74, 181
    child rearing, 158–59
    educational vouchers in, 211–12,
        213
    effect on Third World of
        problems of, 21
    factors revitalizing future society
        in, 136
    family and the child-rearing
        establishment in, 14
    family as a national problem,
        18–20, 197–98
    family renascence of the 1950s
        in, 14–15
    Goshtalk in, 44–45
    heterogeneity of society in,
        83–84, 197–98
    immigrations and, 11–12, 34,
        136
    as the "lead society" in
        modernization, 21

    major alignments on family
        issues in, 20–21, 23
    moral issues dividing, 75–76
    new radicalism of the 1960s and
        the family in, 16–18, 20
    overcoming prejudices via
        children in, 184–85
    as a pluralistic society, 31–32,
        74–75, 183–85, 198
    problems of defining the family
        in, 59–65
    scholastic achievement of
        schoolchildren in, 201
    sociology as tool for solving
        social problems in
    Chicago School, 10–12, 61
    structural-functionalism school,
        13–15, 62, 89–90
    tolerance to newcomers in,
        183–84
    transformation in
        nineteenth-century family
        household, 100–1
    youth culture in, 159–60, 162
U.S. Congress, antiabortion
    movement and, 68
U.S. Constitution
    antiabortion movement and, 68
    ERA and, 57
U.S. Supreme Court, 77
    on abortions, 29, 66–67, 77, 80,
        81
    ban on prayer in public school,
        20, 30
    children's rights, decision on, 70
    on definition of pornography, 45
    First Amendment, 215
    on the right to obtain
        contraceptive material, 28
Universal entitlements, 36
Universal suffrage, 93
Upbringing versus endowment,
    113–14
Upper-middle-class families,
    hyperrationality and, 120
Urbanization, 34, 61, 89, 90

Victorian family (England), 7
Voltaire, 182
Voluntary associations, 183
Voucher concept for social
    services, 212

Weber, Max, 90, 91, 95, 98, 140,
    144, 182
Welfare state, 5, 15, 31, 33
    bureaucracy and, 202
    extension in the 1960s of, 17–18
    minority families and, 206
    needy families and, 19
    public policy (with respect to
        the family) in, 208–10, 214
White House Conference on
    Families (1980), 19, 199
    problems of defining the family,
        59, 63, 64
Whyte, William, 16
Wildavsky, Aaron, 134
Women
    abortion decision as sole
        responsibility of pregnant
        women, 82
    biological differences between
        the sexes, 55–56
    capitalism and the working
        woman, 58
    drafting of women into military
        service, 30, 58
    gender roles and, 55
    in the labor market (1950s and
        1972), 24
    liberation of working-class
        women, 103–4
    as major role in development of
        bourgeois families, 7–8,
        102–3
    "male" work ethic and, 28

marital happiness of, 163, 164,
    167
neo-traditionalist camp and
    women's rights, 55–56
nineteenth-century technological
    inventions for the household
    and, 100–1
as oppressed minority, 24–25
professional camp's changing
    attitude toward, 37–38
role as wife/mother in bourgeois
    families, 101–3
as the superior sex, 58
working mothers, 33, 154
See also Feminist movement
Women's rights. See Equal Rights
    Amendment (ERA)
Woodson, Robert, 215
Woolf, Virginia, 24
Working-class families
    bourgeois families and, 8–9, 37,
        103–4, 115–16, 157
    changing attitudes toward
        woman's domesticity and,
        37–38
    childhood and, 115–16
    hyperrationality and, 120
    language of, 46
    Marxist view of, 9–10
    professional camp and, 104
World War II, renascence of the
    U.S. family after, 15

"Year of the Family" (1980), 59
Yoder v. Wisconsin (1972), 70
Youth culture, 159–60, 162
    liberation cycle and, 180–81

Zero-growth theory, 27, 135
Zero-population theory, 135
Znaniecki, Florian, 11